Speaking through the Mask

A volume
in the series
Psychoanalysis and
Social Theory,
edited by
C. Fred Alford and
James M. Glass.

Inside/Outside Nietzsche:
Psychoanalytic Explorations,
by Eugene Victor
Wolfenstein

Speaking through the Mask: Hannah Arendt and the Politics of Social Identity

Norma
Claire
Moruzzi

CORNELL UNIVERSITY PRESS : ITHACA AND LONDON

Passages from *On Revolution*, by Hannah Arendt, copyright © 1963 by Hannah Arendt, are used by permission of Viking Penguin, a division of Penguin Putnam Inc.

Excerpts from *The Origins of Totalitarianism*, by Hannah Arendt, copyright © 1951 by Hannah Arendt and renewed 1979 by Mary McCarthy West, are reprinted by permission of Harcourt, Inc.

Parts of the preface, "A Story," originally appeared in the essay "Asking the Questions/Telling a Story," in *A User's Guide to German Cultural Studies*, ed. Scott Denham, Irene Kacandes, and Jonathan Petropoulos (Ann Arbor: University of Michigan Press, 1997), used here by permission.

Parts of Chapter 2 originally appeared in an essay titled "National Abjects: Julia Kristeva on the Process of Political Self-Identification," in *Ethics, Politics, and Difference in Julia Kristeva's Writing*, ed. Kelly Oliver, copyright © 1993, are reproduced by permission of Routledge, Inc.

Parts of Chapter 6 originally appeared as an essay titled "Re-Placing the Margin: (Non)Representations of Colonialism in Hannah Arendt's *The Origins of Totalitarianism*," published in *Tulsa Studies in Women's Literature* 10, no. 1 (Spring 1991), used here by permission.

First published 2000 by Cornell University Press

Printed in the United States of America

Library of Congress Cataloging-in-Publication Data

Moruzzi, Norma Claire.
Speaking through the mask: Hannah Arendt and the politics of social identity/Norma Claire Moruzzi.
    p.cm.—(Psychoanalysis and social theory)
Includes index.
ISBN 0-8014-3785-7 (alk. paper)
1. Arendt, Hannah—Contributions in political science. 2. Group identity. I. Title. II. Series.
JC251.A74 M66 2000
320.5'092—dc21

00-010806

Cornell University Press strives to use environmentally responsible suppliers and materials to the fullest extent possible in the publishing of its books. Such materials include vegetable-based, low-VOC inks, and acid-free papers that are recycled, totally chlorine-free, or partly composed of non-wood fibers. Books that bear the logo of the FSC (Forest Stewardship Council) use paper taken from forests that have been inspected and certified as meeting the highest standards for environmental and social responsibility. For further information, visit our website at www.cornellpress.cornell.edu.

Cloth printing   10 9 8 7 6 5 4 3 2 1

FSC FSC Trademark © 1996 Forest Stewardship Council A.C.
SW-COC-098

For Lore and Heddy,
and Romeo

Contents

A Story

Sometimes people ask me, "Why Arendt?" There are several answers to this question, each more or less complete and each used according to the circumstance. The simplest, and maybe the most accurate, is that she makes sense to me. By now, it is hard to determine to what degree she makes sense because she has shaped the way I think; I first picked up *The Origins of Totalitarianism* when I was sixteen. I have been reading Hannah Arendt's writing on and off ever since, a circulation of interest and surprise that has been going on for more than half my life. Given this relationship, the more intriguing question may be, why did Arendt make sense to me in the first place? Why did this particular individual's writing strike me as the best possible way to think about the world in which we live?

It's a world we both have lost and gained. For Arendt, the lost world was obviously the cultural landscape of Europe, the New World the place she landed in 1941 as a refugee. But for me, a postwar child born to first- and second-generation immigrants who believed the Old Worlds were well behind us, history's shadow had a different shape. Firmly foreshortened, minimized by the cheerful lighting of a consumer's paradise, the shadow of history seemed barely to tangle around one's feet. Mostly a matter of recipes and childhood mythology, history was not something that was supposed to get in your way. In our house, my mother never called herself a refugee, although that is certainly what she was when she arrived in New York in 1938. At sixteen, she and her younger sister had been shipped out of Germany to live with American relatives they had never met. Together, they set out to become Americans; when my grandparents did arrive a year later, their daughters would only speak English with them. German was part of the history they felt lucky to have been able to leave behind, a shadow my mother felt she could mostly do without. She got on with her life. When she married my father, mixing ethnicities and religions, they were happy that this was so. They felt free.

For me, ironically, the shadow grew longer. Maybe it was just the passage of time, the shifting of perspective that accompanies the slow turning of the world. Raised as Americans, free to make of ourselves what we wanted, my brother and I pursued different paths: he working to build the present, I fascinated with questions of the past. The absence of certain parts of our history shaped my own life. At sixteen, finished with high school, I left home to spend a year on a kibbutz in Israel where my mother's sister lived. A doctor, she had moved there somewhat skeptically years before, after she had married a fellow German Jewish refugee who was also a Zionist pioneer and a distant relative. On the kibbutz, I worked in the cow shed and read everything I could get my hands on. Mostly, I depended on my aunt and uncle's library. After I had pulled out Salinger, Rousseau, de Sade, and Kazantzakis, my aunt handed me *The Origins of Totalitarianism*. I think she thought it might keep me occupied for a while.

While I was living on the kibbutz, people used to ask me if I was Jewish, and my answer kept changing. In the beginning, I said no. I was as Jewish as I was Catholic, having been raised in neither religion but with the American credo of self-creation. When a double line of my classmates had marched down the hill from the public elementary school to the church that held their catechism classes, and I had been one of what seemed like the few to walk straight home, I had certainly known I wasn't Catholic, and it didn't occur to me that being Jewish was any different. My family didn't practice any religion except a fairly secularized Unitarian Universalism. We hadn't had any religious initiations, and we did celebrate Christmas, but so had my mother when she was growing up, although when we were very small my parents tried a system of giving us one present a day for several days, on the pedagogical theory that too much Christmas buildup was overstimulating for the very young. We were proud to be a mix. But I looked like my mother, who looked like her sister, and people knew I was her niece. They were skeptical when I said I wasn't Jewish, and one day someone did ask me if I was ashamed of it. Of course not! But it suddenly dawned on me that practice had nothing to do with it; this was an identity based on blood.

I suppose I had known that I was Jewish according to religious law, because Jewish national identity is passed on through the mother's line. Nonetheless, I had clung to my mongrel assurance that performance mattered more than pedigree. Now, somewhat confused but accommodating to local custom, I switched my answer. But saying I was Jewish entailed a new set of problems: people expected me to be familiar with holidays and rituals about which I knew nearly nothing. I was suddenly shockingly ignorant about what before I had been proud to know a little. Frustrated, I revised my answer again: when asked if I was Jewish, I gave the somewhat unwieldy but accurate answer that I was Jewish through my mother, and let it go at that.

But I remained puzzled. What exactly did it mean to be Jewish; what did it mean for me to be Jewish? The whole question seemed to me to be completely confused, not just in my own case, but in its larger, theoretical ramifications. My secular, modernist-rationalist kibbutznik relatives almost entirely rejected Jewish religious identification; for them, Jewish identity seemed to be based on an almost superstitious valorization of a

tribal bond, a blood nationalism. The more religious Jews, on whom the
kibbutzniks looked with varying degrees of dislike and contempt, at least
seemed to think that Judaism had to be linked to certain actions and traditions; their emphasis on spiritual practice struck me as possibly more
enlightened than my relatives' faith in bloodline ethnicity. Jewish identity did involve choices, but they seemed to be split between the rituals
of a spirituality I hadn't been raised to practice and adherence to a Zionist nationalism I didn't necessarily believe. In the midst of this quandary,
my aunt lent me Arendt's book, and I started reading history.

At the time, I didn't finish it, but I made my way through the first volume on *Antisemitism*, and well into the second volume on *Imperialism*.
Arendt's work on European Jewish history opened up to me a whole new
way of thinking. Specifically, it allowed me to place my own questionable
Jewish identity within the context of a variegated historical narrative,
instead of finding myself simply confronting the most blunt of that narrative's end results. Reading Arendt's compelling and elaborate account
of European Jewry's troubled relationship with political emancipation
and cultural self-identification, I also came to realize that for me, as for
my mother, Jewish identity had a lot to do with being German.

And what did that mean? For postwar children, German identity could
be a confusing mix of Beethoven, marzipan, and death camps. Unlike
most other sizable American ethnic groups, there wasn't even an available
immigrant identity; the various and powerful German American clubs
and organizations had been disbanded or banned outright during World
War I. German cultural identity, including German Jewish identity, had
to be reconstituted out of a broken past and an anomalous present.

This peculiar lack of historical presence wasn't true of my father's Italian background. We weren't raised to think of ourselves as especially Italian, but we could go to Boston and walk by the house in the North End
where my father had been born. For my father, a reasonably satisfactory
continuity with the Old World existed, something that was after all less
possible for my mother, the emigrant. The quaint traces of cultural practice that are for the second generation the signs of ethnicity are for the
first generation still the remnants of loss. For the refugee, the memory of
that loss is confounded because it is mixed with relief: under the circumstances that necessitate flight, almost any place is better than where
you've been. Nonetheless, the distant memories of childhood always
remain the most familiar. My mother was not the only one to say she
could never go back. One of her duties as a U.S. Army nurse during the
war had been to act as an interpreter for German prisoners; when they
would ask her where she learned her good German, she lied. "In school,"
she said, "in Cincinnati."

So I went back—in part, at least—to study Arendt. A German friend
was studying with a Jewish professor who had finished the war in the
United States, and who had decided, with the strength of age, to return
to teach the new generation. He was running a seminar on Hannah

Arendt, and a study group arranged in the old-fashioned way, with Sunday afternoon meetings at his home and evening gatherings with his venerable friends. I had been reading Arendt through college, her writing on philosophy as well as history and politics, but what I now began to appreciate was her intellectual tone. Both passionate and rigorously disciplined, her writing had a dancer's attack: energy sustaining form. Again, she made sense to me, but she had also become a model of stylistic practice. Her work, her voice, and her context had become familiar, and when I returned to the United States for graduate school, I knew I would write on Hannah Arendt.

I did, and I continue to do so. Arendt has shaped me intellectually, but in other ways as well. Maybe the most honest use we make of others is of the dead, and at some point I became curious about Arendt's own enunciation of a voice, her modeling of another's life as autobiography. Arendt's first independent scholarly project was an investigation of the German Romantics, which became a book on the Jewish salon hostess Rahel Varnhagen. In writing Rahel's story "as she herself might have told it," Arendt tried on another's voice while she detailed that other's story. But Arendt's Rahel is in fact a masquerade; a double narrative of a German Jewish woman's experience of self-creation and assimilation. In writing on and through Rahel, Arendt narrated her own cultural and textual precedent. In writing on Arendt, I found a model for my own exploration of the difficult relationship between the present and the past.

The connection with the past also enables the future. In June 1993, my mother, her sister, and I traveled to Würzburg, the city where they were born. We had all been visitors there before: my aunt in the 1950s, myself during my year in Germany before graduate school, my mother after that. But this trip was in the nature of a pilgrimage. That winter, both my father and my uncle had died after long illnesses; for all of us, but especially for my mother and my aunt, the circumstances of the present had once again been terribly changed, and it seemed the right time to return to an earlier, lost past. Together we retraced paths that were familiar to them, they told stories, and they pointed out sites: the park paths along which they had walked to school; the street where my aunt was bitten by a dog; the bakery to which their mother sent to be baked pastries too large to fit into their own oven; the exact place where their house had stood; the exact place of their grandmother's house, my grandfather's mother, and the only member of the family to die in Theresienstadt. We spoke freely among ourselves, but neither my mother nor my aunt would ever admit, or boast, in conversations with anyone else, that they had lived in this place before.

Certain silences still hold, but it is easier to find the voices that filled them. My mother's cousin rediscovered, translated into English, and distributed a family history written by one of the uncles. Written in German by a man spending his retirement in postwar London, and reflecting the preferences of the family snob, this brief document nonetheless provides a fairly complete account of the extended family, and of their life in Würzburg both before and after the turn of the century. My mother still keeps, but will not catalogue, the extensive collection of her own mother's family photographs. Scenes of swimming, dress-up parties, and picnic outings, they are perfectly ordinary, perfectly foreign. Remnants of another life, the family relics are hoarded, which also means they are hidden away.

I certainly wasn't reading Arendt during our journey to Würzburg. In fact, I was reading Bernardo Atxaga's *Obabakoak* (New York: Pantheon, 1992), a recent novel first published in the always nearly lost tradition of written Basque. But once I was back in the United States, I returned again to her work, and to the manuscript for this book. Reading Hannah Arendt taught me how to think. Writing this book has taught me more than that. In Rahel Varnhagen, Arendt found a precedent for her own self-conscious construction of a German Jewish cultural and intellectual identity. In telling Rahel's story, she also answered certain questions for herself, questions about the relationship between individual self-creation and the claims of personal and political history. At a farther, mongrelized remove, perhaps I have found, through reading Hannah Arendt and writing this book, a way of answering somewhat similar questions for myself.

There are two particular individuals whose advice and friendship have been invaluable to me: Liliane Weissberg, who has persistently called me to take my own work as seriously as she herself was willing to take it; and Kaveh Ehsani, who has always pushed me to think more politically and write more clearly. But this has been a long process, and many others have been a part of it. It is impossible for me to thank everyone adequately, but I can at least try here to give credit to those whose contributions have been especially significant. They are listed as follows in the approximate order in which they became a part of my thinking on Hannah Arendt: Heddy Frank-Blum, Leonore Frank Moruzzi, Romeo Moruzzi, George Kateb, Tracy Strong, Pia Bungarten, Friedrich Friedmann, Richard Flathman, Judith Butler, Neil Herz, Julie Agoos, Kate Forhan, Barry Goldfarb, Laura Trippi, Jessica Reed, Timothy Randolph, Helynn Garner, Abbie Collier, Stephen Engelmann, Sophia Mihic, Zarir Merat, Judit Bodnar, Jozsef Borocz, Lanfranco Blanchetti, Kamran Ali, Ziad Elmarsafy, Sharon Marcus, Susan Maslin, Scott Spector, Lisa Graham, Lynn Schibeci (and family), Agnieszka Sekula Lark, Gayatri Spivak, Sandra Bartke, Isaac Balbus, James Glass, John McGowan, Amalia Pallares, Ron Lake, Shubhra Sharma, Jennifer Rexroat, and Frances Botkin. Costs related to publication were covered in part by a Grant-in-Aid from the Institute for the Humanities at the University of Illinois at Chicago. I would also like to thank my students, whose intellectual energy and curiosity have been a constant source of renewal: Marynel Ryan, Shiera Malik, Sheila Shahriari, Gracja Szafran,

A STORY

Marla Bramble, Andra Folescu, Rita Gondocs, Mahasen Nasser-Eldin, and Julio Garcia. Thanks to you all.

NORMA CLAIRE MORUZZI

Chicago

Arendt Works Cited and Abbreviations Used

Eichmann in Jerusalem (New York: Penguin, 1977), cited as *Eichmann*.

The Human Condition (Chicago: University of Chicago Press, 1958), cited as *HC*.

The Jew as Pariah: Jewish Identity and Politics in the Modern Age, ed. Ron H. Feldman (New York: Grove Press, 1978), cited as *Pariah*.

The Life of the Mind (New York: Harcourt Brace Jovanovich, 1978), cited as *Thinking*.

On Revolution (New York: Penguin, 1986), cited as *OR*.

The Origins of Totalitarianism (New York: Harcourt Brace Jovanovich, 1973), cited as *The Origins*.

Rahel Varnhagen: The Life of a Jewish Woman, trans. Richard Winston and Clara Winston (New York: Harcourt Brace Jovanovich, 1974), cited as *Rahel*.

Speaking through the Mask

One.
The Human
Condition
as Embodied

This book is a political reading of Hannah Arendt. Its purpose is both to read her works against themselves, in order to break down some of the strong distinctions that are often taken to be emblematic of her thought, and to restore the political vibrancy to contemporary understandings of her thinking. Supplementing critical readings of several of Arendt's most significant political texts with the insights of contemporary psychoanalytic, feminist, and social theorists, it reconstitutes the relationship between constructed social identity (whether of gender, religion, ethnicity, race, or class) and political agency. This new relationship is facilitated by a concept of agency as masquerade. Developed out of Arendt's own writings, this concept of the mask can resolve the apparent contradiction between social identity and individual political agency that haunts Arendt's work, and so much of social theory today.

Much good work has been published lately on Arendt. But much of that work, part of the recent rediscovery of her writings, assimilates Arendt's thought to the conventions of other established intellectual discourses. This has been a valuable exercise; indeed, it has been critical in recovering Arendt for a new audience. But Arendt was always adamantly independent, intellectually and politically, and there is a danger in assimilating her too well. In placing her initially within a discourse that might seem entirely foreign, I attempt to free the crux of her thinking for a different political project, at once radically opposed to conventional readings of Arendt's texts and at the same time deeply in keeping with her own writing.

This project involves reconceptualizing Arendt's work as both social and political theory. Arendt's hostility to the social is notorious; it is established through explicit argument in *On Revolution*[1] and underwrites most of her remarks in other texts about gender, race, and class. This apparent hostility to the forms of identity that have been politicized through modern social movements has led to Arendt's thought being regarded as traditionally individualistic and only abstractly relevant to any rethinking of the politics of social power. This is a mistake. Arendt's preoccupations were with the specific leveragings of power in historically defined circumstances. She was fascinated by individuals who re-created political possibility, especially under bleak conditions. If the rhetoric of her argument often pulls one way, toward a definition of the political clarified of any association with social identity, the substance of her analysis pulls in a different direction, toward a conception of political agency that is actually inextricable from the agent's social construction.

This tension can be most directly addressed in *On Revolution*, the text in which Arendt most clearly represents her view of the confrontation between the social and the political. Arendt argues that the social exists as a purely natural essentialism whose overwhelming physicality threatens the fragile artifice of the built political world. But this opposition can be deconstructed when examined through the lens of feminist psychoanalytic theory. Julia Kristeva's writings on abjection interpret the textual dynamic that constructs the social as a natural threat. Joan Riviere's and Mary Ann Doane's works on feminine masquerade amplify the theoretical possibilities implicit in Arendt's own discussion of the public, political mask. These texts open Arendt's work up to new interpretive strategies. By loosening the apparent necessity of Arendt's opposition of the social and the political, these psychoanalytic texts can be used to develop the social applications of a concept (the mask) Arendt had described as limited to the strictly political realm.

Once social identity is redefined as constructed rather than essential, it becomes apparent that Arendt's concept of the mask can have more than just a formally political function. Arendt's recurrent discussions of individuals enacting social roles for political (or personal) purpose gain new significance as examples of action performed through a mask: it is precisely the theatrical quality of the social mask that enables true Arendtian political action in the modern world. I trace these provocative discussions, supplemented with appropriate historical materials, through several of her texts, including *On Revolution, Rahel Varnhagen, The Origins of Totalitarianism, Eichmann in Jerusalem, The Jew as Pariah, The Life of the Mind*, and *The Human Condition*.[2]

Together, these close textual analyses constitute a sustained rereading of Hannah Arendt's writings on the relationship between social identity and political agency, out of which can be developed a theory of (social) masquerade as authentic (political) action. This theory is based on Arendt's writings and insights, although it runs against the grain of her argument. Thus, although Arendtian, this theory of agency is not exactly Arendt's; rather, it offers a theoretical realignment of her conceptual apparatus, and a new way of thinking about social identity and political agency.

The book is composed in something of a circle; it opens and closes with discussions of *The Human Condition*. This is the text that most resolutely restricts the possibility of public, political life to those who are not constrained by their associations with the physical demands of private reproduction, but it is also the text most appropriate to lead us into, and out of, a renegotiation of Arendt's thought. *The Human Condition* is significant in this context precisely for what is left out of it: any specific, detailed analysis of a historical individual functioning as a political actor in the public realm. This absence is remedied in my last chapter, when I reinsert the historical Alcibiades back into Arendt's conception of the Athenian political realm. That chapter closes out this extended discussion by reaffirming masquerade even in the last (or original) refuge Arendt imagined free from it. But to begin with, this first chapter revisits the prologue of *The Human Condition,* in which Arendt founds the rest of her book on a lament for modern technological threats (construed as masculine) to organic, earthly existence (construed as feminine). The prologue is a fairly straightforward, quite poetic piece of writing, but it is significant to this argument because even a cursory reading seems to reveal a sensibility at odds with the rest of her text. For this reason, it is a good place for this argument to begin.

The theoretical core of the book is explicated in chapters 2 and 3, a psychoanalytically informed rereading of Arendt's discussion of the social in *On Revolution.* These chapters present the heart of my argument: the deconstruction of Arendt's opposition of the social and the political, and the development of the concept of agency as masquerade. In chapter 2 I examine Arendt's characterization of the social as essential, threatening, and abject. Julia Kristeva's concept of abjection is used to evaluate the structure of Arendt's distinctions, and their inconsistencies. Although Arendt argues that the American Revolution succeeds as a political project because, unlike the French Revolution, it is not confronted by class-driven demands for social justice, her own argument confounds itself on the issue of race and the contradiction of a freed body politic that still includes slaves.

Chapter 3 is a further analysis of the material on the social in *On Revolution,* but follows the deconstruction (of the social / political opposition) in the previous chapter with a reconstruction of other elements of Arendt's discussion into a theory of agency as enacted masquerade. In particular, I focus on Arendt's analysis of Herman Melville's *Billy Budd,* and her discussions of hypocrisy and the Greek concept of the public persona as a politically enabling public mask. Melville's tale presents a version of political action as speech; hypocrisy threatens the inherent artifice of all constructed politics by offering a myth of authenticity; and the mask offers a dramatic metaphor for the artifice of spoken political agency. These aspects of Arendt's own discussion are supplemented with Joan Riviere's concept of (feminine) masquerade. Riviere's analysis of social identity as a masquerade inflects Arendt's discussion of the artifice of the political role in a new conceptual direction: if social identity can be understood as artifice, the self-conscious enactment of a social role can be a specific aspect of political agency.

The rest of the book traces the political potentials of self-consciously enacted social identities through Arendt's own writings. Chapter 4 is an analysis of Arendt's achievement of an authoritative voice through her assumption of Rahel Varnhagen's persona as an autobiographical and authorial mask. In her first postgraduate book, Arendt tells the story of the Jewish salon figure "as she herself might have told it," yet she splits off this very feminine self-description from the critical affirmation of politicized Jewish identity that concludes that book. *Rahel Varnhagen* is a feminine persona Arendt enacts and then rejects; her validation of Rahel's supposedly self-validated Jewish identity comes at the expense of any possible politicization of gender. For Arendt, feminine experience must remain unique and personal, but Jewish identity becomes a focus for political analysis.

This analysis is carried through in the three volumes of *The Origins of Totalitarianism*, which I examine in four separate chapters. Chapter 5 introduces *The Origins* as the text through which Arendt established her voice as a writer and a political theorist; this is the text in which Arendt struggles to construct her own work according to the lesson of a historically defined, politically aware Jewish identity she had described in the final chapters of *Rahel*. Chapters 6, 7, and 8 each mainly focus on one volume of *The Origins*, and the emblematic figures in each volume who evade the modern limits of political agency through self-conscious self-enactment. Chapter 6 examines Arendt's analysis of the manipulation of the codes of Jewish social identity in *Antisemitism*, considering in particular Benjamin Disraeli's public (Jewish) persona as a successful social masquerade for political purposes. Chapter 7 presents an exposition of Arendt's analysis, in *Imperialism*, of the intersection of race thinking and economic interests in undermining European political possibility. Chapter 8 examines the apparent absence of a recognizable political persona that might give a face to the machinery of totalitarian terror; this chapter links Arendt's insights on collaboration and the agency of self-representation from *Totalitarianism*, *Eichmann in Jerusalem*, and *The Life of the Mind*. These three texts span her entire published career: her first book; the one that made her notorious in much of the Jewish community; and the one she was working on when she died. Together they provide a sustained inquiry, both historical and philosophical, into the possibilities for independent, individual political action, even under the most oppressive, most isolating modern conditions.

The final chapter returns to where the book began, with *The Human Condition*, but with a shifted appreciation of Arendt's oeuvre. If the prologue complicates any simple reading of that text, *The Human Condition* nonetheless remains Arendt's requiem for an idealized context for political action. Arendt considers the polis a historical retreat from contemporary turbulence, and she projects into it her own desires for unproblematic political possibility. But this is nostalgia; in order to indulge it, she elides from her own text any trace of the ambiguous figures who elsewhere provide her with such provocative material for thinking about political agency. Compared to her other writing, *The Human Condition* is a curiously depopulated text, an argument based on the assertion that politics can (most properly) exist without any ambiguity between public role and private life. Left intact, this argument rebukes, with classical authority, the inevitable compromise of modern political and social identity. Yet it can be deconstructed on its own historical grounds, through the figure of Alcibiades—Athens's paramount political actor, an individual who flaunted and confirmed the basic conventions of Athenian identity. In the last chapter of this book, I inscribe Alcibiades back into the context of Arendt's polis. The discussion of his public role as a compelling political actor who manipulated social codes—especially gender— for political purpose provides a deeply Arendtian argument against Arendt's own text, and an example of agency through masquerade even in the earliest political context.

Thus, this book provides a thorough reconceptualization of Arendt's political thought. Using close readings and unorthodox interpretive strategies, it reconstellates her theory of action, her preoccupation with social identity, and her historical groundedness into a theory of (political) agency through (social) masquerade. This is not exactly Arendt's theory, but it is fundamentally rooted in her thought; these are readings against the grain, but they are loyal. In the rest of this chapter, I will discuss the surprising rhetorical formulations in the prologue to *The Human Condition*. As a short introduction, the prologue itself works against the grain of the rest of that text. For those who may be skeptical that Arendt has anything useful to offer contemporary social theory, the prologue is a good place to begin.

THE PROLOGUE

In 1957, an earth-born object made by man was launched into the universe, where for some weeks it circled the earth according to the same laws of gravitation that swing and keep in motion the celestial bodies— the sun, the moon, and the stars. To be sure, the man-made satellite was no moon or star, no heavenly body which could follow its circling path for a time span that to us mortals, bound by earthly time, lasts from eternity to eternity. Yet, for a time it managed to stay in the skies; it dwelt and moved in the proximity of the heavenly bodies as though it had been admitted tentatively to their sublime company.
(*HC*, 1)

The Human Condition is perhaps the most theoretically notorious of Hannah Arendt's books. Although *Eichmann in Jerusalem* would later cause tremendous controversy within the Jewish community, *The Human Condition* is the work that established Arendt as a theorist of the proper distinction between the public and the private. Building from Aristotle's conception of political speech as the highest human good, Arendt claimed to find in the classical polis a public, political life that flourished precisely because it was carefully segregated from the daily concerns of private life, and of work and labor. A privileged few citizens regularly made the transition between the private and the public spheres, but most individuals remained confined within the dailiness of an exclusively private existence. Their efforts—their work and their labor (which Arendt carefully distinguishes)—provided the material conditions that gave the privileged few the freedom to enter the public realm and engage each other as political actors. That the toiling private individuals were women and slaves, defined by their status as necessary to but unfit for the political experience, Arendt blandly acknowledged. Her resolute distinction between a public and a private realm, her advocacy of the traditional hierarchy between them, and her casual relegation of women to an undervalued private sphere have led many contemporary readers, especially feminists, to regard Arendt as something of a traitor to her sex.

Nonetheless, her work provokes our attention. If Arendt is no friend to feminism, neither is she a conventional enemy. Although her political writing defines social issues, and social identity, as a threat to political practice, this book explores the ways in which Arendt's own writings link questions of social identity and political agency.[3] A psychoanalytically informed concept of agency as masquerade facilitates the exploration of that link. But even without the concept of the masquerade, Arendt's distinction between private, gendered bodies and public, political roles may be more pliable than we suppose. Even *The Human Condition*, that most severe of texts in its deliberate reinscription of the traditional exclusion of women from the political realm, begins with an assertion that all political meaning is engendered by the fact of our organic, physical embodiment.

The prologue, which introduces the book and the concerns of the book's author, is a remarkably dense and poetic stretch of philosophical and political prose. Within it, even Arendt's choice of language reveals a preoccupation with the specific and defining boundaries of what it has always meant to be physically, commonly human. The prologue is about the transgression of those boundaries, and other, inhuman ones. It is about the sending into orbit of an artificial satellite around the earth, an action that at once challenges our temporal and spatial location in an infinite universe. The satellite, or the language Arendt uses in presenting us with the image of the satellite, emphasizes our known, shared existence as beings circumscribed by the temporal context of our common natality and mortality, located upon "this fragile earth, our island home."[4]

Further on in *The Human Condition*, and elsewhere, Arendt writes about the connection between natality and the political act of founding or making a new beginning: natality as freedom. For the most part, she carefully distinguishes the concept of natality from the labor of giving birth.[5] However, even a reader who would adamantly oppose a gynocentric, resolutely embodied interpretation of natality must be struck by the premise enunciated in the prologue: that all political meaning and possibility is founded on our earthly, natal existence.[6] If the political concept of natality is, for Arendt, not really equated with the physiological fact of birth, the prologue establishes that the concept and the fact are nonetheless fundamentally linked. Political subjects are the founders of political beginnings, but such subjects are themselves always also birthed, physical beings.[7]

The first paragraph of the prologue (quoted above) is also the first paragraph of the larger text of *The Human Condition*. There is no other preface, no acknowledgments. Although it is rather stunningly Heideggerian in its poetic evocation of technological intrusion on the harmony of the natural landscape,[8] it is more than that. In this case, the natural landscape is evoked but also given sexual definition; the transgression is upon space, time, and sexuality / gender.

This technological transgression against a gendered natality is stated in the first line. Specifically located in time (the first phrase is a date, "In 1957," which provides some kind of temporal placement), the contradiction within the nominative phrase signals a cultural alienation perhaps more profound than any remarked upon in Heidegger's writings. The alienation of modern culture from nature by technology is a recognizable contemporary philosophical problem. But Arendt, in 1958, writes of "an earth-born object made by man," an object that cannot but be an abomination, since it is made by the masculine *homo faber* (man-the-maker) and born (of the feminine earth) and yet avoids natality. This object of unnatural origin inserts itself not among human bodies, but among celestial ones.[9]

In describing the satellite as artificial and "man-made" rather than naturally occurring or natally engendered, Arendt emphasizes the violation of gender-specific difference and human embodiment. The satellite is an object, born of the earth and made by man, that intrudes itself among the most perfect of natural bodies: those that are celestial, heavenly, and sublime. At once, the human, the godly, the earthly, and the celestial are all confused by the confrontation between natality and artifice, as though creativity suddenly tempted chaos. It is as though, for Arendt, the satellite's successful orbit represents the ultimate combination of threats against a natural, known ordering.

In all likelihood, Arendt herself considered "man" a generic term for humankind, rather than a specifically masculine referent. But by so thoroughly emphasizing the gender-specific aspects of the satellite's origin and identity, she brings the issue of embodied gendered difference to the foreground of her description of the satellite as an artificial intruder among natural bodies and natural orders. In this opening paragraph of *The Human Condition*, she immediately involves the issues of gendered identities and the construction of the body itself in the beginnings of her own political narrative.

The next sentence of the opening paragraph emphasizes our mortality, the finite time that we, as humans, have for our creations and experience, as opposed to the undifferentiated revolutions of a changeless eternity. The satellite, man-made, is not eternal. It can move for us in spheres we could never dream of reaching, but its reception among the sublime company is indeed tentative; made by mortals, it is itself neither eternal nor natural. But it is not subject to natality; man-made, it cannot begin, and so it is fundamentally apolitical. This surrogate evasion of natality, however, is political, in that it threatens our earthly worldliness, our human condition of creative physicality that is also the necessary condition for politics.

Arendt is Heideggerian enough to recognize that a described image can perhaps most completely present our world to us, and also that the human world is grounded in the natural earth.[10] This Heideggerian understanding of the intersecting relationship between earth and world enables Arendt to question any enunciated wish to sever our earthly ties; she cannot help but understand such a wish as also putting in jeopardy our ability to create and maintain a world for ourselves. Without explicitly stating the philosophical connection between earth and world, Arendt, in the prologue's second paragraph, points out how curious were the emotions surrounding this technological triumph. As mistaken as she might have felt it to be for modernity to have responded to the event by glorying in the technological prowess and domination of the natural order,[11] she presents as more disturbing still the response that came soon after: "relief about the first 'step toward escape from man's imprisonment to the earth'" (HC, 1). This expressed desire to achieve, through technology, an escape from our naturally located human condition resonates for Arendt as a desire to transcend one of the few facts that all humanity shares: that we are all earthly creatures. To wish to escape the earth is also to wish to be alienated from the only world we know (together), and it is in this sense that Arendt calls the expression of such sentiments "strange," "extraordinary," indeed, almost perverse (HC, 1). To transcend this fact of our earthliness is to transcend one of the few binding features of our plurality, and therefore also to subsume our worldliness, and to disregard the political. To declare, as did "one of Russia's greatest scientists: 'Mankind will not remain bound to the earth forever'" (HC, 1) is to wish that we could leave the burden of our physical bodies behind, and soar like the Platonists to the realm of the Truth. Arendt, whose polis may be a bit too ideal for historical accuracy, nonetheless prefers a worldly public space open to political actors to a utopia supervised by philosopher kings.[12]

This (political) escapism from earthly and worldly experience is apparently the attempted evasion of spatial and temporal location. But Arendt's language describes a modern desire to escape from the physical body's gendered specificity. In the first line of the prologue, she identifies the earth with the feminine and natality ("earth-born" versus "man-made"). She goes on to describe the attempt to escape from "the earth as a prison for men's bodies" (HC, 2) in terms of a rebellion against the body of the feminine, the symbolic mother. She writes, "Should the emancipation and secularization of the modern age, which began with a turning away, not necessarily from God, but from a god who was the Father of men in heaven, end with an even more fateful repudiation of an earth who was the Mother of all living creatures under the sky?" (HC, 2).

8

Rebellion against the law of the Father can occur as a recognizable flaunting of language and order. Repudiation of the body of the Mother, however, is also repudiation of the body of the self, if that self can be said to exist. It would seem, without being essentialist, that the minimal coherence necessary to contour the fragments of the self would be the given (physical) metabolism of a body; yet in Arendt's text, the body is itself defined through its shifting construction in the narrative. Nonetheless, an attempt to escape the body threatens the premise of self, narrative, and politics. The body contours the self, but the definitions of the body are variously constructed in narratives, and those narratives—and the body that is present in them—shape the discursive world of politics. The attempt to escape the body, then, is a political issue: the repudiation of all known and all possible human experience.

This concern that a rejection of humanity's shared spatial and temporal location is also a rejection of embodied gendered difference, not in favor of a less sexually prescribed set of relations, but in order to reject and abandon the gendered and specifically feminine body, extends throughout the opening paragraphs of the prologue's description of alienation. An artificial body trespasses among celestial ones, its flight signaling the possibility of escape from the (feminine) body of the natural earth, rather than merely a (masculine or asexual) technical mastery. Arendt writes that "the earth is the very quintessence of the human condition" (*HC*, 2), and escape from that condition may also become exile from the humanly created world. Artifice, which creates the world, now threatens to undermine its construction out of the earth: just as technology offers to relieve us of the only common home we know, it teases the other shared limits of our physicality, the supposed facts of birth and death:

> For some time now, a great many scientific endeavors have been directed toward making life also "artificial," toward cutting the last tie through which even man belongs among the children of nature. It is the same desire to escape from imprisonment to the earth that is manifest in the attempt to create life in a test tube, in the desire to mix "frozen germ plasm from people of demonstrated ability under the microscope to produce superior human beings" and "to alter [their] size, shape, and function"; and the wish to escape the human condition, I suspect, also underlies the hope to extend man's life-span far beyond the hundred-year limit.
> (*HC*, 2)

Hannah Arendt, in 1958, describes the loss of the mother's body and the parental function as being at least as important as the extension of the limit of mortality. Although tampered with, a natural finitude remains; but it is the threatened technological rejection of natality, of natural, bodily, gendered beginnings, that Arendt identifies as "a political question of the first order" that "can hardly be left to the decision of professional scientists and professional politicians" (*HC*, 3), groups that would be implicitly, predominantly, male.

9

This threat to the known physical body, which is also a threat to worldly, political beginnings, presents itself initially as a lack of language. Unlike psychoanalytic interpretations in which lack and loss of the (mother's) body allows for language, Arendt describes a lack and loss of language that would accomplish the loss of the defined and delimited body. Technology is almost no longer accessible to language, in that "we, who are earth-bound creatures and have begun to act as though we were dwellers of the universe, will forever be unable to understand, that is, to think and speak about the things which nonetheless we are able to do" (*HC*, 3).[13]

This lack of language is perhaps better understood by Arendt as the loss of the ability to narrate, to tell stories. It is therefore also the loss of the ability to create meaning and to act or think politically:

> Wherever the relevance of speech is at stake, matters become political by definition, for speech is what makes man a political being. . . . Men in the plural, that is, men in so far as they live and move and act in this world, can experience meaningfulness only because they can talk with and make sense to each other and themselves.
>
> (*HC*, 3–4)

Thus, the possibility of technology's outdistancing (political) discourse suggests a future situation such that we will be able to do things for which we have no description, and which cannot therefore truly be understood as action, although we transform and abandon world, earth, and body.[14] It is a vortex of progress, in which the fate of meaningful language and the fate of the body are inextricably linked.

Conversely, Arendt worries in the prologue that a body that has already been separated from meaningfulness will suddenly become overwhelmingly prominent. Although its opening pages discuss the threatened loss of the laboring, gendered, physical body and its political potentials, the last section of the prologue briefly predicts a society in which the laboring body has been severed from its labor but has gained integration in nothing else. Automation, in 1958, seems to offer relief from the burden of productive and reproductive necessity: mass escape from a condition of toil. But again, this probable escape from the presence of bodily necessity implies a change in the understood human earthly and worldly condition we may not care to anticipate. This technical evasion of the body's use does not necessitate a concomitant emphasis on the body's pleasure or the mind's activity; in fact, Arendt fears quite the opposite:

> It is a society of laborers which is about to be liberated from the fetters of labor, and this society does no longer know of those other higher and more meaningful activities for the sake of which this freedom would deserve to be won. . . . What we are confronted with is the pro–spect of a society of laborers without labor, that is, without the only activity left to them.
>
> (*HC*, 5)[15]

Technological usurpation of the body's function thus threatens, if not loss of the body, then loss of the body's meaningfulness and perhaps also of meaningfulness *per se*.

Yet loss of the body's function also presents the prospect of a remnant physicality that is both aimless and useless. This body, freed from the constraints of productive or reproductive labor, could no longer be relegated to the hiddenness of the private realm, the realm of necessity, since the conditions of human necessity would have been separated from the work of the body. Having no need to remain hidden in privacy, the formerly laboring body would intrude upon the public, the realm of discourse, action, and self-disclosure among peers. But equals are not necessarily peers, and modern mass culture having reduced peers to equals, Arendt seems to fear that the intrusion of the relieved, formerly laboring but now meaningless body upon the political space would destroy political possibility. This aimless physical appearance in the public space would disrupt the fluent theatrical quality Arendt values in political action and discourse. It is the body's meaningfulness that provides for natality, language, and politics. The severing of worldly meaning from the earthly physicality of the human condition doubly threatens worldliness: with the loss of the physical ability meaningfully to begin anew, and with the overwhelming of the possibility for meaningfulness with sheer physical presence. Or so it would seem.

In response to the "preoccupations and perplexities" (*HC*, 5) introduced in the prologue, Arendt presents the rest of her text. She proposes "to think what we are doing," and she writes that because she wants to limit her discussion to those activities that are most generally accessible, she will not examine thinking, but will limit herself to a discussion of the (bodily) activities of labor, work, and action (*HC*, 5). She wants, then, to think and write about the present and historical worldly role of the body, without specifically discussing either the body or the mind. She writes that she will confine herself "to an analysis of those general human capacities which grow out of the human condition and are permanent, that is, which cannot be inextricably lost so long as the human condition itself is not changed" (*HC*, 6). Yet her entire prologue has warned of the imminent loss of the permanence of the human condition. In other words, she intends to think about the condition of our active embodiment, at a moment when the presupposition of our embodiment, which is the condition of our activity and our thinking, is no longer so easily presumed.

Within the structure of the larger text, embodiment seems to play a different role. Since the categories of labor, work, and action are hierarchically structured, Arendt's privileging of political action, which is the category traditionally reserved for an elite class of propertied male citizens, seems also to indicate an accompanying privileging of that embodied class of masculine actors. This may or may not be the case; our concern here, however, has been to recognize the foundational role embodiment, in its various aspects and representations, takes throughout and in relation to the narrative construction of this political text.

For Arendt, mortality and natality bracket the human condition of plurality and worldly being. Natality she links with action and beginning(*HC*, 9), mortality with the ability to end and complete or tell a life-story (*HC*, 19). These physical facts, in their fundamental significance, provide for all the rest of our activities and Arendt's theoretical conceptualizations. Despite this, it would seem that an overt appreciation for the necessary human condition of embodiment is absent from the rest of the book.

This apparent exclusion of the emphatically physical body from the structure of Arendt's political discourse stems from the character of the distinction she makes between public and private. Although *The Human Condition* is an analysis of labor, work, and action, it is also a discussion of presocial forms of productive, cultural, and political relations. Society, for Arendt, is that strange and modern amalgamation of the public and the private that destroys the virtues of both.[16] Society publicly valorizes the economic calculations that were hidden in the household; in doing so, it subverts the protected, private sphere of intimacy and intimate bodily functions, and also the contained public space of self-disclosure and the embodied stories of political action. More than any of her other writings, *The Human Condition* is a study of the supposedly ideal separation between public and private, a separation she identifies as having existed in the classical polis, before society, a mistranslation by the Romans (*HC*, 23), could even be said to exist.

The historical problematic of such clear distinctions, even in classical Athens, will be addressed in the last chapter. For the moment, it is worth inquiring into what Arendt wishes to gain from her conceptual discriminations: the public, the sphere of discourse and action, becomes an ideal space of transcendent self-disclosure.[17] Released within that space from the household confines of cramped necessity and anonymous bodily function, the political actor is free to represent himself, to himself and others. He can create for himself an appearance and a role, stepping beyond the private limits of simple human physical existence. This quality of a defined space of transcendental freedom is so remarkable, and so important for Arendt, that it would almost seem to justify any necessary bodily exclusion. But Arendt creates this possibility of a transcendental political freedom by specifically excluding that which she considers to be antipolitical: not just physical necessity, but the force and violence of household despotism, which she associates with the urgencies of the body.

But is free, enacted agency necessarily restricted only to those who can emancipate themselves from the demands of the body? Arendt proffers an understanding of political enactment that depends on certain exclusions. Nonetheless, she premises even this highly restricted version of political agency on an understanding of the political as fundamentally embodied, although some bodies are apparently more privileged, more performative, and less essentialized than others. Arendt presumes that these embodied political actors can achieve their agency only within the restricted space of a defined political sphere. But is this necessarily so? Can others, whose bodies have been perceived to be more defining of their roles, also enact themselves as agents? And if so, does their enactment not challenge the construction of their supposedly determinate identity, and the fixed borders of the political sphere itself?

Two.
The Social
Question

If *The Human Condition* is premised on human embodiment, it is in *On Revolution* that physical bodies directly confront the political. Except for the prologue, most of *The Human Condition* maintains a firm distinction between the private realm of physical necessity (and the bodies that mitigate it), and the public realm of free political subjects. Much of Arendt's attraction to the classical model seems to be based on the way it provides matter-of-fact closure to certain particularly vexing modern topics, like gender and class.[1] But in *On Revolution* she acknowledges that modern politics has been complicated by these very issues, and she makes room in her own narrative for what she calls "The Social Question." If the prologue of *The Human Condition* provides an intriguing counterweight to the development of the book proper, *On Revolution*'s chapter "The Social Question" provides a whole alternative discourse through which to approach the rest of her work.

To deconstruct Arendt's argument about the impossible relationship between the social and the political, it is necessary to attend to the way her metaphors and tangents pull against her narrative structure. *On Revolution* is an explication of a political possibility that is ever proffered and ever lost: the pure politics of (revolutionary) speech and action. Arendt bemoans the "lost treasure" of a revolutionary politics distracted by the concerns of the body, but in her own work this distraction becomes an opportunity for a remarkable discussion on the politics of theatrical representation. Most of this is contained in chapter 2, "The Social Question," although some of her statements about social intrusions into political practice spill over the chapter borders she sets for herself. Like the all-too-present gendered and impoverished physical bodies she accuses of disrupting the possibility of pure political practice, the chapter on "The Social Question" interrupts the book's evolving narrative of revolution as founding. Arendt's interpretations of the political roles of compassion, hypocrisy, and the mask are all developed around and in this one chapter, and it is on this relationship in her text between (bodily) representation and (political) writing that I concentrate my discussion of *On Revolution*.

I focus on two related aspects: Arendt's representation of an abject body emerging into the political space and political attention, and her ensuing discussion of representation as it is variously enacted and recognized. In this chapter I examine how Arendt describes the essentialist body of physical necessity breaking through the secure borders of the political space, a breaking through she conceives of as a breaking down of all possibilities for (political) identity, freedom, and action. The threat this body poses to the defined borders of the political is the threat of the abject; in this discussion I rely particularly on Julia Kristeva's *Powers of Horror: An Essay on Abjection*.[2] In chapter 3 I explore the significance of the subjects that Arendt is prompted to address in her own discussion of the body and the social question, especially the political significance of artifice, (self-) representation, and the mask. By referring to Joan Riviere's "Womanliness as a Masquerade," I extend Arendt's discussion of the representation of (political) truth through the role and the mask back to a differentiated discussion of the representation of the feminine through (public) masquerade. Together, these two chapters provide a deep reworking of Arendt's material on the relationship between embodied identity and political practice, and make that material newly accessible to an alternate discourse of political agency and social identity as masquerade.

ON REVOLUTION: THE VIOLENCE OF BEGINNINGS

On Revolution is one of the most typically Arendtian texts, in that it is marked by careful and provocative conceptual distinctions. It is not, however, as elegantly structured by them as are many of her other texts. Rather, Arendt develops her argument of what revolution is, in contradistinction to what it is not, as a slow elaboration of possibility and failed attempt. The book is a comparative analysis of two revolutions: the American and the French. One revolution is pure, one corrupted. In Arendt's presentation, the American Revolution is apparently successful because it remains purely political, while the French Revolution fails as a political endeavor because it is intruded upon by the social question: the miserable body and its immediate needs.[3] But if the French Revolution is distracted from its pure political purpose by social issues, so is Arendt's text. From its first pages, *On Revolution* complicates any pure political practice, or pure political narrative, by introducing the problem of bodies.

On Revolution begins with an introduction titled "War and Revolution." As in the prologue to *The Human Condition*, Arendt begins this historical project with an account of contemporary crisis; she locates the origin of her argument in the present, before she removes it to the past. Again the contemporary crisis is metaphysical and physical—a crisis of political ideology brought on by the technologically achieved possibility of total human destruction. But if *The Human Condition* develops from its prologue into a political meditation on an ideally disciplined past, *On Revolution* is less serene. An analysis of modern politics cannot avoid violence.

In the very first paragraph of the book, Arendt announces that the twentieth-century erosion of ideology has resulted in a political preoccupation with freedom achieved through war and revolution. Thus, violence has become the predominant practice of modern politics (*OR*, 11). Nonetheless, Arendt still insists that violence is inherently destabilizing, a shaky beginning for any truly political thought or practice:

> Yet, however needful it may be to distinguish in theory and practice between war and revolution despite their close interrelatedness, we must not fail to note that the mere fact that revolutions and wars are not even conceivable outside the domain of violence is enough to set them both apart from all other political phenomena. It would be difficult to deny that one of the reasons why wars have turned so easily into revolutions and why revolutions have shown this ominous inclination to unleash wars is that violence is a kind of common denominator for both.
> (*OR*, 18)

Although she has asserted the centrality of war and revolution as contemporary political issues, Arendt still tries to distinguish between an Aristotelian politics of speech and action, a politics that is definingly human, and the fundamentally antipolitical mute force of violence:

> Where violence rules absolutely, as for instance in the concentration camps of totalitarian regimes, not only the laws—*les lois se taisant*, as the French Revolution phrased it—but everything and everybody must fall silent. It is because of this silence that violence is a marginal phenomenon in the political realm; for man, to the extent that he is a political being, is endowed with the power of speech. . . . The point here is that violence itself is incapable of speech, and not merely that speech is helpless when confronted with violence.
> (*OR*, 18–19)[4]

Despite the confusions of violence and politics that inevitably occur in any discussion of war and revolution, Arendt attempts from her own text's beginning (itself marked off as an introduction) to keep (bodily) violence separate from (the discourse of) the political.

This is, however, impossible, and the introduction concludes with the problem of beginning, and the violent origins of political and narrative beginnings. Whereas in the prologue to *The Human Condition* beginning was associated with a feminine, earthly body and with natality, in the introduction to *On Revolution* beginning is associated with violence, fratricide, and narrative. This is a negative, explicitly masculine metaphor of beginning[5]:

> . . . Cain slew Abel, and Romulus slew Remus; violence was the beginning, and, by the same token, no beginning could be made without using violence, without violating. . . . The tale spoke clearly: whatever brotherhood human beings may be capable of has grown out of fratricide, whatever political organization men may have achieved has its origins in crime.
> (*OR*, 20)[6]

Although Arendt will, immediately after the introductory discussion of violence, begin to emphasize the political continuity inherent in any successful revolution, that emphasis presupposes a violent origin that shadows any further discussion. In *On Revolution*, narrative beginning is introduced as already compromised, and violence is acknowledged to accompany, and even to engender, the political endeavor. Arendt will attempt to limit its appearance in her text, but it will appear nonetheless.

After the introduction, Arendt's text is ordered into six chapters, which build an argument of deftly accumulating comparisons. Chapter 1, "The Meaning of Revolution," formally begins the text with an emphasis on revolution as political beginning rather than mere restoration or civil strife. Chapter 2, "The Social Question," considers social and political realities, and compares those that determined the French Revolution to the political intentions of the American Revolution, which is characterized in chapter 3, "The Pursuit of Happiness." Chapters 4, "Foundation I: *Constitutio Libertatis*," and 5, "Foundation II: *Novus Ordo Saeclorum*," compare the distinct practices of liberation and foundation. The book culminates in chapter 6, "The Revolutionary Tradition and Its Lost Treasure," in which Arendt mourns the evanescent appearances of democratic, participatory, political spaces in the postrevolutionary situation: the councils, *soviets*, and assemblies that inevitably spring up after a revolutionary liberation, and are almost as inevitably put down in the process of founding the new state.

In Arendt's conception of political practice and identity, the body as such, with its immediate physical needs and attendant social demands, is to be kept hidden in the dark shelter of the private realm, away from the public gaze. Only those who have freed themselves from the necessity of the body's demands, and from the apparent specificity of their embodied identity, are fit to enter the public world of political practice. Yet when this forbidden body, the body of those whose identity seems physically defined rather than freely constructed, finally makes its appearance in the political realm, it does so violently. Its self-presentation is a shock to a whole tradition of political conceptualizing. This description, which intrudes itself into the discussion of rebellion and revolution in chapter 1, "The Meaning of Revolution," is a harbinger of the bodily intrusion that will be more fully discussed in chapter 2, "The Social Question":

> Behind these words, we still can see and hear the multitude on their march, how they burst into the streets of Paris.... And this multitude, appearing for the first time in broad daylight, was actually the multitude of the poor and downtrodden, who every century before had hidden in darkness and shame.... [So that] the public realm—reserved, as far as memory could reach, to those who *were* free, namely carefree of all worries that are connected with life's necessity, with bodily needs—should offer its space and its light to this immense majority who are not free because they are driven by daily needs.
> (*OR*, 48)

Using a trope that will become common in her description of the socially marked body's intensely physical intrusion into the political space, Arendt describes the masses as having "burst" into the street and the light of day. Reading this passage, one would almost believe that "the poor and downtrodden, who . . . had hidden in darkness and shame" had previously been confined to the cellars, perhaps creeping out only occasionally to scavenge in the dead of night. Arendt's verb is transitive without being passive: the poor and downtrodden are not hidden by others who are ashamed of them; they hide themselves because, seemingly, they are themselves ashamed. One would think that no poor person had ever been seen in Paris on the street at midday. Arendt seems to assert that indeed none ever had; despite whatever daily physical presence they may have had, the poor had never been seen as political actors, until they "burst" into the street and onto the scene.[7]

The violence Arendt ascribes to the multitude's entering into the political scene is specific to her writing, but the descriptions of darkness and shame are not. Arendt emphasizes the violence of the undeniable claim poverty made on politics, but her characterization of poverty as having previously been hidden and shameful is remarkably like John Adams's, which she directly quotes a bit later:

"The poor man's conscience is clear, yet he is ashamed. . . . He feels himself out of the sight of others, groping in the dark. Mankind takes no notice of him. He rambles and wanders unheeded. In the midst of a crowd, at church, in the market . . . he is in as much obscurity as he would be in a garret or a cellar. He is not disapproved, censured, or reproached; *he is only not seen*. . . .

(John Adams, quoted in *OR*, 69)

For Adams also, the poor are not political, not public, and therefore not seen. The difference is that in Adams's vision, the invisible poor remain in their invisible place. For Arendt, the poor have indeed become dramatically visible, but their appearance threatens the structure of politics and of (political) performance.

This violent entrance is not merely that of a new group of actors. In Arendt's analysis, the bursting of the masses into the free space of the political (a space defined as free because it is cleared of social necessity and social demands) is a transgression of elemental boundaries. It is as though the entire theatrical metaphor of the political (the metaphor of actors appearing within a context dedicated to discourse rather than physical obligation—a metaphor to which Arendt is extremely attached) were in danger of losing its meaning. In this case, it is not the audience who have rushed the stage, spectators whose participation might be disruptive but informed; rather, it is as though the cleaning staff of a theater, the invisible selves who sweep up refuse, had with desperate insolence intruded their economic demands into the middle of the drama. If they refuse to retreat back into the darkness with their needs and obligations, pure (political) performance as such cannot go on.

For Arendt, this bursting in of the masses depoliticizes revolution; it abolishes the political context, and political space, in which men can be free among themselves. Instead they are overwhelmed by a natural force: "The various metaphors in which the revolution is seen not as the work of men but as an irresistible process, the metaphors of stream and torrent and current, were still coined by the actors themselves, who, however drunk they might have become with the wine of freedom in the abstract, clearly no longer believed they were free agents" (OR, 49). What bursts back into the public space with the multitude is precisely that from which the political self originally sought to distinguish itself: the overwhelming presence of the natural and necessary body. This body, by its appearance, transforms the political into the social, a new, mixed category within which private needs become matters of public policy.[8] Within Arendt's own narrative, this metaphor of the body's demanding intrusion upon politics is paralleled by the intrusion of her own compelling reflections on "The Social Question" into her discussion of revolution as liberation and founding.

"THE SOCIAL QUESTION": ABJECTION

In chapter 2, "The Social Question," Arendt enters fully into a discussion of the threat the body poses to revolution and politics. The organic process of our physical existence is now set in opposition to our ability to act: the body's necessity becomes historical necessity. This is from the first page of chapter 2: "The less we are doing ourselves, the less active we are, the more forcefully will this biological process assert itself, impose its inherent necessity upon us, and overawe us with the fateful automatism of sheer happening that underlies all human history" (OR, 59).

Within this same first paragraph, Arendt goes on to link "the image of the revolving, lawful, and necessary motion of the heavenly bodies" with the image of "the poor, driven by the needs of their bodies, (who) burst on to the scene of the French revolution" (OR, 59). The astronomical metaphor that in The Human Condition linked the natality of founding to the natality of the body is now used to imply that (human) bodies are a (transgressive) law unto themselves. Human action used to be justified by reference to heavenly necessity; in the modern age, according to Arendt, bodily necessity becomes the motivation, and thus the substitute, for human action.

It is not just that physical needs and the problem of class become political issues. The problem is that they carry an emotional as well as a physical necessity, and once they have been acknowledged they cannot be denied. Reduced to its needs, the body cannot rise above them, and the demands of physical necessity replace the luxury of political choice; questions of food and shelter, questions of social welfare, replace a discourse of self-determination. Not only for the individual citizen, but for the entire tradition of conscious human action and history, the body poses an immanent threat. This body is abject.

Arendt uses this term very briefly, as a description of a condition of acute and downtrodden misery. But in her writing, the miserably abject creatures who confront the political with the social question(s) do so with a notable degree of violence, and the threat they pose seems much more profound than merely an appeal to charity. For Arendt, the abject poor are the prisoners of their bodies, and the threat they bring to the political realm is that of the abjected body's claim to recognition.

Arendt writes that what is abject is poverty: "Poverty is more than deprivation, it is a state of constant want and acute misery whose ignominy consists in its dehumanizing force; poverty is abject because it puts men under the absolute dictate of necessity as all men know it from their most intimate experience and outside all speculation" (*OR*, 60).[9] Poverty is dehumanizing because it makes the body's immediate needs more absolute than any other human capacity. In Arendt's reading, poverty is the subjugation of human creative possibility to human physical necessity. Although she obviously intends to use "men" in the generic sense for human, the question of whether women can ever escape the condition of abjection is here rather moot. To be abject is to be servile, degraded, cast down; it is also to be cast off, cast out, rejected. It is by attending to these latter meanings of abjection that we may become better able to recognize the deep familiarity of the body's threat, which Arendt assigns to poverty. For Arendt, poverty is not merely material want or lack; it is a state of subjugation to the most immediate forms of necessity and desire, of being without subjective capability. The abject poor can conceive of neither freedom nor individuality; they are so oppressed by the immediacy of their own bodies that they seem almost to be without language, and therefore, for Arendt, without any political capacity.

Why is Arendt so vehement? Others have commented on her rather extraordinarily negative description of the "social" and the extent to which it is associated with the maternal feminine.[10] In reading Arendt's description of abject poverty, I was struck by the resonances between Arendt's language, and the vehemence behind it, and Julia Kristeva's analysis of bodily abjection in *Powers of Horror*. Once Kristeva's explication of abjection is read back into Arendt's discussion of those who are abject, the intensity of Arendt's analysis becomes not eccentric but politically profound.

ABJECTION: KRISTEVA

In *Powers of Horror*, Julia Kristeva distinguishes the abject from both the subject and the object, and her discussion helps to clarify the apparently inordinate vehemence of Arendt's writing. The threat of the abject, according to Kristeva, is precisely that threat of regression into the overwhelming presence of the maternal that Hanna Pitkin has linked to Arendt's description of the social. Kristeva's work does not deal with Arendt, but she does deal deeply with the peculiar nature of the inescapable but repressible threat the immanent physical body presents to the constructed individual self. According to Kristeva, the abject is that which constitutes and opposes the self, that which most confounds the self's boundaries. This is a psychoanalytic threat, not a political one:

> There looms, within abjection, one of those violent, dark revolts of being, directed against a threat that seems to emanate from an exorbitant outside or inside, ejected beyond the scope of the possible, the tolerable, the thinkable.... Unflaggingly, like an inescapable boomerang, a vortex of summons and repulsion places the one haunted by it literally beside himself.
>
> (Kristeva, *Powers of Horror,* 1)[11]

Drawing on Lacanian psychoanalytic theory, Kristeva poses the dynamic of abjection as the acknowledgment that there are no pure boundaries. In Arendt's language, Kristeva is telling us that from our (contemporary) perspective the public and the private really have (always) been merged into the social.

For Kristeva, the abject is that which, although intimately a part of early experience, must be rejected so that the self can establish the borders of its unified subjectivity. This rejection (abjection) of certain aspects of physical immediacy is the act that establishes subjective identity, but this act also establishes that identity as a prohibition, and as lacking an earlier bodily continuity. The subjective self, therefore, is always haunted by the possible return of the abject that was a part of presubjective experience. This threatened return, which would dissolve the self into undifferentiable physicality, is both desired and feared.[12]

This self-splitting, a self-abjection, is the quality that makes abjection such a threat. Abjection contradicts the self's claim to its own unity and knowledge, but this contradiction is so profound precisely because it emerges from the gestures with which the self attempts to assert such a claim: "I expel *myself,* I spit *myself* out, I abject *myself* within the same motion through which 'I' claim to establish *myself*" (3). Abjection confuses the bounds between the subject and the object; it blurs the usually clear distinction between the self and the other that constitutes identity. But abjection does not provide a reconciliation of meaning. Instead, the abject is that which seems to confound the possibility of meaning, its presence threatening a chaos that must be withheld:

> The abject has only one quality of the object—that of being opposed to *I.* If the object, however, through its opposition, settles me within the fragile texture of a desire for meaning, which, as a matter of fact, makes me ceaselessly and infinitely homologous to it, what is *abject,* on the contrary, the jettisoned object, is radically excluded and draws me toward the place where meaning collapses. ... And yet, from its place of banishment, the abject does not cease challenging its master.
> (1–2)

The self abjects that which is most necessarily inescapable and rejected: the bodily reminders of physical dependence and necessity. Kristeva writes of the two distinct threats the abject poses to the self's free agency:

The abject would thus be the "object" of primal repression. . . . . The abject confronts us, on the one hand, with those fragile states where man strays on the territories of the *animal*. Thus, by way of abjection, primitive societies have marked out a precise area of their culture in order to remove it from the threatening world of animals or animalism, which were imagined as representatives of sex and death.
(12–13)

In order to attain language and culture, the (human) self must differentiate from the (animal) body. Instead of politics and civilization, however, the abject would drag us back into bestiality.

This version of the abject would seem to correspond with Arendt's descriptions of the dehumanizing force of overwhelming bodily necessity, a necessity without language or law. When, in Arendt's text, those subjugated by this necessity finally appear in the political space, they are visible but they do not speak. They are as mute and demanding as animals, and their mere presence expresses their needs and their total lack of regard for the niceties of political distinctions.

The second threat the abject presents to the distinctly human self and body involves gender. After undermining the supposedly clear separation of human and animal nature, the abject draws us back to a confusion of the boundaries between the self and the mother's body. The abject thus also represents a threat to natality as clearly defined human beginning, a blurring of the moment of origin and identity: "The abject confronts us, on the one hand, and this time within our personal archeology, with our earliest attempt to release the hold of *maternal* entity even before existing outside her, thanks to the autonomy of language" (13). Unlike Arendt, Kristeva emphasizes the enveloping power of the maternal, which both engenders us and precedes a separation of (our)self and other at the earliest conscious stage.[13] In Arendt's writing the abject poor are without political language or law, but in Kristeva's text the abject is beyond the paternal law and language. Kristeva is relying here on a Lacanian model of psychoanalytic development.[14] Before language and the symbolic, linked with the father / the law, intrude a third party into the mother-child dyad, the symmetry of that relationship obscures any absolute claim to a proper division between two physical bodies as separate selves.

This confusion of the self with an animal or maternal body generates a deep unease relative to that self's ability to function productively or reproductively as a free adult. This confusion is what Arendt sees the wretched multitude as having brought with them when they burst upon the political scene. The abject subverts the political possibility of natality, so that the metaphor of political beginning as birth must be explicitly refused: "When they appeared on the scene of politics, necessity appeared with them, and the result was that the power of the old regime became impotent and the new republic was stillborn; freedom had to be surrendered to necessity, to the urgency of the life process itself" (*OR*, 60). Once the abjected body is reintroduced into the realm of the public and political self, the possibilities for freedom and power (which for Arendt are products of the shared experience of participatory action) recede, but this is described in terms of sexual and reproductive failure. Faced with the return of the abjected body (whether represented by the miserable poor, or representative of the bestial or maternal body), the self can neither sustain its creative attempts nor bring them to fruition. It becomes impotent, and the future stillborn.[15]

Kristeva's theorization of the abject allows us to recognize that the threat Arendt perceives in the abject poor is a familiar psychoanalytic construct given political application. By emphasizing the threat of the abject, Arendt highlights the traditional problem of marking the boundaries of citizenship and political participation: the determination of which bodies, already present in the body politic, are to be defined as external to it.[16] The difficulty here is that these (politically excluded) bodies are not just physically present, they are themselves necessary. No state can function without women, or without workers. The problem of identity, whether political or personal, is that boundaries must be defined, but they must be defined precisely because no complete separation is possible. The need to distinguish differences arises from the recognition of similarities.

Arendt's writing on the social question seems idiosyncratic in the extreme until read in conjunction with Kristeva's writing on abjection. Kristeva's main figure is Louis-Ferdinand Céline, the early twentieth-century French antisemite. But the disapproval, as much aesthetic as political, with which Arendt regards the miserable poor is comparable to the disgust with which Céline regards European Jewry. These are the excluded ones whose very presence seems to insult the claims to identity made by the state or the nation, claims that are themselves premised on their own violability. The abject always threatens a return because its separation is always somewhat hypothetical. As Arendt acknowledges at the beginning of *On Revolution*, the founding of a political project, the natality of beginnings, is almost always also a violent disavowal of other claims.

THE ABJECT RETURNS: SLAVERY

Arendt characterizes the political beginnings of modern Europe, and especially the French Revolution, as corrupted by the bursting in of the newly visible but abject poor. She characterizes the American Revolution as another story, and a supplement: America as having the physical abundance and narrative political exuberance the Old World lacks.[17] For those like John Adams in America, the poor remain abject but supposedly invisible, postponing the violence of a confrontation with the social question until some later date. This role will be undermined, however, when Arendt reintroduces the local supplement to America's glorious national history: the fact of black slavery in the United States.

In "The Social Question," while dealing with the American Revolution, Arendt rather uncomfortably acknowledges the injustice of a politics of bodily exclusion while she acclaims the success of its (limited) political practice. In Arendt's terms, the American Revolution is a political success because it excludes the social question of poverty, which it is able to do because "the predicament of poverty was absent from the American scene" (OR, 68). But she also acknowledges that despite America's happy social complacency, "the absence of the social question from the American scene was, after all, quite deceptive, and . . . abject and degrading misery was present everywhere in the form of slavery and Negro labour" (OR, 70).

In this text, the fact of slavery in America presents a nearly unresolvable contradiction: political beginning and narrative are always inseparable from bodily violation; the political always either involves or represses the social. Arendt has presented the American Revolution as politically successful because its actors kept to political issues and avoided social questions. Yet she must also acknowledge that their avoidance was the result, not of easy circumstances, but of forceful rejection and repression, and that the American Revolutionary beginning was as uneasy as any other. In the French Revolution, the issues of material and social equality intruded themselves into political developments: the body and also the emotions became political. In the American scene, such issues were not absent but were decisively kept out of public politics. They could not, however, be kept from private awareness, although Arendt notes with some satisfaction that the American revolutionaries were disturbed by this exclusion for practical, political reasons, rather than for reasons of emotion:

> For if Jefferson, and others to a lesser degree, were aware of the primordial crime upon which the fabric of American society rested, if they "trembled when [they] thought that God is just" (Jefferson), they did so because they were convinced of the incompatibility of the institution of slavery with the foundation of freedom, not because they were moved by pity or a feeling of solidarity with their fellow men.
> (OR, 71)

In America, the abject was knowingly kept outside the space of political appearance, which was thus temporarily cleared of the disruptive presence of the emphatically physical body. The political reality and violence of black slavery in America would not be generally admitted to be of political relevance until much later. Once the morality of race politics became a recognizable political issue, however, the secure foundations of traditional American political identity could no longer be maintained.[18]

Yet Arendt does try to maintain a realm of pure politics separate from abjected bodies and any related social issues. She does this most famously in *The Human Condition*, where the apologia for the exclusion of women and slaves from the public and political life of the *polis* is embedded in the structure of an argument about the necessary distinction between the private and the public spheres. According to the argument, this distinction must be maintained if meaningful political life is to exist. In Arendt's view, the distinctions between private and public, between labor, work, and action are all successfully maintained in the Athenian *polis*, and this view is reflected in the organization of *The Human Condition*. *On Revolution*, however, is a comparative text about success and failure, a political text into which the social more successfully and inevitably intrudes.

The apologia in *On Revolution*, unlike the one in *The Human Condition*, is neither so simple nor so easily confined to its proper sphere.[19] In *On Revolution*, the apologia occurs in the chapter "The Social Question," the textual context in which the abject intrudes itself back into the political, prompting a response. Arendt's response to this acknowledged corruption of her supposed modern American political ideal will be her discussion of compassion, hypocrisy, and the mask.

Arendt characterizes the intrusion of the social as destructive of the political, and perhaps it is, if the political is defined as exclusive of social concerns. In Arendt's terms, the American Revolution was initially politically successful precisely because the nation was without abject free labor and was able to assign the social question of slavery to the blackness of oblivion. Obviously, however, the issue is not so simple, the repression not so complete. To return for a moment to Kristeva:

> The abject is the violence of mourning for an "object" that has always already been lost. The abject shatters the wall of repression and its judgements. It takes the ego back to its source on the abominable limits from which, in order to be, the ego has broken away—it assigns it a source in the non-ego, drive, and death. Abjection is a resurrection that has gone through death (of the ego). It is an alchemy that transforms death drive into a start of life, of new significance.
> (Kristeva, *Powers of Horror*, 15)

What Arendt will name, in chapter 6, the "Lost Treasure of the Revolutionary Tradition" has always already been lost. Abjection is the denial and reminder of that loss. The acknowledgment that the American Revolution's political success was founded on the abjection of American slavery returns Arendt's discussion, in "The Social Question," to an originary point from which an alternative discourse can proceed.

Three.
The Mask and
Masquerade

This chapter is a further discussion of Arendt's chapter "The Social Question" in *On Revolution*. My preceding chapter provided a psychoanalytically informed deconstruction of the role of abjection in Arendt's writing and concluded with her acknowledgment that the abject is indeed present from the beginning of the American polity in the form of race slavery. Within the structure of her chapter, this acknowledgment of historical complicity also becomes the anchoring point for a set of discussions about political action that pull against the argument of the rest of her text. That argument is based on the split between compromised (French) and dedicated (American) revolutionary politics. But in the rest of "The Social Question," Arendt explores the possibility that all political action is by nature compromised and that the fundamental threat to political identity is not abjection but the search for a specious public authenticity. Politics is artifice, and artifice is the achievement of public life in spite of the knowledge that we are all already abject. Thus her chapter, and my discussion of it, breaks in two: first the horror of the abject, and then the possibility that politics is the public world we sustain among ourselves once we have acknowledged our own and each other's abjection.

Arendt's exploration of this possibility—that political action is always an assertion by a compromised, constructed identity—is developed through three related discussions: on *Billy Budd*, Herman Melville's political parable of violence and virtue; on hypocrisy; and on the political mask. Together these three discussions trace a provocative line of thought, but they remain incomplete as a theoretical alternative, and by the end of her chapter Arendt segues back to abjection and its imperative necessity. Yet her trajectory remains. She reaches toward an explicitly constructed version of political identity; she offers the political possibility of a persona, a public mask that artificially coheres the chaos of the private self so that self can speak forth as an authentic political actor; but then she hesitates regarding its modern application. Who wears the political mask in our contemporary world? What is its personification?

In this chapter I refer to Joan Riviere's 1929 article "Womanliness as Masquerade" to supplement these questions and Arendt's incomplete theoretical trajectory.[1] Riviere's essay, based on her own analytical practice, interprets stereotypical, seemingly inappropriate feminine behavior as a strategic masquerade, a compensatory gesture in a subtle negotiation for power. This power is both social and political, and its negotiation involves both terrains. Riviere's work displays femininity, the demarcation of the female gender, as a practice rather than an essence. Read back against Arendt's writing on (feminine) abjection, Riviere's insight reveals the women marching on Versailles to be agents mobilizing the specific construct of their gendered identity and experience for political purpose rather than simply bodies publicly proving their necessity.

Riviere's essay on feminine masquerade provides the conceptual link between Arendt's own writing on the public mask as a source of political agency and her suspicion that political action requires the transcending of any nondominant social identity. But whereas Riviere writes of a specifically feminine masquerade, I apply her theory of strategic enactment more broadly. Feminine masquerade is a masquerade of social identity; other social identities can be enacted as well. In chapter 4 I discuss Arendt's own textual masquerade through her narrative of feminine Jewish experience in *Rahel Varnhagen* and her reasons for resisting the politicization of the feminine but not the Jewish aspect of that experience. In subsequent chapters I examine her preoccupation with individuals who successfully masquerade a religious or ethnic social identity as a political strategy. But in this chapter I concentrate on tracing out Arendt's own thinking on political action as moral artifice (against a utopian ideal of natural virtue and vice) and then extending that line of thought into a theory of political action through social masquerade.

THE RETURN OF THE ABJECT / ALTERNATIVE BEGINNINGS

When Arendt acknowledges that abjection is present from the beginning of the American polity in the form of race slavery, she also implicitly acknowledges the tension pulling at the structure of her own narrative. Slavery's exclusion from political consideration guarantees the consolidation of American national identity. But the abjection of a fundamental aspect of American social reality also guarantees its return: the return of the abject. In spitting out the abject, the (political) self seeks to consolidate a clearly defined and public identity, an identity that is accomplished through the exclusion of certain bodily, functional parts of the self. The return of the abject does not unify the split self, but disrupts it; the abject does not reintegrate within the borders of identity, but throws those borders into question. The return of the abject is thus a return to a moment of origin before the creation of a unified self and a replacement of the achieved single voice with a sense of differing and vagrant identities.

Writing in the mid-twentieth century, Arendt recognizes that the return is already here and that it has compromised the categories of her narrative from its beginning. No theoretical analysis of modern revolution can presume a pure political endeavor uninflected by social realities; no evaluation of the modern political subject can presume a wholly unified subjectivity, undivided in its intentions or desires. Later, in her chapter 6, Arendt mourns the loss of the mode of political self-representation that seems, in the glimpses possible during its brief historical appearances, to have been perfectly authentic and sincere. In this chapter, however, she offers accounts of political self-representation that recognize the shifting and fragmented voice of a different political self.[2]

In *On Revolution*, Arendt acknowledges that if the political voice begins with speech and narrative, the political story is predicated on violence. In her introduction, Arendt described the intimate relations among originary violence, revolution, and political narrative:

> The relevance of the problem of beginning to the phenomenon of revolution is obvious. That such a beginning must be intimately connected with violence seems to be vouchsafed for by the legendary beginnings of our history as both biblical and classical antiquity represent it. . . . The first recorded deeds in our biblical and our secular tradition, whether known to be legendary or believed in as historical fact, have travelled through the centuries with the force which human thought achieves in the rare instances when it produces cogent metaphors or universally applicable tales.
>
> (*OR*, 20)

At this much later point in her text, confronted with the social contradiction inherent even in American Revolutionary politics, Arendt again reasserts the centrality of violence in the political space of speech and action. Instead of attempting to secure an exemplary model of revolution free of the originary force of violence, she turns her attention to the presentation of a political story, a narrative type that is always and essentially at odds with any notion of pure virtue or perfect good.

The textual bridge between Arendt's discussion of American slavery and narrative political representation is a brief analysis of the insidious effect Rousseau's doctrine of general will and selfless virtue had on French Revolutionary thought and practice. Arendt's ensuing remarks on compassion, virtue, hypocrisy, and the mask can be read as elaborations of her discussion of Rousseau, but as such they are out of scale and only questionably appropriate, since Arendt makes no reference at all to Rousseau's own work on theatricality and politics, the *Lettre à M. d'Alembert sur les Spéctacles*. In reversing the convention that would find in Rousseau a more natural figure of political critique than Billy Budd, I have tried to make room in Arendt's text for her own interpretation of the problem of truth and representation.

SPEAKING ANOTHER'S VOICE: ARENDT AND MELVILLE

Arendt's primary political narrative, as illustrative of political representation, is Herman Melville's *Billy Budd*.[3] Melville's story, according to Arendt, is a political realist's response to the sentimentality and misplaced compassion of Rousseau and the French Revolution: "Melville . . . knew how to talk back directly to the men of the French Revolution and to their proposition that man is good in the state of nature and becomes wicked in society" (*OR*, 82–83). Yet although *Billy Budd* is proffered as an interpretive antidote to the social excess of the French Revolution, the politics it represents is deeply implicated in a violence no less real for its avoidance of sentimentality. For Arendt, *Billy Budd* illustrates the recognition that within the purposefully constructed context of political deliberations the sincere impulsiveness of the pure innocent can be even more overtly destructive than the devious plottings of the cynic. Implicitly, Arendt's discussion of *Billy Budd* is itself about the relation between narrative and political origins—narrative being the means through which fraternal violence is stabilized and incorporated as a founding tradition.[4] Above all, *Billy Budd* is, and is explicitly presented by Arendt as, a narrative about the difficult relation between speech and violence, and the necessary relation between politics and speech.

That this section of Arendt's text is about narrative rather than simply the events being narrated is made clear through her curious introduction to the discussion of *Billy Budd*. Arendt not only emphasizes the narrative qualities of Melville's story; she herself assumes the voice of the storyteller. Although she speaks as though through Melville, this is her own apostrophe to the audience as intellectual sympathizers with the French Revolution:

> Let us assume you are right and your "natural man," born outside the ranks of society, a "foundling" endowed with nothing but a "barbarian" innocence and goodness, were to walk the earth again—for surely it would be a return, a second coming; you certainly remember that this happened before; you can't have forgotten the story which became the foundation legend of Christian civilization. But in case you have forgotten, let me retell you the story in the context of your own circumstances and even in your own terminology.
>
> (*OR*, 83)

Through the persona of Melville, Arendt allows herself to speak those traditional opening words: let me (re)tell you a story. She enunciates those words through Melville's mouth, but they are her own.

Arendt's use of Melville as a role through which to pronounce the truth of her own interpretation is thoroughly in keeping with her writing later in the chapter on the role of the mask. It is worth noting, though, that she is here already putting into textual practice the political action (as dramatic or narrative representation) she is preparing to theorize. It is also worth noting that Arendt's use of Melville as a mask conforms to her own understanding of the mask as a public persona in that Melville is a recognized public figure and a man. Arendt's problematic use of the persona of Rahel Varnhagen as a mask through which to tell a more intimate, personal story will be explored in chapter 4.

Not only is Arendt's discussion of *Billy Budd* thus introduced with the storyteller's opening line "let me tell you a story," but the apostrophe also serves to link Melville's story to the long tradition of founding political and social narratives. In this strange announcement to her audience, Arendt explicitly refers to the foundation myths that present the eventual emergence of a new social order out of a (presocial) individual's conflict with original law. She mentions "Christian civilization," associating the figure of Billy Budd with that of Christ, but in describing his "'barbarian' innocence and goodness" one is reminded more of Adam and, by extension, in the violence and innocence of Billy Budd's actions, of Cain and Abel. Although the foundation legend Arendt has Melville mention is a version of the Christian second coming, what she seems to have in mind, through her political contextualization of the words she ascribes to him, are the fratricidal myths of political origination she named in her introduction: Cain slew Abel; Romulus slew Remus. Whatever the explicit or implicit associations, however, Arendt, through Melville, identifies *Billy Budd* as a postrevolutionary political foundation legend.

By emphasizing that *Billy Budd* is a traditional and political story-myth and by opening her discussion of it with a slight revision of the familiar "let me tell you a story," Arendt marks this point in her text as a new beginning. The reemergence of the abject (through the acknowledgment of slavery's abjection) into the political scene disrupts the ordered structure of Arendt's political text because it reintroduces the violence the narrative had repressed. This disruption prompts her to embark on an alternative narrative of political possibilities. Arendt's introduction to *Billy Budd* emphasizes the story's modernity and traditionalism; it is a new return to an old original style, and so it is in her sense revolutionary.[5] For Arendt, *Billy Budd* is a political story in which violence plays an unusually prominent role precisely because violence appears but fails to speak politically.

As Arendt presents it the story is about "goodness beyond virtue and evil beyond vice" (*OR*, 83),[6] and the contradictory relationship between speech and violence: Billy Budd, the innocent who stammers and cannot speak, answers the liar Claggart's spoken evil by absolutely silencing him—with a single deadly blow. Arendt expresses even less hesitation over condemning Billy's natural but inarticulate goodness than does Captain Vere; for her, Billy Budd's fundamentally antipolitical crime is that he resorts to violence when he cannot manage speech. Being without language, he is without politics and is confined to the bodily expression of physical violence. His violence, which is a response to another man's words, serves only to silence any possibility of dialogue. In his frustration with his own limitations and the other's calculated accusation, Billy Budd attacks Claggart physically. In doing so, he may preserve his honor, but he destroys the possibility of a political engagement between himself and another. Locked into the immediacy of his body, Billy Budd's violence destroys both the space between persons that is necessary for speech and the embodied existence of his opponent. His goodness is pure, immediate, and unworldly; for Arendt, it is opposed to worldliness and to the political, the two values she holds most dear.[7]

In Arendt's view, the ambivalent hero of the story is Captain Vere, the unsentimental political man whose fairness and kindness do not prevent him from deciding to hang Billy Budd, despite his knowledge of the sailor's essential purity and goodness. Captain Vere's mastery of speech and of the mechanisms of violence make him resolutely political: he is neither confined to the violent necessities of his body, as is Billy Budd, nor is he evasive of the bodily responsibilities of spoken action, as is Claggart. Although Captain Vere's goodness is compromised by his political resolution, Arendt finds his worldly acknowledgment of human limitation admirable. One of her few actual quotations from Melville is of Captain Vere's words: "Claggart was 'struck by an angel of God! Yet the angel must hang!' The tragedy is that the law is made for men, and neither for angels nor for devils" (*OR*, 84). Arendt in effect congratulates Captain Vere for being a Machiavellian political actor; he may be tempted by compassion, but he does not abandon the virtue of his role in the political world for the moral purity of a supposedly higher one. He may eschew violence, but he is also capable of ordering it. Captain Vere permits violence within the political sphere, but only as a result of public determination.

Despite the moral righteousness of his violence against Claggart, Billy Budd violates the respect for persons and their bodies that Arendt wants to preserve for the public realm. Captain Vere, who himself orders punitive violence against Billy Budd (an act that, as Melville makes clear, Billy speechlessly forgives), does not in doing so violate the rule of language in the public realm, because for him violence is definitely subsumed by speech. In particular, Arendt applauds Captain Vere for holding fast politically by not giving in to the emotion of compassion.

The danger of compassion is that, like spontaneous or unregulated violence, it destroys the conventions of political space: "Because compassion abolishes the distance, the worldly space between men where political matters, the whole realm of human affairs, are located, it remains, politically speaking, irrelevant and without consequence" (*OR*, 86).[8] Arendt very clearly blames compassion for the violent excesses of the French Revolution; its irrelevance is political, not historical. Compassion can be of no political consequence because it is more akin to mute violence than to speech:

> As a rule, it is not compassion which sets out to change worldly conditions in order to ease human suffering, but if it does, it will shun the drawn-out wearisome processes of persuasion, negotiation, and compromise, which are the processes of law and politics, and lend its voice to the suffering itself, which must claim for swift and direct action, that is, for action with the means of violence.
> (*OR*, 86–87)[9]

For Arendt, compassion, which she associates with Melville's Billy Budd and Dostoevsky's Christ (and not with Captain Vere or the Grand Inquisitor), has no capacity for the kind of stable political foundation with which she is concerned in *On Revolution*.[10]

Unable to speak for himself, Billy Budd is cut off from politics, the realm of speech, and resorts to violence. Captain Vere judges him accordingly; although he recognizes Billy's goodness, he is constrained by his own responsibility as a political actor to protect the public realm with its rule of law and language from spontaneous eruptions of violence in its midst. Billy Budd's crime is that he replaces speech with force: he would end the narrative, in particular and in general. At the close of her discussion of the story, Arendt emphasizes precisely this narrative problem and again speaks through Melville:

> Clearly, Melville reversed the primordial legendary crime, Cain slew Abel, which has played such an enormous role in our tradition of political thought. . . . It is as though he said: Let us suppose that from now on the foundation stone of our political life will be that Abel slew Cain. Don't you see that from this deed of violence the same chain of wrongdoing will follow, only that now mankind will not even have the consolation that the violence it must call crime is indeed characteristic of evil men only?
> (*OR*, 87–88)

Even though the myths of political foundation may be inevitably fratricidal, Arendt emphasizes the terrible importance of the proper narrative assignment of the fratricidal roles. Goodness enacted publicly as compassion and violence invites chaos into the story, and Arendt indicates that within the narrative structure, political virtue must reject violence and choose speech, even if the choice necessitates the actor's or another's death.

HYPOCRISY: THE DENIAL OF ARTIFICE

Arendt's discussion of *Billy Budd* is about the silencing of speech. Her discussion of hypocrisy is about its perversion. The bridge between the two is pity, which she writes "may be the perversion of compassion" (*OR*, 88). If compassion is a dangerous, mute passion akin to love and violence, pity is a sentiment: compassion debased by speech. Pity implies condescension rather than solidarity, which she identifies as the political alternative to pity and a relative of compassion. In writing about pity, Arendt once again resorts to a metaphor of intrusion and the bursting of (political) boundaries (*OR*, 90–91). Yet what has intruded into her discussion is not violence, which has already been acknowledged, but falsity.

At this point in "The Social Question" Arendt begins to acknowledge that although speech is the fundamental political practice, it is not necessarily inherently political, virtuous, or truthful. Narrative especially is artifice, and thus artificial. Once mute emotion veils itself in the sentiments of pity, no natural relation between truth and speech can any longer be assumed: speech is recognized as artifice, and everywhere provokes suspicion. (The parallels implicit here between spoken truth and gendered authenticity will be further developed later in this chapter in the discussion of Joan Riviere's "Womanliness as a Masquerade.")

The evil of hypocrisy, and "the passion for its unmasking" (*OR*, 98), are given remarkable weight in Arendt's writings and are treated very carefully. Initially, Arendt rather fastidiously distances herself from the witch-hunt mentality of those who, be they political actors or historiographers, take up the passion for political unmasking. She minimizes their obsession: "Was not hypocrisy, since it paid its compliment to virtue, almost the vice to undo vices, at least to prevent them from appearing and to shame them into hiding? Why should the vice that covered up vices become the vice of vices? Is hypocrisy then such a monster?" (*OR*, 101). These questions, rhetorically asked, pose a problem that Arendt might very well be interested in. Hypocrisy prevents that which ought not to appear from appearing and shames it into hiding. In this way it is very much like Arendt's traditional distinction between public and private, which kept the poor and the abject ashamed and out of sight. What is so wrong, she seems to ask, with a minor vice—a little hypocrisy to our ideals—if it secures for us a coherently ordered space in which to appear and a proper appearance?[11] In trying to resolve the problem of hypocrisy, Arendt seems also to be attempting a resolution of the contradictions in her own political ideals.

Rather than argue the relative merits of democratic or elite politics, Arendt works toward this resolution by reexamining the metaphysical relation between being and appearance as described by Socrates and Machiavelli. Note that she again speaks through their publicly recognized and authoritative (and masculine) personas:

> Socrates, in the tradition of Greek thought, took his point of departure from an unquestioned belief in the truth of appearance, and taught: "Be as you would wish to appear to others," by which he means: "Appear to yourself as you wish to appear to others." Machiavelli, on the contrary, and in the tradition of Christian thought, took for granted the existence of a transcendent Being behind and beyond the world of appearances, and therefore taught: "Appear as you may wish to be," by which he meant: "Never mind how you are, this is of no relevance in the world and in politics, where only appearances, not 'true' being, count; if you can manage to appear to others as you would wish to be, that is all that can possibly be required by the judges of this world."
>
> (*OR*, 101)[12]

Both these positions, as Arendt presents them, hold that the truth as we know it is that which is seen, whether by a personal or a worldly audience. This appearance is implicitly recognized to be a construction; the truth of appearance is not merely the sight of the natural body (although that body's appearance has its own political significance and truth when it does intrude within the public realm) but the more elaborately constructed presentation of a self. Thus neither truth nor self is taken to be essential. Instead, they are what we encounter in the world, and are therefore necessarily multiple and in flux.[13]

By placing her discussion of hypocrisy within the philosophical context of being and appearance, Arendt shifts her argument from the presumed contradiction between essential truth and worldly practice to a reevaluation of the relation between them: the only truth we know becomes performative.[14] In order to appear, and therefore to be, truth requires an audience, and she worries particularly, as she says Socrates and Machiavelli do, about "the problem of the hidden crime," the nature and agent of which are never perceived (*OR*, 102).[15] Yet if the definition of truth is subtly shifted from the essential to the worldly, there remains a break between the two that hypocrisy is able to exploit. In fact, hypocrisy is such a serious issue for Arendt precisely because it undercuts the truth of worldly appearance rather than of essentiality. It is because she so highly values worldliness and the artifice of worldly representation that Arendt so definitely condemns, although on her own terms, the modern vice that, by pretending to essentiality and thus provoking suspicion, betrays the dramatic truth of performance and presentation.

The whole crux of Arendt's thinking bears down on her discussion of hypocrisy. Like Robespierre and the French revolutionaries, Arendt identifies hypocrisy as an elemental threat, but her reasoning is entirely different. Arendt condemns hypocrisy within the political space even more than she fears the intrusion of the abject within that space, because the hypocrite actively practices what the abject can only by its presence imply: the disintegration of the worldly reality of performative truth. The hypocrite destroys the (human) truth of dramatic action because the hypocrite pretends to the (absolute) truth of essentiality. Whereas the abject threatens an intrusion of the forgotten and the repressed on the political space (of appearance), the hypocrite threatens to corrupt the very premise of performance itself, and therefore also the premise of the political space.

It is not simply that the hypocrite lies; lying has always been a fact of political practice within the public space. The political liar has always tried, as skillfully as possible, to fool the political audience. The hypocrite is something new, the inevitable product of a modern political attitude that emphasizes purity of intention as much as if not more than efficacy of result. The hypocrite fools himself; he confuses the artifice of a worldly role with an elusive truth of being:

> Yet hypocrisy is not deceit, and the duplicity of the hypocrite is different from the duplicity of the liar and the cheat. The hypocrite, as the word indicates (it means in Greek "playactor"), when he falsely pretends to virtue plays a role as consistently as the actor in the play who also must identify himself with his role for the purpose of play-acting; there is no *alter ego* before whom he might appear in his true shape, at least not as long as he remains in the act.

(*OR*, 103)[16]

The hypocrite is a playactor who no longer recognizes the limits of his own performance. In confusing performance with essence, the hypocrite asserts the fixed, absolute qualities of essentialism as the scale of value for performance. Thus the hypocrite disbelieves agency, the ability to make a judgment and assert it in the world, in favor of a self so unified that its responses would be utterly unthinking. Self-convinced, without knowledge of self or others, the hypocrite cannot conceive of a capacity for original action or worldly performance. In fooling himself, the hypocrite becomes a parody of an actor.

The return of the abject may destroy the boundaries of the public space and the dramatic conventions of political performance, but the hypocrite abolishes the distinction and distance between actor and observant audience:

> Psychologically speaking, one may say that the hypocrite is too ambitious; not only does he want to appear virtuous before others, he wants to convince himself. By the same token, he eliminates from the world, which he has populated with illusions and lying phantoms, the only core of integrity from which true appearance could arise again, his own incorruptible self. . . . As witnesses not of our intentions but of our conduct, we can be true or false, and the hypocrite's crime is that he bears false witness against himself.
> (*OR*, 103)[17]

The appearance of the abject, miserable body may drag the achievement of a public world back toward a natural bestiality, and compassion in the political sphere may lead all too easily to unrestrained violence. But hypocrisy denies the worldly achievement of artifice by insisting on a false and unobtainable naturalness, a naturalness that would deny the very capacity for thinking itself. Arendt began her discussion of hypocrisy by referring to Socrates and Machiavelli, two worldly thinkers who emphasized the duality of thoughtful existence: I appear to others, and I appear to myself. The difference between the two performances is the gap that makes self-consciousness possible. The hypocrite denies this duality, insisting that all appearance, to self and others, is one seamless reality. In doing so, the hypocrite abandons "the core of integrity" that is, ironically, the space of critical self-perception.

Hypocrisy is artifice that would deny itself, is ashamed of precisely that self-consciously performative quality that is the highest public achievement: the knowing presentation of a dramatically viable self. It is the threat hypocrisy presents to the performative quality of public politics that causes Arendt to revile it so adamantly: "What makes it so plausible to assume that hypocrisy is the vice of vices is that integrity can indeed exist under the cover of all other vices except this one. Only crime and the criminal, it is true, confront us with the perplexity of radical evil; but only the hypocrite is really rotten to the core" (*OR*, 103).[18] This accusation of rottenness may be the most unmitigated condemnation in all of Arendt's writing. Even the political criminal remains a recognizable if unself-conscious political actor. Only the hypocrite betrays the conscious practice of politics itself.[19]

SPEAKING THROUGH THE MASK: ARENDT

For Arendt, political practice, especially revolutionary political practice, is inherently theatrical.[20] After her discussion of hypocrisy as a threat to the necessary artifice of public performance, Arendt extends her thesis of politics as dramatic representation to a discussion of truth and the mask. Since for Arendt truth is worldly, public, and performative rather than essential or private, the theatrical mask provides a metaphor of political significance:

> The profound meaningfulness inherent in the many political metaphors derived from the theatre is perhaps best illustrated by the history of the Latin word *persona*. In its original meaning, it signified the mask ancient actors used to wear in a play. . . . The mask as such obviously had two functions: it had to hide, or rather to replace, the actor's own face and countenance, but in a way that would make it possible for the voice to sound through. At any rate, it was in this twofold understanding of a mask through which a voice sounds that the word *persona* became a metaphor and was carried from the language of the theatre into legal terminology.
>
> (*OR*, 106–7)[21]

The mask represents and creates a public role for the speaking self: a persona. The mask provides the private ego with a stable public representation that is artificial, enabling, and salutary. For Arendt there is no contradiction in this; the public realm and our shared worldliness are the achievements of human artifice. Truth, and especially political truth, can be known only in that worldly realm, and the recognizable individual who enters it and speaks the truth through the appropriate public persona is necessarily also an achievement of craft and artifice.

Arendt emphasizes that the stably recognizable mask of public performance is separate from the private or natural self: the public persona stabilizes a particular representation of the shifting variations of the private self, but these modulations of identity and desire continue beneath the mask. The existence of worldly truth, and of identities that we know among ourselves in public, presumes the existence of an embodied private self whose personal manifestations are as real and as transient as the body's daily needs. This relation, between the private body and the natural self on the one hand, and the recognizable and specifically public dramatic mask of the actor on the other, is critical to Arendt's conception of truth and politics:

> The point of this distinction and the appositeness of the metaphor lie in that the unmasking of the "person," the deprivation of legal personality, would leave behind the "natural" human being, while the unmasking of the hypocrite would leave nothing behind the mask, because the hypocrite is the actor himself in so far as he wears no mask. He pretends to *be* the assumed role, and when he enters the game of society it is without any play-acting whatsoever. In other words, what made the hypocrite so odious was that he claimed not only sincerity

but naturalness, and what made him so dangerous outside the social realm whose corruption he represented and, as it were, enacted, was that he instinctively could help himself to every "mask" in the political theatre, that he could assume every role among its *dramatis personae*, but that he would not use this mask, as the rules of the political game demand, as a sounding board for the truth but, on the contrary, as a contraption for deception.

(*OR*, 107–8)

Hypocrisy is the denial of artifice, the insistence that the self is stably fixed in the public role or mask and entirely identifiable with it. The distinction between the artifice of any achieved public self-representation and the fluidity of the natural or private self is not seen by Arendt as a contradiction. Rather, it is what provides for the worldly performance of political truth because it provides the space between private self-consciousness and the performance of the public role that makes room for agency. Because the hypocrite insists on the conflated, unified identity of the public role, the public person, and the natural, private, bodily self, no one of those can really be said to exist, and the truth of the entire performance is reduced to a single flat dimension. The hypocrite deceives himself. He wears the mask, only to forget that the mask exists to be worn.[22]

The discussion of hypocrisy is the dramatic culmination of "The Social Question." The short section that concludes the chapter is again about violence: the unrestrained violence whose principle is rage. Arendt associates rage with a kind of thoughtlessly desperate drive for self-preservation, whether it be that of the miserable poor or that of the corrupt and hypocritical upper classes, and she writes that the violence of the French Revolution, which was a conflict between those two rages, "swept away rather than 'achieved in a few years the work of several centuries' " (*OR*, 111).[23] Because it is an explosion of uncontrolled passion, rage, even more than compassion, destroys the artifice of the political world. In Arendt's view of the raging social contest that was the French Revolution, the miserable poor had never achieved artifice, and those in the hypocritical court culture denied even to themselves that they employed it (Marie Antoinette's infamous "Let them eat cake" being a prime example of the hypocrisy of those who no longer recognize the artifice of the world they create and in which they live).

For Arendt, the French Revolution was destroyed by the social question because the question was embodied rather than represented. When the miserable poor burst into the public world, they did so with the irresistible force of the abject, and the bodily necessity that is the abject was embodied in the women's march on Versailles:

No doubt the women on their march to Versailles "played the genuine part of mothers whose children were starving in squalid homes, and they themselves afforded to motives which they neither shared nor understood the aid of a diamond point that nothing could withstand."

... It is indeed as though the forces of the earth were allied in benevolent conspiracy with this uprising, whose end is impotence, whose principal is rage, and whose conscious aim is not freedom but life and happiness.

(*OR*, 112–13)[24]

For Arendt, the women's march for life and (private) happiness cannot compare with Jefferson's affirmation of life, liberty, and (public) happiness. One instance carries the physical threat of feminine *jouissance* and masculine impotence, the other the orderly restraint of masculine politics.[25] Arendt continues: ·

Where the breakdown of traditional authority set the poor of the earth on the march, where they left the obscurity of their misfortunes and streamed upon the market-place, their *furor* seemed as irresistible as the motion of the stars, a torrent rushing forward with elemental force and engulfing a whole world.

(*OR*, 113)

At the conclusion of her chapter, Arendt again invokes metaphors of a natural and irresistible physicality to convey the sense of the social threat to the political world. Eliding any larger discussion of the complex historical changes that resulted in the "breakdown of traditional authority," she describes the political appearance of the poor and abject as an image of Mother Nature enraged. Feminized and physicalized, the social question can finally be understood, in the context of this text, only as an overwhelming threat to the political.

Unlike *The Human Condition*, in which natality and embodiment play a positive and fundamental role (at least in the Prologue), *On Revolution* locates the origin of politics in the admittedly much more violent act of fratricide, and in its narrative retelling. In *On Revolution*, natality has been left behind, and if it reappears at all, as it does (as the maternal) in the exceptional chapter "The Social Question," it is characterized entirely as a threat. In *On Revolution* the realm of representation that is the political has no positive connection to the private experience of the body. The appearance of the abjected and feminine body within the political can be understood only as essentially destructive because Arendt cannot conceive of this body as capable of representing itself.[26] Supposedly without any artifice, the feminine body marching on Versailles is apparently a natural force rather than a self-conscious actor and therefore is outside of political significance. Arendt makes no allowance for any kind of representation of the body or the feminine within the political. Indeed, the body and the feminine are so closely identified as to be almost interchangeable, and both are then abjected from the realm of speech and action. They ought not even to be spoken of, which would give them a token of political credibility, and their inevitable problems ought to be organized and resolved by the inhuman artifice of technology.[27]

In Arendt's writing the body is often associated with necessity and labor rather than with speech or artifice, and women in particular are identified with the body's laborious necessity. Insofar as the laboring body is responsible for the daily reproduction of human life, it can be associated with natality and beginning, as it is in *The Human Condition*. But in *On Revolution* the maternal body is no longer laboriously occupied / in labor. Rather, it looms on the edge of the political realm as an overwhelming presence that would negate any attempted representation of an independent self: the chastising mother figure who always calls us back to who we "really" are. When it appears, the wretchedly abject body that bursts back into the space of the political has the treacherous strength of the feminine other: the seductive threat of a *jouissance* that is at once immediate and abysmal, the other and the same.

Without boundaries, without distinctions, the body in *On Revolution* is not utterly hypocritical but the opposite: utterly essential. The feminine can only be conceived as the body itself, totally determined by its physical essentiality. Thus the women marching on Versailles are, for Arendt, the epitome of a social intrusion into political affairs because they *are* the abject (feminine) body of necessity rather than its representatives. Locked in their abjection, they are as dangerous as the hypocrite, incapable of the mask.

SPEAKING THROUGH THE MASK: RIVIERE

At this juncture of the argument, let us consider the possibility that the feminine other is wearing a mask. Arendt has explicitly argued that the mask provides the amorphous self with a stable public role for representing and speaking the truth. Implicitly, the body, insofar as it is feminine, cannot assume the mask, because the feminine body and the feminine role are apparently the same, a fixed and essential reality incapable of self-representation and artifice. The significant problem then is whether the feminine body has the capacity to represent itself.

In Arendt's writing there is never an explicit suggestion that the feminine may itself be masquerade. But within the discourse of contemporary feminism, this conception of femininity as a performance rather than an essence has gained increasing influence. Much of the significant theoretical work on the spectacle of a femininity that is performed for the (masculinist) viewer's gaze came out of feminist film theory and practice, particularly Mary Ann Doane's influential 1982 essay, "Film and the Masquerade: Theorising the Female Spectator." A few years later, in response to published discussions prompted by her first essay and to relate further clarifications in her own thinking, Doane published "Masquerade Reconsidered: Further Thoughts on the Female Spectator."[28] In both essays Doane explicitly locates her theoretical analyses of femininity and masquerade within a classically psychoanalytic context, and in both essays the key to her conceptual apparatus is Joan Riviere's 1929 essay, "Womanliness as a Masquerade."[29] Although Doane is critical of Riviere's apparent acceptance of the psychoanalytic definition of feminine masquerade as pathological (while the definition of normal femininity remains a lack—of subjectivity, agency, and the phallus), she credits Riviere with innovating a fundamental shift in the theorization of the feminine, a shift that can be differently appropriated:

To claim that femininity is a function of the mask is to dismantle the question of essentialism before it can even be posed. In a theory which stipulates a claustrophobic closeness of the woman in relation to her own body, the concept of masquerade suggests a "glitch" in the system. What I was searching for, in the 1982 essay, was a contradiction internal to the psychoanalytic account of femininity. Masquerade seems to provide that contradiction insofar as it attributes to the woman the distance, alienation, and divisiveness of self (which is constitutive of subjectivity in psychoanalysis) rather than the closeness and excessive presence which are the logical outcome of the psychoanalytic drama of sexualized linguistic difference.

(Doane, "Masquerade Reconsidered," 37)[30]

Doane appropriated Riviere's psychoanalytic account of feminine masquerade to a psychoanalytically informed discussion of feminine representation and filmic practice. But Riviere's account of feminine masquerade can also be deployed within a psychoanalytically informed consideration of feminine political subjectivity and agency. Both Doane and Arendt are concerned, although differently, with the question of feminine (self-) representation. Doane uses Riviere's essay to structure her own interpretive work; I am using Riviere's essay to deconstruct Arendt's interpretive resistance to the problem of feminine political agency.

Although Arendt is not herself working within a psychoanalytic context, her analysis of the abject and of feminine, bodily essentialism is psychoanalytically loaded. Kristeva's analysis of abjection located the threat of the abject within the psychoanalytic, rather than the political, sphere, whereas Arendt (mis)places it in the political. Arendt's further displacement of feminine identity outside political possibility is dependent on her conviction that feminine identity is essential and complete; it cannot be enacted or performed; it is too fully genuine to be available to the artifice of political self-representation. But a psychoanalytic account that detaches the feminine from its supposed essentiality can also be used to loosen the prohibition Arendt has placed between (essential) femininity and political identity.

Through reading Riviere, it becomes possible to reread Arendt and reconfigure the relationship she presumes between the political metaphor of the actor speaking through the mask and those social identities whose bodies are presumed absolutely to define them. As Doane points out, conceptualizing femininity as masquerade empties out the question of essentialism from the beginning. What is left is a different understanding of feminine agency and self-representation, which allows Riviere's concept of social masquerade to be matched up with Arendt's concept of the political mask.

Riviere's essay is based on the case study of an analysis of a successful professional American woman. Heterosexual, happily married, a proficient housewife, the analysand's work involved public speaking of a "propagandist nature" (Riviere, "Womanliness," 36). This would seem to indicate that her work was explicitly political. The immediate problem for analysis was the woman's consistent experiences of nervousness after having given a speaking performance and her need, after her own presentations, to gain reassurance, both professional and personal, from men who were recognizable father figures:

> To speak broadly, analysis of her behavior after the performance showed that she was attempting to obtain sexual advances from the particular type of men by means of flirting and coquetting with them in a more or less veiled manner. The extraordinary incongruity of this attitude with her highly impersonal and objective attitude during her intellectual performance, which it succeeded so rapidly in time, was a problem. (36)

In other words, this woman veered between a problematic and coquettishly sexual femininity and an appropriately impersonal, objective, or masculine professionalism. The essay does not attribute her success to these feminine wiles; rather, it questions the recurrent eruptions of femininity within the public context and through the professional, masculine persona this woman seemed to have successfully mastered. In Arendt's analysis, such behavior might be seen as the bursting through of the social into the public realm. Riviere, however, addresses the various assumption of two separate roles by the same actor.

The woman in question assumes the feminine role not as a natural regression into essentiality but as a propitiatory gesture to her male colleagues:

> Analysis then revealed that the explanation of her compulsive ogling and coquetting—which actually she herself was hardly aware of till analysis made it manifest—was as follows: it was an unconscious attempt to ward off the anxiety which would ensue on account of the reprisals she anticipated from the father-figure after her intellectual performance. The exhibition in public of her intellectual proficiency, which was in itself carried through successfully, signified an exhibition of herself in possession of the father's penis, having castrated him. The display once over, she was seized by a horrible dread of the retribution the father would then exact. Obviously it was a step towards propitiating the avenger to endeavor to offer herself to him sexually. . . . Thus the aim of the compulsion was not merely to secure reassurance by evoking friendly feelings towards her in the man; it was chiefly to make sure of safety by masquerading as guiltless and innocent. It was a compulsive reversal of her intellectual performance; and the two together formed the "double-action" of an obsessive act, just as her life as a whole consisted alternately of masculine and feminine activities. (37)[31]

The feminine role is assumed by this woman, in her masculine context, as a mask. She is a woman masquerading as such; representing herself as personal and feminine in order to minimize the transgression of her successful representation of herself as publicly impersonal and masculine. Having successfully entered the public and masculine realm as a (masculine) woman, she then takes pains to emphasize that she is seemingly just a (feminine) woman after all. She resorts to the role of the feminine in order to disguise her enactment of the role of the masculine.

Riviere's analysand is relying on androgyny, through the overlapping of distinct roles, to consolidate her public position and command of the public gaze. Yet within the analysis itself there seems to be an evolution from hypocrisy to performance. The analysand is first a hypocrite because she conceives her own behavior to be an inappropriate eruption of natural truth that compromises the validity of her public self; analysis allows her to see herself as an actor and thereby to gain interpretive distance from as well as public control over her own actions. Femininity then becomes a role, and the analysand recognizes the significance and theatricality of this role through dreams of the mask. Riviere describes her analysand's dreams of masks and death:

> Before this dream she had had dreams of people putting masks on their faces in order to avert disaster. One of those dreams was of a high tower on a hill being pushed over and falling down on the inhabitants of a village below, but the people put on masks and escaped injury!
>
> Womanliness therefore could be assumed and worn as a mask, both to hide the possession of masculinity and to avert the reprisals expected if she was found to possess it—much as a thief will turn out his pockets and ask to be searched to prove that he has not the stolen goods. (38)[32]

Femininity, then, can be assumed as a mask, especially by those who are already participating in public power. Certainly the abrupt role-switching of Riviere's analysand emphasizes the artifice of (her) femininity. At this point in her discussion, Riviere shifts from analyzing compulsive feminine behavior to theorizing the possibility of a strategic feminine masquerade.

Yet even as she reveals that femininity can be a mask, Riviere herself uses the technique to hedge the question of a distinction between an essential femininity and a feminine mask. Like Arendt, who supports her own provocative arguments about truth and the mask by speaking through the personas of Melville, Socrates, and Machiavelli, Riviere utilizes the technique of feminine masquerade within her own essay as a way of propitiating her own (masculine) psychoanalytic critics:

> The reader may now ask how I define womanliness or where I draw the line between genuine womanliness and the masquerade. My suggestion is not, however, that there is any such difference; whether radical or superficial, they are the same thing. The capacity for womanliness was there in this woman—and one might even say it exists in the most

completely homosexual woman—but owing to her conflicts it did not represent her main development and was used far more as a device for avoiding anxiety than as a primary mode of sexual enjoyment. (38)

Having just described a radical new understanding of traditional femininity, in which specifically sexual behavior in a public context is interpreted as a negotiation of power relations rather than as a distressingly inappropriate eruption of private, feminine bodily behaviors, Riviere proceeds to negotiate her way as a woman writer within the psychoanalytic intellectual community. She explicitly defers to more conventional (and masculinist) conceptions of femininity. Riviere first asserts that "genuine" or essential womanliness is the same as womanliness as a masquerade. Given that this statement is part of the conclusion of her description of her analysand's use of femininity as a mask, Riviere would seem to be indicating that essential femininity is no different from what we now can recognize as femininity as a masquerade: that what we used to regard as essential is in fact artifice.

But she immediately follows this statement with a sentence that emphasizes womanliness as a universal female "capacity," a "main development," and "a primary mode of sexual enjoyment" rather than "a device for avoiding anxiety" or using power (38). This statement would seem to indicate that femininity is an inherent quality in all women, one that usually develops naturally and relative to sexuality and the body rather than artificially and relative to anxiety and power. Thus Riviere, while asserting that there is no difference between an essential femininity and the feminine mask, nonetheless asserts that her analysand's masquerade is a deviation (in quality rather than in degree) from the norm of essential or natural femininity.

However, Riviere immediately cites other instances of womanliness as a masquerade, examples taken from "everyday observation" rather than psychoanalytic inquiry (39). A "capable housewife" admits she finds herself " 'acting a part,' she puts on the semblance of a rather uneducated, foolish and bewildered woman" in order to best manage the builder, the upholsterer, the butcher, and the baker (39). A "clever woman, wife and mother, a university lecturer in an abstruse subject" wears particularly feminine clothing when lecturing to colleagues (but not to students), and her manner with them becomes "flippant and joking" (39). In each of these cited examples, competent adult women shift to a foolish or coquettish feminine role with powerful men in public situations, and they do so in order to finesse the power relationship, shifting it in their own favor by seeming to abdicate any challenge or claim. Even if the men in question are tradesmen, they have access to some resource the women need, which they can share more or less willingly depending on the relationship between the man and the woman involved. Riviere does not assert that all or most instances of feminine behavior are a mask, but she does establish that womanliness can quite often and ordinarily be recognized

43

as a masquerade in relations of power, and that power saturates daily life. Feminine masquerade is not necessarily only a neurotic compulsion; given the extent to which gender inflects the structure of power in almost any relational field, feminine masquerade can seem to be quite ordinary, practical good sense.

The situation that remains significantly unmentioned is that of relations between men and women in private. Here, by implication, femininity is real and natural, rather than a masquerade. Given that the women she describes use a feminine masquerade as a way of brokering power with men in public situations, and given that women have traditionally been dependent for their power and position on private and personal relations with men within the household, is it so far-fetched to conjecture that women may have used femininity as a masquerade to broker power in those relations as well?

Riviere holds back from this. She stops short of supposing that all or most instances of feminine behavior are a mask, in part, at least, because the psychoanalytic structures within which her theory is located insist that what is behind the mask is sadism (38–40). The spectacle of a negative and hostile emotion masquerading as ordinary womanliness, and indistinguishable from and perhaps identical to what is supposed to be normal feminine masochism, is too much even for Riviere, and she stages a retreat from it. Whether or not her retreat is genuine is open to question; she backs off from the Freudian implications of her work, implications that are only necessary if the Freudian understandings of gender and identity development are subscribed to fully. The question of what is behind the mask remains.[33]

Yet this retreat leaves Riviere with the apparent trivialization of her own work, and a very traditional return:

> These conclusions compel one once more to face the question: what is the essential nature of fully developed femininity? What is *das ewig Weibliche?* The conception of womanliness as a mask, behind which man suspects some hidden danger, throws a little light on the enigma. (43)

Riviere here actually masks the independence and originality of her own work behind gestures of deference to the father figures of the psychoanalytic establishment. After having presented her own intellectual performance, she minimizes its theoretical significance by resuming a deferential and innocent role: her work can only throw a little light on the surface of the feminine enigma, an enigma whose essential nature seems to be a masculine perplexity. By reasserting the primacy of the traditional questions male psychoanalysts had been asking about women, rather than the knowledge female psychoanalysts may ha⋅ ⋅ been gleaning about other women or themselves, Riviere masks the power of that knowledge and the challenge it could present to the dominant men. She masquerades as the dutiful daughter to the psychoanalytic establishment, reaffirming the significance of their question as a compensation for the threat of her own work, which is that the question is irrelevant. The danger behind the womanly mask is perhaps not the projected masculine fear of female sadism but the radical possibility of feminine agency.

SPEAKING THROUGH THE MASK: THE SOCIAL BODY IN THE POLITICAL SPACE

Riviere's work offers the mask and masquerade as an alternative to the seeming dead end of feminine essentialism, despite her return at the conclusion of her essay to the old (masculine) question of what woman is really, i.e., behind the mask. For Arendt, of course, the essentialist problem is uninteresting. She is not so much concerned with what is behind the mask of artifice as with whether or not a body is capable of using the mask for the double process of hiding and representing itself.[34] She asserts nearly the same point as Riviere but without the rhetorical hesitation: "In politics, more than anywhere else, we have no possibility of distinguishing between being and appearance. In the realm of human affairs, being and appearance are indeed one and the same" (*OR*, 98). Yet in her writing, women are typically seen as incapable of this self-conscious performance.

Despite the ambiguities of her text, Riviere makes clear that women are capable of artifice and that the feminine role that seems to preclude self-representation may itself be highly and self-consciously artificial. If one reads this insight of Riviere's back into Arendt's theoretical structure, while applying Arendt's validation of the mask back into Riviere's conception of womanliness as masquerade, the texts work to illuminate each other. Considered together, they provide a degree of liberation from the confinement of traditional political and social assumptions about the essential nature of truth, the feminine, and the validity of self-representation through masquerade.

Arendt's theorization of the mask as a stably achieved public identity through which an amorphous, private, and unknown self can speak the truth, when reconstellated with Riviere's theory of feminine masquerade, provides for an escape from the debilitating preoccupations with essentialism. Rather than continually pursuing the question of *das ewig Weibliche*, a question that re-creates its own reification each time it is asked, Arendt's work, like Riviere's, emphasizes that the significant issue is the masquerade itself, not the supposedly essential truth it conceals. Since Arendt describes truth as that which is presented through the mask—as performative—feminine masquerade can be understood to be true (performative) femininity, as Riviere in part concludes. The essential capacity for the feminine, which Riviere further asserts exists in every woman (a statement with which Arendt might not disagree), is probably the performative capacity of the physical body itself.[35]

For Arendt, the supreme threat to the political space comes from the intruding abject body, especially the feminine body, which is unable to represent itself but is forcefully and immediately present. According to

45

Riviere, womanliness can be observed to be a masquerade: the female body representing itself. Since the work Riviere's analysand performs is identified as "of a propagandist nature, which consisted principally in speaking and writing," it can be supposed to be political in Arendt's terms (Riviere, "Womanliness," 86).[36] Through Riviere's analysis, the analysand's feminine public behavior is recognized to be a masquerade. But if her behavior were to be observed without benefit of Riviere's interpretation, it would be quite possible to presume that it was simply the eruption of an otherwise successfully excluded (private) femininity within the boundaries of the political space.

Riviere's analysis allows us to recognize artifice when we see it, including when it appears as a social intrusion within the public realm. Without the analysis, we would suspect that the analysand's femininity was what was revealed behind the mask, rather than the mask itself. We would accuse her of a hypocritical lack of public authenticity, rather than recognizing the performance of a (series of) role(s). More significantly for the problem of social identity and the political, the analysis also allows us to reconsider the supposed inability of those traditionally excluded from the public realm to represent themselves within it.

Those who have only recently entered the public realm, who have come from a previously excluded or marginalized group or class, may very well choose to represent themselves by emphasizing the otherness that still marks them.[37] They may wear the mask of the other, as does Riviere's analysand, but they do so precisely in order to manage for themselves the terms of their acceptance within the public and political space. This masquerade, which may either go unrecognized or be scorned as devious maneuvering, can be acknowledged, when reconsidered through the theoretical insights of Arendt's work, as truly political activity.

In combination, Riviere's and Arendt's analyses provide for a different interpretation of the women's march on Versailles. Arendt, without the benefit of Riviere's insight into feminine masquerade, can only understand the women's blunt appearance as a force of nature intruding into the human world of truth and artifice. Riviere's analysis, however, allows us to conceive that the women may very well have known exactly what they were doing in representing themselves as female and wretched before the public gaze. Given Arendt's own validation of the mask or persona as a valid means of self-representation, the women's march can be reinterpreted as authentic political action, instead of mobile chaos.

On Revolution is a chronicle of the historical degeneration of the public space, which is threatened by the intrusion of the abject body—what Arendt calls the social question. She fears that the intrusion of this body, which she identifies with the poor and the feminine, will destroy the possibility of the recognized artifice of truth and self-representation, which she locates in the political space. Yet other writers have reconsidered the essentiality of womanliness, and have observed that seemingly inappropriate social and feminine behavior that emphasizes a woman's associa-

THE MASK AND MASQUERADE

tion with her gender and her body may very well be extremely politic. If so, the naturalness of a formerly marginal or excluded group's behavior cannot be taken for granted once its members have begun to perform for the public gaze.[38] Although the integrity of the political space may be said to have been broken down by the participation of the physical body, the body cannot be presumed to be incapable of artifice simply because it is subject to specific social markings, be they of class, gender, or race. Those markings, displayed within the public space, may be differently understood to indicate a high degree of self-conscious political self-representation. In fact, precisely those figures who are best able to manipulate an ambivalent or controversial persona of the body may have the best possibilities for dramatic political success.

Arendt herself tried an early version of this form of masquerade. When she wrote her book on Rahel Varnhagen, she was as much writing her own story, through Rahel's persona and Rahel's words, as she was writing a version of Rahel's Enlightenment Jewish travails. Although Arendt wrote her private truth through Rahel's public persona, Rahel's was a specific mode of feminine, personal representation that Arendt was then to reject—without, however, ever rejecting the masquerade itself. Within the context of this study, Arendt's masquerade with Rahel Varnhagen is more important as a methodology of agency than as a rejected experiment with *écriture feminine*. It is also a text that, when read as a masquerade, provides some explanation for Arendt's strong distinction between public and private experience, and her insistence that specifically feminine experience is private rather than political.

Four.
Speaking
as Rahel:
A Feminine
Masquerade

> It was never my intention to write a book *about* Rahel. . . . What
> interested me solely was to narrate the story of Rahel's life as she
> herself might have told it. She considered herself extraordinary,
> but her views of the source of that quality differed from that of
> others. She attempted to explain this feeling in innumerable
> phrases and images which retain a curious similarity throughout
> her life as they strive to formulate the meaning of what she called
> her Destiny. . . . All that remained for her to do was to become a
> "mouthpiece" for experience, to verbalize whatever happened.
> This could be accomplished by introspection, by relating one's
> own story again and again to oneself and to others; thereby one's
> story became one's Destiny: "Everyone has a Destiny who knows
> what kind of Destiny he has."
> HANNAH ARENDT, *Rahel Varnhagen*, xv–xvi

This chapter applies the theory of masquerade to analyze the parallels
between Arendt's private life and her first independent scholarly project:
Rahel Varnhagen: The Life of a Jewish Woman (originally published in England as *Rahel Varnhagen: The Life of a Jewess*).[1] It is also an investigation
of Arendt's early, contradictory attempts to establish an authorial voice.
Much has been written of Arendt's peculiar identification with Rahel
and of the degree to which the twentieth-century writer found in her
nineteenth-century counterpart a friend and a model for living in an
increasingly hostile world. Since the revelation of Arendt's student affair
with her married teacher Martin Heidegger, the book is often read as an
empathic exercise through the discovery of a historical confidant.[2] It is
also often noted that the book is different, in both style and content, from
any of Arendt's other published writing. In this chapter, I argue that the
difference is owing to the book's being a feminine masquerade. But as a
project to stabilize an authorial voice, the masquerade falls short: this text
is the site of Arendt's own resistance, for personal reasons, to the theorizing of feminine personal experience.

In 1929 Arendt had finished her dissertation (on "The Concept of Love
in Augustine") and was living in Berlin with her new husband, Günther
Stern-Andrews. Searching for a new topic, she decided to research the
German Romantics, and then narrowed her focus to an investigation of

a single personality, the Jewish salon hostess and woman of letters, Rahel Varnhagen. Arendt learned from Rahel, and the book is considered a testimony to Rahel's lesson of Jewish pariah identity and self-respect. It is usually assumed that Arendt found in Rahel what she was looking for, and that what she was looking for was a model of Jewish pariah self-consciousness. But the text itself contradicts this assumption. What Arendt was initially looking for, and what she found in Rahel, was a representation of her own painful personal experience as a feminine parvenu.

Arendt's *Rahel Varnhagen* is itself a divided text. For most of the book, Arendt struggles to tell Rahel's story "as she herself might have told it" (*RV*, xv), but the story she tells, so empathetically that it could be her own, is that of a Jewish woman parvenu. Only in the book's last two chapters does Arendt break out of the claustrophobic uniqueness of this personal history to develop the notion of pariah consciousness she uses to give the story a (politically) satisfactory ending. The book is usually treated as a unified whole, as a coming-to-consciousness of a politicized Jewish social identity. But Arendt herself acknowledged that the last few chapters were written under different circumstances and different influences than the rest of the manuscript.[3] Most of the book, like its original title, is the feminine story of a "Jewess," while the last chapters are about Jewish identity. What is abjected, stylistically and theoretically, is the concern with Rahel's specific experience as a woman.[4]

Arendt claimed for Rahel the status of pariah rather than parvenu: one who consciously holds herself aloof, rather than one who seeks acceptance by behaving as a sycophant. But Rahel was, for most of her life, a Jewish woman desperately seeking not just acceptance but love from particular Gentiles, who failed her. Arendt used Rahel's story to change her own, to free herself from the shame of (parvenu) rejection, and to move beyond that personal abyss to achieve the clear authorial voice of the pariah. Only by writing of, and speaking through, Rahel could Arendt eventually transform the (feminine) parvenu's private and social pain into the (Jewish) pariah's public and political independence. Speaking through the constructed mask of Rahel's story, told as Rahel supposedly would have told it, Arendt made her own transition from speaking in the voice of the parvenu—Rahel's voice, preoccupied with the pain of excessive individual burden—to speaking in the voice of the pariah—her own mature voice, with its strangely individual authority.[5]

ARENDT/RAHEL: A PERSONAL MASQUERADE

Despite her remarkable and controversial ability to theorize Jewish identity as a politicized social construct, Arendt refuses to politicize feminine experience. Without a conception of gender, femininity can only be essential, and (any) woman's experience can only be personal. For Arendt, the feminine masquerade of *Rahel Varnhagen* fails because she can never recognize it as a masquerade, only as a (displaced) exposition of personal truth. In speaking as Rahel, Arendt can write the personal truth of her own story through the mask of Rahel's experience. She can even recognize Rahel as a model of Jewish (woman's) experience, and use the last few chapters of the book, like the final stages of a psychoanalysis, to gain a critical distance on this model of narrated behavior. But Arendt never seems willing, either publicly or to herself, to acknowledge Rahel as a model of a (Jewish) *woman's* behavior, and she never gains the same kind of critical distance on the social construction of femininity. Instead, after using Rahel as a public mask through which to speak her personal truth, Arendt simply leaves both behind. She takes up the powerful, nearly masculine authorial voice she will use in all of her other public, political writings, and she keeps secret, until after her death, the very feminine story of chosenness and seduction that would seem, for her, to betoken glory and shame, rather than any possibility for agency and emancipation.

The revelation of Arendt's youthful affair with her teacher Martin Heidegger has been the abject whose return has haunted recent Arendt scholarship. Despite all the attention it has received, no one knows quite how to manage it.[6] Arendt's writing was controversial, but her image as an intellectual Pallas Athena seemed unassailable.[7] Like Athena, Arendt was a woman who did not seem vulnerable in the ways that women often are: she relied on her mind as her shield and her sword. But this impressive, autonomous identity was based on the abjection of the Heidegger affair, and the return of the affair as public knowledge has made Arendt's image vulnerable in a specifically feminine way.

The return of the abject can be defensively denied in order to maintain the integrity of a self's boundaries, or it can be obsessively fixated upon as proof that the self's integrity was always contaminated and its project hypocritical. To some extent this alternation has characterized scholarly dealings with the revelation of the Arendt/Heidegger affair. As a biographical fact, it can be segregated from Arendt's intellectual achievements, or treated as a truth that confirms or undermines them. Perhaps not surprisingly, the *Rahel Varnhagen* text has for the most part been treated in a parallel way. As a book that doesn't seem to fit, in style or content, with Arendt's other published writings, it was often ignored by political theorists, who segregated it out as a youthful aberration from the accepted Arendt canon; and literary scholars and historians interested in the German Romantics, eighteenth-century urban salons, or Rahel Varnhagen herself didn't necessarily try to place it in the context of Arendt's political writings.[8] Although the renewal of interest in Arendt has begun to change this for both the oeuvre and the identity, the return of the abject requires a (re)integration that is neither a toleration nor a capitulation, but a new inscription of meaning that comes from a shift in the pattern of the whole.

In this chapter, I use the interpretive strategy of a masquerade to evaluate the extent to which Arendt used her narrative of Rahel Varnhagen to tell the story of her own affair. But if Arendt eventually brought a political formulation of Jewish identity to bear on Rahel's life and on her own, as evidenced by the book's last chapters, she never managed to do the same with feminine identity. She never managed the maneuver of claim and distance of Riviere's analysand and of her own work on Jewish pariah / parvenu consciousness. Riviere's analysand enacts her masquerade of femininity within the context of her professional, political sphere, just as Riviere notes that the housewife who plays the mild coquette with the butcher is masquerading within her own professional context. For Arendt, the professional context is her published work as a writer and a scholar, and the feminine masquerade is her book on Rahel Varnhagen. But whereas Riviere's patient practices a feminine part as compensation for the threat of her competent professional, political (and implicitly masculine) role, Arendt tries to combine the two. Her feminine masquerade is not a strategic enactment, but the public personification of a specifically private feminine pain.

In writing *Rahel Varnhagen*, Arendt collapsed the distance between public persona and private self, and risked being trapped by the norm of immobilizing authenticity that she identified with the social question. Because she could not or would not conceptualize the structures of her own feminine experience, preferring to keep them private and therefore unique, she leaves her textual masquerade theoretically incomplete. It is her own history that prompts her to abject the feminine from the political, while she politicizes her identity as a Jew. A theory of masquerade enables a reading of Arendt's affair with Heidegger and her narrative of Rahel as parallel stories; a recognition of the stories' parallels shows why her feminine masquerade is never fully conceptualized either in the *Rahel Varnhagen* text or as a theoretical possibility in any of her other published writings.

HANNAH ARENDT: A LIFE

Arendt was born in 1906, the only child of a solidly middle-class, assimilated German Jewish couple in Königsburg. Her father was institutionalized with the tertiary stages of syphilis in 1911; he died in 1913. Her mother was a social democrat, sympathetic to the Spartacists, and an admirer of Rosa Luxemburg; Hannah Arendt grew up in a bourgeois, secular, and Left-politicized household. She was intellectually precocious, but she seems not to have been particularly impressed by her mother's politics. She was drawn instead to philosophy, and in 1924, at the age of eighteen, she moved to Marburg to begin her university studies. In Marburg she became a student of Martin Heidegger's, and during the following year they had an affair.

This affair was first made public in Elizabeth Young-Bruehl's biography, and received renewed attention with the publication of the new material in Elzbieta Ettinger's study.[9] Part of what made the revealed relationship so fascinating was its secrecy. Despite the significance it had held for both parties, it was not publicly known, and the inaccessibility of the partners' correspondence allowed rude biographical fact to retain its shroud of romantic mystery. This significance has been fairly well established: Heidegger was not in the habit of conducting affairs with his students, and Arendt understood that their relationship was exceptional and an indication of her own exceptionalness.[10] The fact of the affair selected her out as special, unique; it validated her worth as a thinker and affirmed her feminine status as a (Jewish) woman. But it also locked her into secrecy: all this exceptionality could not be made public.[11]

Their intimacy was sexual and intellectual, but Heidegger was not only her teacher—he was married, with two children, and his wife was openly antisemitic. Although this relationship provided a singular validation of Arendt's intellectual and personal worth, it also placed her scholarly career in jeopardy; public knowledge of her uniquely privileged position would completely compromise her. She had become exceptional, a young Jewess chosen by an Aryan intellectual prince, but this specialness had to remain private knowledge. She had achieved an impossible identity: the relationship that most proved her success as a parvenu would, if known, most guarantee her role as a pariah.[12] Both she and Heidegger were uncomfortable with the dual relationship, and in 1926 Arendt moved to Heidelberg to write her dissertation, a philosophical exploration of worldly desire and transcendent overcoming, under Karl Jaspers.

In Heidelberg Arendt led a productive if relatively unexceptional student life. She was intellectually successful, and she was socially admired; she became involved in relationships with several well-respected and eligible men. But the affair with Heidegger had left Arendt with a secret, and with a terrible schism between her private and public lives, which nonetheless overlapped. Although she had physically and formally distanced herself from Heidegger, she continued to meet him. She was unable to break the relationship until 1929, when she finished her dissertation and moved to Berlin. There she reencountered Günther Stern, whom she had known in Marburg, married him, and began work on her new project on the German Romantics, which soon became a project on the Jewess Rahel Varnhagen.

RAHEL VARNHAGEN: A TEXT

This project became a very strange book. Stylistically and conceptually, the Varnhagen text is much more personal than Arendt's other intellectual work: it doesn't fit. Scholars who have tried to evaluate this work within the context of the rest of Arendt's writings have often tried to assimilate it to her other discussions of Jewish identity, and have usually interpreted its oddity as an indication that she was still working through ideas that would later become clear.[13]

The peculiar style of the *Varnhagen* book becomes even more striking when it is compared to the tone of a short essay Arendt published on Rahel in 1932, at the beginning of the project. First published as "Berliner Salon" in *Deutscher Almanach für das Jahr 1932* (Leipzig), the essay is an examination of the evolution of Berlin salon society, from Henriette

Herz's League of Virtue, which Arendt characterizes as entirely a product of the Enlightenment, to Rahel's circle of unconventional Romantic personalities, through the Christian-German Table Society, which was anti-Enlightenment and excluded Jews, Frenchmen, philistines, and women. Arendt positions Rahel as the most admirable and open-minded of the salon figures, but the essay places her firmly within a clearly defined historical, cultural, and political context. This short, early article also discusses the public living of private life that took place in Rahel's salon. In comparison with the book manuscript, most of which was written in 1933, the article shows that Arendt chose, through style and content, to present a very different kind of narrative in *Rahel Varnhagen*, a narrative that was peculiar to the book and not necessarily to her research on Rahel.[14]

The version of Rahel represented in Arendt's book is overly emotional, sentimental, melancholy, and abstracted, and because the text attempts to replicate the experience of Rahel's life, it is itself heavy and oddly without reference. At the end of the book Arendt does include a chronology of Rahel's life, but its linear detail of dates and events is strikingly at odds with the emotive textual account. Early reviews described it as suffocating.[15] To tell Rahel's story "as she herself would have told it," Arendt relied on extensive quotation; she seems to be attempting to crawl inside her heroine's words. But Arendt's interpolations only emphasize Rahel's interiority, her vulnerability, and her uniqueness.[16] According to Arendt, Rahel is nothing but her naive, uneducated sensibility; one needs to read other sources to learn that she studied languages, that her family granted her a remarkable degree of financial and spatial independence, and that her husband, the Gentile and eventually aristocratic August (von) Varnhagen, was not simply an adoring dupe.[17] This text is a highly stylized, exquisitely empathized version of a particularly Jewish and feminine attempt at self-realization, but it is eventually unclear exactly whose attempt is being represented.

Through the mask of Rahel's story, Arendt is writing her own. But it is a story that cannot be spoken clearly. Arendt emphasizes Rahel's uniqueness, and her unhappiness, but the text, and the figure it represents, remain strangely muffled. Although Arendt asserts that Rahel had an original wit, none of it comes through. Instead of the salon hostess, the woman who lived her life through passionate friendships, Arendt's Rahel is a woman who lives her life through a series of futile, unhappy love affairs. She is continually trying to redefine herself, guarantee her exceptionality, and erase the taint of her Jewishness by winning true love, acceptance, and a marriage proposal from a socially prominent Gentile. Yet her desperate attempts to escape herself end in failure and personal agony: she is confined to an abyss of interiority. Even tragedy, when it is reduced to a purely personal account, becomes melodrama. Rahel becomes ridiculous; it is a life of shame. She is abject.

Yet this is the version of Rahel's life that Arendt tells, because it is the version that most allows her to speak her own story. Of course this story cannot actually be described in its factuality, and will not be until both Arendt and Heidegger are dead. Instead, Arendt, through Rahel, attempts to speak the personal truth of a life entirely subjectively. Everything is interior, emotionally exquisite and emotionally adrift, because the specific references cannot be mentioned. In public, a forbidden, failed affair would become ordinary and shameful.[18] Only in private can the depths of romantic futility be fully indulged.

TWO WOMEN / ONE VOICE

Although both Rahel and Arendt may intellectually link the failure of their romances to the problem of their Jewish identity in a society in which antisemitism is still deeply conventional, the personal pain they both experience is simply heartbreak: the conviction that all joy is over because that one who is most important, whatever his traits, has chosen and abandoned this one, oneself. Although anyone can have a broken heart, the gendered conventions of the romantic genre specify different inflections of the experience. For women, heartbreak can seem to mean the very end of experience, because for women experience has traditionally been defined as being chosen by a man. Thus, heartbreak can be both the end of emotional life and its defining event: the experience that defines a woman as being both worthy of choice and specially marked by the loss of that worthiness. Both Arendt and Rahel feel passed over by life and by love, but they cling to their misery because it is all they have left of their having been chosen; without it, each would be just herself, a woman alone.

This is Arendt's description of Rahel's reaction after the failure of her first love, her engagement to the Prussian noble Karl Finckenstein. The empathetic style, incorporating quotation to the extent that Arendt seems to be speaking through Rahel's actual words and through the words she would have spoken, is typical of the whole book:

"Disgraced by destiny, but no longer susceptible to disgrace."

Everything was over; only life, stupid, insensitive life, went on. One did not die of grief, of unhappiness. Day after day, one awoke, behaved like other people, went to sleep. In these "absurd regularities" greater misfortunes than being jilted had faded away to nothing.
(*Rahel*, 53)

A few pages later, Arendt continues in the same vein:

She fled abroad from Berlin because she could no longer endure the disgrace. Because she was condemned to go on living, to enjoy every new day with the natural "innocence of all creatures." But it was no longer innocence when one knew "thoroughgoing unhappiness," "when anguished by grief, humiliation, in *despair*, one would gladly give up life in order not to be capable of pain; when one has thought everything, *all* of nature, cruel." Natural as gladness was, it had become inappropriate, a pleasure she could no longer allow herself, to which she merely succumbed.
(*Rahel*, 67)

These passages mirror Arendt's own private writing on her experience. They are descriptions of intense shame combined with a deep resentment at having to make do with ordinary life. Compare Arendt's descriptions of Rahel's emotional state with her earlier writings about her own heartbreak:

All good things come to a bad end; all bad things come to a good end. It is difficult to say which was more unbearable. For precisely this is what is most intolerable—it takes one's breath away if one thinks of it in the limitless fear which destroys reticence and prevents such a person from ever feeling at home: to suffer and know, to know every minute and every second with full awareness and cynicism, that one has to be thankful even for the worst of pains, indeed it is precisely such suffering which is the point of everything and its reward.

(Young-Bruehl, *Hannah Arendt*, 57)[19]

Writing about herself, Arendt describes an abstract catastrophe that nonetheless confirms her specialness. For both women, heartbreak implies a particular emotional punishment: not just the loss of the social prestige attachment to these men guaranteed but also the mortification of having been put in one's place when one doesn't think one should have to be there. The fact of romantic failure emphasizes the parvenu aspirations.

By figuring Rahel's romantic and empathic emotionalism in her own narrative, Arendt can claim to speak as Rahel and can openly tell a story for which she cannot otherwise find the words: her own story of Jewish, feminine vulnerability through social aspiration and rejection. Through this masquerade, speaking as Rahel, Arendt can even express ambivalence at the success of the performance:

Apparently Rahel had not wanted them to fall prey to her magic; rather, she had hoped that someone would ask how things stood with her. The possibility of fascination was inherent in her situation, and, after all, how were all these others to know that she had wanted them to break through this fascination in order to get at herself—that is to say, at what had happened to her? Each of them had enjoyed the "spectacle" which she offered to all; none had wanted to accept the truth which she had always been ready to scream out at the slightest provocation.

Her desire had been to tell the truth at all costs; instead she had made herself impenetrable.

(*Rahel*, 67–68)

Of course, Arendt herself was not ready to scream out the details of her relationship with Heidegger. But by speaking the emotional truth of that relationship through Rahel, Arendt can share her particular pain while also remaining impenetrable. For a young woman with a shameful, glorious secret, it is a perfect strategy.

SPEAKING A LIFE / THEORIZING AN IDENTITY

But while it provides for the safe exploration of the meaning of the personal story, this feminine masquerade doesn't fully achieve a critical perspective on it, and the book itself is deeply fractured.[20] In chapters 1 through 11 Arendt indulges that purely personal experience, and splits her own burden with the heroine of her text. Both she and Rahel are locked into a resolutely subjective perspective, straining between alien-ation and aggrandizement. For most of the book there are no politics in the text, and antisemitism is a personal, individual experience, mediated through specific relationships. But in the last two chapters Arendt gains a different perspective, on Rahel and on the text. She gains a voice of her own as she begins to theorize a historical and political consciousness that is emphatically Jewish, but not necessarily feminine.

Unlike the rest of the book, which was completed by 1933, the last two chapters were written in 1938, after history and politics had begun to assert a stronger claim on individual lives. In 1933 Arendt fled Germany for France, where she worked in refugee organizations and became more involved with Zionism. By 1936, her thought was being shaped as much by her practical experiences, her friendships with Kurt Blumenfeld, Walter Benjamin, and Heinrich Blücher (the former communist who would become her second husband) as by her academic training in phi-losophy.[21] She began to see herself, and think of herself, as an individual within history, and she began to see Rahel this way as well. In chapters 12 and 13 Arendt no longer speaks through Rahel—she writes about her and about politics.

In chapter 12 Arendt begins to theorize the notion of the Jew as pariah that she develops further in essays written in the 1940s, and in *Antisemi-tism*, volume 1 of *The Origins of Totalitarianism*, published in 1951.[22] Instead of a lone woman seeking a personal solution, a Romantic, Arendt begins to think of Rahel as a Jew, an individual whose identity participates in sociological, historical, and political realities. The parvenu Jew is an outsider who seeks an assimilation that can never be complete, but the self-conscious pariah affirms her minority identity and the social exile it costs her, and cultivates her powers of observation. When fully developed in the essays, it is clear that the self-conscious pariah is a politicized iden-tity. But at this stage in her writing Arendt's conceptualizations are not so precisely defined, and Rahel is an individual whose story blurs clear-cut definitions. At points in the last two chapters Arendt uses the terms almost interchangeably to describe her:

As a Jew Rahel had always stood outside, had been a pariah, and dis-covered at last, most unwillingly and unhappily, that entrance into society was possible only at the price of lying, of a far more generalized lie than hypocrisy. She discovered that it was necessary for the par-venu—but for him alone—to sacrifice every natural impulse, to con-ceal all truth, to misuse all love, not only to suppress all passion, but worse still, to convert it into a means for social climbing.
(*Rahel*, 208)

The self-conscious pariah claims the referents of a social identity that is larger than her purely personal experience of its effects. Although for most of her life Rahel treats her pariahdom as a curse and is a resolute, almost desperate parvenu, her deathbed affirmation that being a Jew defined the worth of her experience allows Arendt, with a bit of editorial finesse, to rescue her from parvenu shame and celebrate her as a self-conscious pariah.[23]

Arendt discovers Rahel as a pariah when she discovers the possibility for herself, when she begins to understand the interior life as contextualized within a public world. The parvenu's world is entirely social, but her social experience is entirely personal, so the social world is understood by her to be a world of personalities. The pariah understands that personalities are shaped within a political landscape, that social constructs are political constructs and are therefore available for politicization. Although early in the text of *Rahel Varnhagen* Arendt credits Rahel with more than "mere worldliness" (*RV,* 33) because she lives a life of sensibility rather than either frivolity or sense, incipient in the final two chapters is the positive notion of "worldliness" that will become one of the defining tenets of Arendt's political philosophy. "Worldliness," for Arendt, became the ability to see oneself as an individual within the shaping patterns of a larger world; not to forgo uniqueness, but to credit experience with a political and historical context.

For Arendt, however, this also meant shifting perspective from Rahel's feminine experience as a woman to her sociological experience as a Jew.[24] Intent on her need to transform her story of Rahel's (feminine) parvenu consciousness, Arendt developed the notion, and the voice, of the (Jew as) pariah. For Arendt, a self-consciously Jewish identity seemed to be the political means to climb out of the seductive morass of feminine subjectivity. Rahel's story, as Arendt first tells it, is a story with which one can empathize, but it is fundamentally subjective. For Rahel, and for Arendt, the personal is not political, if the personal is conceptualized as the private experience of uniqueness: the pure interiority of personal experience must be transcended if the individual's experience is to be politicized. Yet for Arendt, as for Rahel, identity as a woman and identity as a Jew were intimately related, and there is nothing intrinsic to Arendt's methodology that would necessarily exclude a complete paradigm of feminine pariah and parvenu consciousness.[25]

THE POLITICS OF MASQUERADE

The lesson of *Rahel Varnhagen* is not simply the lesson of being the pariah; rather, it is the complex lesson of becoming (incompletely) the pariah, through the enactment of a masquerade (albeit incompletely realized). In the last chapter of the book, Arendt describes masquerade as the behavior of the parvenu:

> For the latter, being condemned to lead a sham existence, could seize possession of all the objects of a world not arranged for him only with the pseudoreality of a masquerade. He was masked, and consequently

everything that he touched appeared to be masked; he concealed his true nature wherever he went, and through every hole in his costume his old pariah existence could be detected.

(*Rahel*, 225)

This writer, who will later base her conception of political being and action on a theory of appropriate artifice, is here still committed to a norm of naturalness. In this early version, a masquerade, her feminine masquerade, is understood not as artifice appropriate to agency but as hypocrisy to be abandoned. The woman must remain inherently a parvenu; only as a Jew can Rahel, or Arendt, approach self-conscious pariah status.

But *Rahel Varnhagen* is an early, ambivalent text. Arendt's later work provides a stylistic model of a woman's voice that speaks through an assumed mask of somewhat androgynous authorship, one that attempts to avoid the binary opposition of either feminine subjectivity or masculine logic. For every author the question of voice is fundamental. Every new text challenges the sufficiency of all those that preceded it; every author must summon the authority to claim a new voice. The voice writes the author into history; before the voice has been established, the author has no perspective, no place.

Arendt apparently resolved the problem of voice quite successfully. She is the only woman generally accepted into the canon of modern political theory, and her work has always been independent of any school or party affiliation. Furthermore, she established for herself a powerful authorial voice that combined a tone of objectivity with a highly subjective style of political analysis. She wrote as a woman, but she did not write in a particularly feminine, let alone feminist, voice. She has been criticized for her masculinist perspective on politics, yet her husband, Heinrich Blücher, noted that in all their circle of friends, only her mother "simply and thoughtlessly" took her for a man.[26]

Contemporary theorizations of feminine writing (*écriture feminine*) have usually opposed its absences, fragmentation, and interiority to the linear constructions of traditional (masculinist) prose. These discussions have also usually proposed that this style was the only viable way for a woman writer to find her voice as a woman, rather than speaking the style, and the truths, of masculine power.[27] Arendt's rejection of this (feminine) style of writing, which she utilized in *Rahel Varnhagen*, suggests that such a style may be useful up to a point: it is effective for the expression of feminine experience and emotional truth. But if écriture feminine is taken to be the natural or essential mode of expression of women's experience, it risks segregating that experience from possibilities of political analysis.

Écriture feminine can only provide for political agency when it is considered as a strategy, a masquerade like any other, not a more immediate conveyance of the essential truths of feminine being. To provide for political agency, the (feminine) masquerade needs to be recognized as employing effects that are not natural, but social constructs with political implications. But Arendt was not able to recognize écriture feminine as a strategy, since that would also have required theorizing the politics of feminine experience, which would in turn have meant recognizing her affair with Heidegger as both more and less than a purely personal event. Arendt resisted this; she resisted categorizing her own experience as a woman in political (that is to say, socially constructed) terms. Instead she constructed her text as the natural expression of someone else's voice and experience: Rahel's. Rahel's truths were real, absolute, feminine, and Arendt shared them. But because she would not claim the generality of feminine experience, for Arendt feminine writing could not lead to feminist politics: politics meant transcending the feminine, moving from the interior truth of emotional empathy to the worldly truth of shared experience. To the extent that she began to interpret Rahel's life in political terms, Arendt characterized that life as defined by its Jewish identity, and split off the political analysis from the representation of its feminine interiority. By abjecting feminine experience from her theorizing of the political, Arendt managed both to consolidate her conception of political identity and to save the intimate secret of her own abject history. Écriture feminine, feminine writing, feminine experience thus remained for Arendt personal and unique, but separate from the possibility of political agency.

While she was writing the Varnhagen book in 1933, Arendt published one of the few pieces she ever wrote that explicitly dealt with feminism: a critical but fairly positive review of a book dealing with the psychology of contemporary women from a socialist-feminist perspective.[28] Arendt emphasizes that the family, rather than the individual, should be the appropriate unit of analysis for a study of the problems of contemporary women, and she seems to say that working women's inequality has little to do with the ideology of the women's movement. This review, like the Varnhagen book, lacks a political conception of women's social identity (studying the family is not the same as studying women in the family). Since Arendt never understood gender as a social construct, she never understood Second Wave Feminism as anything other than an insistence on the universality of purely personal experience, most narrowly conceived.

That experience always feels unique, but in order to be made socially meaningful, to be shared in common, it must be contextualized. Yet placing personal experience in the sociological field threatens the original sense of one's uniqueness: general categories dispute private truths. Although Arendt adamantly affirmed Jewish pariah identity, she never managed an equivalent analysis of feminine (i.e., women's gendered) experience.[29] Instead she evaded any sociological examination of gender by focusing on other aspects of social identity; her version of Rahel's Jewish pariah status ultimately escapes the question of her feminine subjectivity. Without any notion of gender, Arendt found that the only appropriate approach to specifically feminine experience must be psychological: when writing about Rahel's experience as a woman, Arendt emphasized her interiority; when considering her as an individual with a self-consciously affirmed social identity, she wrote about Rahel as a Jew.

Although she rejects the theoretical exploration of feminine identity and subjectivity, Arendt is not finished with the masquerade. In her later work Arendt modifies her terms: she develops a concept of the mask as a political persona, and represents the enactment of a masquerade as the construction of a social identity. Although *Rahel Varnhagen* was Arendt's first independent scholarly project, it was not published until 1957.[30] Her first published book, and the one that made her reputation, was *The Origins of Totalitarianism*. In that text Arendt explored masquerades that were more explicitly self-conscious: strategies through which individuals enact roles not just to achieve personal transformation, but in which personal transformation is also a masquerade for the disposition of political power.

Five.
Finding a Voice:
The Author and
the Other in
The Origins of
Totalitarianism

This chapter functions as an introduction to the second half of the book, which itself involves a shift in theoretical focus. In the first half of the book, the aspect of social identity that is most significant is gender. The feminist psychoanalytic theories of Kristeva and Riviere are used to investigate Arendt's constructions of feminine identity and her exclusion of it from her political analyses. But in *Rahel Varnhagen* Arendt herself shifts focus, moving from an explication of feminine personal experience in the first eleven chapters to a theorization of Jewish political identity in the last two. In chapter 4 I traced that shift. In this chapter I continue that line of inquiry but consolidate it around an investigation of Arendt's concern with enacted social identities of ethnicity and race.

After *Rahel Varnhagen*, Arendt's next major project was the three-volume *Origins of Totalitarianism*, published in 1951. This work is Arendt's attempt to "think what we are doing" and to make some sense of the disastrous events of the preceding few years. For Arendt, this means thinking systematically and historically about the politics of social identity as ethnicity and race: not just Jewish identity and antisemitism but also the race thinking that legitimized the practices of colonialism and imperialism. What is most brilliant about *The Origins* is that Arendt, writing immediately after the war and outside any particular political or intellectual school, makes this link. She realizes that the recent history of Jewish genocide cannot be separated from the modern, rationalized subjugations of whole peoples by the colonial powers and their delegates. And she further realizes that these problematic social identities, be they ethnic or racial, are not given but are constructed over time by both individual actions and larger sets of circumstances.

For Arendt, part of the tragedy of totalitarianism is its reduction of political possibility and agency to a system in which each individual's role is absolutely predetermined. Socially contructed identity is reduced to a biological fact, and the plurality that provides for political action is transformed into radically isolated categories. *The Origins* tracks this slow transformation, but in each of the first two volumes there are emblematic figures who evade the process by enacting a masquerade. Benjamin Disraeli constructs himself as a flamboyantly Oriental Jew; T. E. Lawrence plays the part of the heroic Arab nationalist so well that he himself loses track of his role as a British agent. Themselves deeply implicated in the politics of European imperial expansion, these figures nonetheless offer models of political self-enactment that break down the rigid categorizations of identity through which the imperial project functions. Their masquerades make room for agency even as the system in which they act becomes increasingly closed to the possibility. Even under full totalitarianism, agency is preserved by those individuals who are able to conceive of themselves as still representing themselves, although the plurality that enables this self-representation may exist only in the mind.

In the next three chapters I follow Arendt's own investigation of the relationship between agency and social(ly constructed) identity through the three volumes of *The Origins* and to some extent through discussions in *Eichmann in Jerusalem* and *The Life of the Mind*. Building on the theories of abjection and masquerade already introduced, I detach Arendt's problematic Eurocentrism from her very provocative thinking about the social constructions of subaltern identities.[1] Her preoccupation, in *The Origins* and in much of her later work, was with the possibilities for political action and agency. Over and over again she circles around the question of who acts; over and over again she resolves upon individuals who find freedom in their own lack of a fixed identity, who discover in their own plurality the possibility for enacting alternatives in the public world.

This refiguring of Arendt's thinking on action depends on extremely close readings of Arendt's texts. The emblematic figures who masquerade a social identity for political purposes usually appear as distractions from a narrative of inevitable political closure. To refigure their significance, it is necessary to locate these specific historical analyses in the context of her larger discussions. Just as the feminist analysis of the previous chapters depended on close textual interpretation, the postcolonial analysis of the next three can only be credible if based firmly on an alternate, but faithful, reading of the texts.

In this chapter I also continue the previous chapter's discussion of the problem of authorial voice. In *Rahel Vanhagen* Arendt shifts from a feminine masquerade to a discussion of Jewish pariah identity and takes on this role for both herself and Rahel. But *The Origins*, written after the experience of war and exile, describes a process through which the European self is reduced to a body without a mask: an individual whose identification with the immediacy of the social role precludes the self-conscious distance necessary for political agency. Arendt rejects this, yet she must find a way to reformulate her own relationship to the cultural and political context she describes as lost. To write her text, Arendt must defy her own narrative and project her voice through a public persona she reconstructs through the writing of the text itself.[2]

THE JEW AS OTHER: WRITING THE ORIGINS

The Origins was Arendt's first published book (other than her thesis on Augustine) and the work through which she achieved a widely recognized intellectual voice.[3] Written in the United States after the war, it operates from a backward-looking vantage point, a position from which the future is impossible to know, and the present nothing but exhaustion and wreckage. This is the opening of the Preface to the first edition:

> Two World Wars in one generation, separated by an uninterrupted chain of local wars and revolutions; followed by no peace treaty for the vanquished and no respite for the victor, have ended in the anticipation of a third World War between the two remaining world powers. This moment of anticipation is like the calm that settles after all hopes have died. We no longer hope for an eventual restoration of the old world order with all its traditions, or for the reintegration of the masses of five continents who have been thrown into a chaos produced by the violence of wars and revolutions and the growing decay of all that has still been spared. Under the most diverse conditions and disparate circumstances, we watch the development of the same phenomena—homelessness on an unprecedented scale, rootlessness to an unprecedented depth.
>
> (*The Origins*, vii)

This historical perspective owes much to Walter Benjamin's image of the angel of history who, appalled, faces the accumulating wreckage of the past, all the while being drawn inexorably backward into the unknown disasters of a future that is called progress. Benjamin provided Arendt with more than the image of her historical perspective. He also provided her with the theory of a historical methodology: a narrative that seeks to give meaning but not to explain and remains intentionally fragmentary.[4] She cannot explain totalitarianism; if she tried, she could only remain as silent as Billy Budd. But if she acknowledges her own subjective relation to the history she is writing (by emphasizing comprehension and a Benjamin-style relation with the past and the project of history), then she can simply try to begin to stammer out the pieces of her story.

In the same pattern she will follow in many of her subsequent writings, Arendt introduces her text by locating it in the present. *The Origins* is more than usually suspended in that moment of contemporary crisis; although the text looks backward, it is itself the attempted means of bridging the impossible split between past and future. Homeless, rootless, but herself safe on the American shore, Arendt attempts to retell the past in order to make the present and provide for the future. The empty, anticipatory moment of the present is to be occupied by the text itself.

That this particular text is an extremely personal one is borne out by Arendt's own emphasis on bearing the burden of the present:

> The conviction that everything that happens on earth must be comprehensible to man can lead to interpreting history by commonplaces.

Comprehension does not mean denying the outrageous, deducing the unprecedented from precedents, or explaining phenomena by such analogies and generalities that the impact of reality and the shock of experience are no longer felt. It means, rather, examining and bearing consciously the burden which our century has placed on us—neither denying its existence nor submitting meekly to its weight. Comprehension, in short, means the unpremeditated, attentive facing up to, and resisting of, reality—whatever it may be.

(*The Origins*, viii)[5]

This invocation, in the preface, to shoulder the burden of the present, and to acknowledge and resist it, helps to revolve the text upon itself. We begin and end in the present, but by the time we finish, we are not where we were when we started. Something has been achieved—in this case the telling of a story, the finding of a voice.

But Arendt has a great deal of trouble telling this story. The recent social and political history of antisemitism is most familiar to her, most nearly her own, and, since it is placed in the first volume, it would also seem to be the originary point for the narrative as a whole. Critics have wondered at the universal relevance of historical antisemitism to the totalitarian phenomenon and why Arendt gave it such emphasis.[6] But it is no accident that the title of *The Origins of Totalitarianism* is in the plural; there is no single originating point, except the moment of the present, which is itself always moving and slipping away. Even Jewish history is of concern here only insofar as it relates to the development of modern antisemitism: the discussion is limited spatially to Central and Western Europe and temporally to the period between the rise of the court Jews and the Dreyfus affair.[7] Considered differently, Arendt is attempting to describe the Jewish participation in modernity, while also asserting that neither that participation nor modernity exists any longer in any recognizable sense. Since she herself is a product of that lost existence, she is implicitly faced with the task of creating herself, of writing herself into the history of which she is both author and product.

That effort results in a stammering text. Although she prized her own critical distance from the emotionalism of modern Jewish history, Arendt has great difficulty with the beginning of *The Origins*, because the story she is telling is her own. The social and political phenomenon of antisemitism is not presented as the single and causal origin of totalitarianism, and there is likewise no single moment of origin, except the present, from which to begin the volume on *Antisemitism*. Rather, finding herself with a horrifying modern result, Arendt attempts to jump into a description of historical circumstance, not to explain what has happened, but to make it somehow meaningful. She forces herself to begin somewhere, and rather arbitrarily, and she is too implicated in that history to be able to make her narrative smooth: she hesitates, she hedges, she stammers.

The early site of Arendt's struggle to voice her own story was *Rahel Varnhagen*, but that text was defined by a different set of personal, cultural, and linguistic experiences. It was a book in German about an Enlightenment German Jewess, written in Weimar Germany by a young German Jewish woman struggling as much with issues of feminine identity as with issues of Jewishness. *The Origins* was written from the perspective of America; it was Arendt's first major work, her first major work to be published here, and her first major work in English, despite the editing that her manuscripts always required, and her own assertion that "After all, it wasn't the German language that went crazy."[8] It provided her with a new and also an original beginning, since she did not have an established intellectual past. Nonetheless, that beginning is quite self-consciously the result of incredible loss and an attempt to review and come to terms with it.[9]

In *Rahel*, the loss and pain were personal, inflected by larger social issues but also carefully individualized. The masquerade in that text is intended as much to veil experience as to enunciate it. By the time she is writing *The Origins*, Arendt's personal experience has necessarily become much more politicized, the stammering author is all too close to being a silent victim, and Arendt's investment in the story is her own need to tell it. In articulating a voice, Arendt forcibly identifies herself with those who inhabit the world of politics as she understands it, as a world of language, and not with those who are silent or silenced. She identifies herself with the free men who are political actors, rather than with women or with the abject, feminine poor—with the speaking Captain Vere, and not with the silent, stammering Billy Budd.[10]

This standpoint of intellectual observation, rather than emotional identification, got Arendt into public difficulties, especially with *Eichmann in Jerusalem*.[11] It was this text that provoked Gershom Scholem's accusation that she had an insufficient amount of *Herzenstakt* ("tact of the heart," or nicety of feeling) for the Holocaust sufferings of her fellow Jews.[12] Arendt publicly defended her apparent coldness by reiterating her belief that compassion corrupts the integrity of the political realm. In response to Scholem, she wrote:

> Generally speaking, the role of the "heart" in politics seems to me altogether questionable. . . . I cannot discuss here what happens when emotions are displayed in public and become a factor in political affairs; but it is an important subject, and I have attempted to describe the disastrous results in my book *On Revolution* in discussing the role of compassion in the formation of the revolutionary character.
> (*Pariah*, 247)

The section of *On Revolution* that deals with the role of compassion in politics is of course the discussion of Billy Budd. In that discussion Arendt identifies Captain Vere as the model of political responsibility, the individual who refuses to give in to any feeling of compassion that would interfere with his duty to see that the rituals of worldly justice endure. Captain Vere may know that Billy is like " 'an angel of God' " (Arendt quoting Melville); nonetheless " 'the angel must hang!' " (*OR*, 84). By explicitly referring, within the context of the Eichmann controversy, to this discussion of compassion, Arendt is putting herself in the position of Captain Vere, asserting her own identity as the one who speaks rather than as one who is calumnied or silenced.

Given that *Eichmann in Jerusalem* was subjected to what Arendt, writing to Scholem, called a "campaign of misrepresentation," it is noteworthy that she implicitly reemphasized her own affinity with the figure of Captain Vere rather than Billy Budd. Even in a situation in which she might very well have felt intellectually victimized by the "Jewish 'establishment,'" Arendt was careful to locate herself in the position of the pained but disinterested observer. She willed herself to be the one who speaks, the one who can "be frank about it" (*Pariah*, 247–48).

Her own position, however, is more ambiguous. As much as she wished for the authority of Captain Vere, she was more in the position of one faced with a great wrong done to her. As a Jew who had managed to escape the Holocaust, the emigration that provided her with some physical and intellectual distance is precisely what marks that distance, temporally and spatially, as the sign of loss, and Arendt's displacement is a sign of her own involvement in the story. She wills herself to speak as clearly as (the masculine) Captain Vere, precisely because she finds herself, at the moment of writing *The Origins*, in a position much more analogous to (the more feminine) Billy Budd's. She too finds herself having to tell her own story, as an explanation for a wrong that has occurred to her, and she too has difficulty in finding a voice.

Yet although Arendt would will herself into the position of Captain Vere, the more obvious model of voice available to her as a Jewish woman writing about antisemitism is less the august tone of masculine authority than the more emotionally charged and feminized staccato of a voice attempting to recount its own crisis while avoiding its own abjection.[13] In *The Origins*, Arendt committed herself to telling the story from a perspective distant enough to allow for evenhanded treatment of the historical and political circumstances, even if this commitment meant suppressing her own emotional involvement in the narrative. She did this by politicizing her understanding of her identity as a Jew. This standpoint of specifically political intellectual analysis, rather than personal emotional identification, is precisely what defines the difference between the last two chapters of *Rahel Varnhagen* and the rest of that text, and what most strongly characterizes the voice Arendt develops through the three volumes of *The Origins*.

Six.
The Charlatan:
Benjamin
Disraeli

The latter problem Englishmen have been rather slow to see in
its true perspective. Gladstone was not in all respects a typical
Englishman, but he was extremely English in his judgement that
Disraeli was fundamentally a false man. That was, and still partly
is, the view of a plain Englishman, even of Disraeli's own party.
But more and more it is coming to be seen that all this was *not
insincerity* but something else, a thing which he thought and
talked all his life—*race*. He could not speak a plain truth like an
Englishman because he was an oriental.
      D. L. MURRAY, "Disraeli," quoted in Boris Segalowitsch,
Benjamin Disraelis Orientalismus (Berlin: Verlag Kedem, 1930), 8–9

In this chapter I begin the process of tracing Arendt's own investigation
of the relationship between political agency and the self-conscious
enactment of social identity through the three volumes of *The Origins of
Totalitarianism*. This is the text that most clearly lays out the questions
and methods Arendt will pursue for the rest of her life. Rather than the
purely philosophical question "Why is there something rather than
nothing?" Arendt asks "Why is there this, and not something else?" Hers
is a deeply historical approach, attentive to the details and the inherent
contingency of the present. From the postwar perspective of her American refuge, Arendt asks "How did we get here? What did we do to deserve
this?" For Arendt these are not moral questions, nor are they strictly
political. They are the fundamental questions that arise from her absolute commitment to worldliness: the recognition that we are in and of this
world, no matter what our religious faith.

   In *Antisemitism* Arendt explores the modern history of the European
Jewish community. This is a history of assimilation, which means it is as
much a history of the community's changing self-perception and self-
representation as it is a history of social and political emancipation. In the
text of *Antisemitism*, and in the concept itself, social and political factors
are inextricably combined, but in this case Arendt does not find that such
a combination precludes political action. Instead, she explores the extent
to which a self-conscious enactment of (Jewish) social identity becomes

an effective strategy for political agency. She explores the political possibilities of social masquerade.

Antisemitism is divided into four chapters, which are arranged as an introduction to and narrative of the eventual tragedy of the Jewish role in Europe. The first chapter, "Antisemitism as an Outrage to Common Sense," introduces the actual textual beginning of *The Origins* with a further hedge on the whole project. Chapter 2, "The Jews, the Nation-State, and the Birth of Antisemitism," provides a historical and political background to the modern phenomena of Jewish emancipation and antisemitism. If the first chapter is a final moment of textual resistance, the second chapter is strangely unstructured and disjointed. But the third chapter is tightly organized. Titled "The Jews and Society," it is itself divided into three sections: "Between Pariah and Parvenu," "The Potent Wizard," and "Between Vice and Crime." That some of Arendt's most original insights into antisemitism are explored in her chapter on "The Jews and Society" should by now come as no surprise. Just as in *On Revolution*, the textual space devoted to social issues becomes an opportunity for theoretical innovation about the politics of social identity. This is the most densely theorized section of her analysis of antisemitism, and the section I will concentrate on. Chapter 4, "The Dreyfus Affair," concludes the volume, and provides an analysis of an assimilated community whose desperately apolitical outlook makes it all the more vulnerable to race prejudice and antisemitic victimization.

In "The Jews and Society," Arendt investigates Jewish reactions to antisemitism, including the successful Jewish masquerade of Benjamin Disraeli. Sandwiched between a discussion of the pariah and the parvenu and a discussion of hypocrisy and vice, Arendt describes Disraeli as the British Jew who fashioned himself as an Oriental, the self-styled exotic other who masqueraded as such in order to dominate the national political life of the international British empire. This masquerade is about race, not gender. But like Riviere's analysand, Disraeli performs the characteristic behaviors of a seemingly inappropriate identity in a public, political context, and he deploys this performance in order to finesse the opposition his embodied social identity would otherwise provoke. Disraeli's flamboyant Jewishness confounds those who would accuse even the baptized Jew of a hidden but essential Jewish identity, just as the analysand's feminine coquetry disarms those who would inevitably distrust a woman in a man's role. Both pariah and parvenu, Disraeli plays the strange role of hero and antihero combined, and he too functions in Arendt's text as an "Outrage to Common Sense."

In this chapter, I locate Disraeli as an emblematic figure in Arendt's text. I also investigate the implications of his role, both for Arendt's larger consideration of antisemitism and for Disraeli's own political negotiations. The key to Disraeli's significance is his recognition that ethnic or racial identity is a social construction rather than an essential physical fact. His Jewishness is a self-conscious mask, but no less real for being performed rather than inherent; the performance of the characteristics of ethnicity, like the performance of the characteristics of gender, returns the freedom of self-definition to the problematized self. Disraeli's insight that he can freely access the characteristics of Jewish social identity in order to create himself as a Jew becomes the basis for his formal role as a self-constructed Jewish political actor.

In *Antisemitism*, Disraeli's masquerade of Jewish social identity for political purposes overshadows other possibilities for Jewish political agency; Arendt's discussion of the Dreyfus affair emphasizes Jewish pettiness, while nearly eliding the significance of Bernard Lazare's self-conscious role as a Jewish pariah. In his own political career, Disraeli's Jewish masquerade is played out in a context of British imperial practice. For both Arendt and Disraeli, the confluence of antisemitism, Jewish identity, and imperialism occurs in Zionism. At the end of her discussion of the Dreyfus affair Arendt gestures toward Zionism as an appropriate political response to European antisemitism; although she doesn't mention it, Disraeli was himself implicated in a plan for a Jewish homeland and British protectorate in Palestine. At the end of this chapter I examine the extent to which Disraeli's Jewish masquerade and his notion of Jewish nationalism complicated and constructed each other; Disraeli's Zionist project becomes the bridge that connects Arendt's own history of *Antisemitism* to her discussion of *Imperialism*.

IDENTITY IN THE NATION-STATE

The Origins begins like a nested set of boxes with a paradox at their center: the book opens with part 1, *Antisemitism*, and *Antisemitism* opens with chapter 1, "Antisemitism as an Outrage to Common Sense." To emphasize the irrationality of antisemitism as a political movement Arendt points to the relative powerlessness of the Jews (*The Origins*, 5) and the blatant but believed forgery of "The Protocols of the Elders of Zion" (*The Origins*, 6–7). Antisemitism is outrageous; the "Protocols of the Elders of Zion" was a blatant forgery in a tradition of blatant forgeries. Nonetheless, that forgery acquired the significance of a foundation myth, the banality of its clichés notwithstanding:

> The point for the historian is that the Jews, before becoming the main victims of modern horror, were the center of Nazi ideology. And an ideology which has to persuade and mobilize people cannot choose its victim arbitrarily. In other words, if a patent forgery like the "Protocols of the Elders of Zion" is believed by so many people that it can become the text of a whole political movement, the task of the historian is no longer to discover a forgery. Certainly it is not to invent explanations which dismiss the chief political and historical fact of the matter: that the forgery is being believed. This fact is more important than the (historically speaking, secondary) circumstance that it is a forgery. (*The Origins*, 6–7)[1]

In Arendt's text, this reference to the "Protocols" further emphasizes the contingency of her own narrative and the historical construction of anti-semitism as a political movement.

In chapter 2, "The Jews, the Nation-State, and the Birth of Antisemitism," Arendt begins to investigate a theme she explores throughout the book: the tension between the cultural and social aspects of national identities and the political rights associated with nation-states. In the nineteenth century individual nation-states began to provide for a more general social and political assimilation of some of their Jewish populations, and only then did the Jews become significantly marginalized Europeans.[2] The state's legal emancipation of certain Jews was selective; Arendt makes clear that legal rights were by no means granted to Jews in general but rather only to those Jews who were financially valuable to the new nation-states. This preferential early emancipation broke down the solidarity of the traditional Jewish communities without effectively integrating all of their members into the national communities of the nation-states:

> Thus, at the same time and in the same countries, emancipation meant equality *and* privileges, the destruction of the old Jewish community autonomy *and* the conscious preservation of the Jews as a separate group in society, the abolition of special restrictions and special rights *and* the extension of such rights to a growing group of individuals.
> (*The Origins*, 12)

This partial assimilation began to transform Jewish identity as it was perceived and experienced. Emancipated as individuals, Jews became vulnerable to parvenu attitudes because their status was determined by their relations to the state and not to the nation.

Arendt's point is that the eighteenth- and early nineteenth-century Jews were legally emancipated without being nationally assimilated:

> It is still one of the most moving aspects of Jewish history that the Jews' active entry into European history was caused by their being an inter-European, non-national element in a world of growing or existing nations. . . . It is not without historical justice that their downfall coincided with the ruin of a system and a political body which, whatever its other defects, had needed and could tolerate a purely European element.
> (*The Origins*, 22–23)

Implicated in the workings of the state but not the nation, Jews were caught in the paradox of the nation-state. In her historical description, the fate of the European Jews and the fate of politics in Europe are combined: the scourge of antisemitism was its subversion of the entire body politic, not just the bodies of the Jews.

Arendt's famed hostility toward economic explanations of sociopolitical events originates here, in her examination of the institutionalization of race-based ideologies and the concurrent decline of political possibilities in the nation-state:

> Europe was much too busy expanding economically for any nation or social stratum to take political questions seriously. . . . The enormous

growth of industrial and economic capacity produced a steady weak-
ening of purely political factors, while at the same time economic
forces became dominant in the international play of power. Power was
thought to be synonymous with economic capacity before people discovered that economic and industrial capacity are only its modern pre-
requisites.

(*The Origins*, 51)

She writes of "Europe" here as though it were an entirely unified, unself-
conscious, and bourgeois entity. Although Arendt is critical of the bourgeois tendency to identify political prerogative with economic power, she
seems to overlook completely the degree to which economic class
became a political issue during the period of economic expansion; she has
no conception that class can become the perspective from which to challenge bourgeois economic politics. Her hostility to a bourgeois view of
politics as the means to implement economic policy thus never really
acknowledges a socialist critique. Without a conception of class identity
that can be anything other than bourgeois or *ressentiment*, she is left to
challenge the bourgeois perspective from a bourgeois position, conceptualized as a kind of antiliberal, democratic, premodern reaction.[3]

Given Arendt's failure to theorize either class or gender, it is striking
that she is so sensitive to the significance of race (inclusive of ethnicity).
She is clear that race became a defining factor in the ideology of imperialism, which itself functioned as the political justification for European
policies of international economic expansion. She also makes clear that
antisemitism prepares for the racism of imperialism by introducing race
thinking into the politics of the nation-state. But most important, she
realizes that race-based ideologies themselves help construct the identities to which they supposedly respond, in that individuals and communities must position themselves relative to a negative social representation
of their own identity. Her thinking on this matter, as provocative as some
of her theorizing on "The Social Question" in *On Revolution*, is contained
in *Antisemitism* in her chapter "The Jews and Society."

PARIAHS AND PARVENUS

The first section of chapter 3 is titled "Between Pariah and Parvenu."
These are terms Arendt had already begun to utilize in *Rahel Varnhagen*,
but here they are much more fully developed as political conceptions.
Arendt uses them to define possible responses to a particular situation of
minority self-representation that is based on a principle of exceptionalism.[4] When social and / or political discrimination prevents the civic and
social assimilation of a particular group into a national community, a
policy of exceptionalism may develop, such that selected individuals may
be allowed political rights or social access, insofar as they are exceptional
members of the otherwise despised community. Thus, in order to
become acceptable to the dominant group, minority individuals must go
out of their way to show that they are not like whatever is assumed to be

the common nature of their group. If they strive for this kind of accept-ance, they choose the role of the parvenu. This is a kind of cultural pass-ing, and all too often requires both the internalization of the standards of this provisional social acceptance and the extension of those standards through a rejection of any solidarity with less-than-exceptional minority counterparts. Those who reject this policy of tokenism while affirming their right to be accepted as legitimate members of a minority identity have chosen the role of the pariah.

Both pariah and parvenu are preoccupied with the problem of a domi-nant group's acceptance of a minority identity, and the potential for a wider social and political integration. The difference is that the parvenu takes a purely individual perspective and is therefore willing to accept dis-criminatory standards in a personal effort to transcend them. The pariah, on the other hand, realizes the political dimension of discrimination, in that it is applied arbitrarily and impersonally to an entire group. The pariah therefore rejects the individualism of the parvenu, in solidarity with the common position of the community.[5]

In *Rahel Varnhagen* and later essays Arendt lauded the pariah type.[6] In "The Jews and Society," however, her attention is caught by decidedly ambiguous figures, who like the social itself often combined a number of categories: Rahel Varnhagen, Benjamin Disraeli, Marcel Proust. This is a varied assortment: a woman, a "charlatan," a homosexual.[7] In *Antisemi-tism*, Rahel is mentioned only briefly. Since Arendt had already written, but had not yet published, the Varnhagen manuscript, it is striking that Rahel is given so little attention here. She is highlighted as a moment of hope in the social and cultural world of the salons, but her complex iden-tity as a Jewish woman was simply too privately complicated a matter for Arendt to try to incorporate in this context. For this text, and this section on "The Jews and Society," she concentrates on problematic men, and especially on the social and political charmer Benjamin Disraeli.[8]

DISRAELI: THE POLITICS OF MASQUERADE

Disraeli, as a baptized Jew, provides Arendt with a figure who has a rela-tionship with the Jewish community different from her own. Disraeli's relationship with his Jewishness was self-consciously self-constructed, elaborated not out of religion but out of race. Arendt titles her discussion of Disraeli "The Potent Wizard,"[9] and he is, by her description, a sort of marvelously gifted alchemist who is able to transform the lead weight of his Jewish identity into the golden glow of social success and power. Dis-raeli is the only figure in *Antisemitism* who retains a kind of glamor: the supposed heroes of this volume—the Dreyfusards—appear as a dedi-cated, earnest lot. Only Disraeli, in Arendt's presentation, has an unmis-takable aura—the aura of romance and exoticism that will be carried over, and more fully developed, in volume 2, *Imperialism*.

Disraeli captures Arendt's imagination because he not only emphasized his Jewishness but also appropriated it as a personal origin out of which to create his own identity and voice. He accomplished a masquerade of Jewish identity that allowed him to achieve a recognized political role, combining Arendt's concept of the public mask through which to speak the truth with Riviere's conception of a strategy of social masquerade. Arendt does not exactly endorse this intermingling of the political and the social, but this is a chapter on society, and she is captivated by his success and by his charm:

> Benjamin Disraeli, whose chief interest in life was the career of Lord Beaconsfield, was distinguished by two things: first, the gift of the gods which we moderns banally call luck, and which other periods revered as a goddess named Fortune, and second, more intimately and more wondrously connected with Fortune than one may be able to explain, the great carefree innocence of mind and imagination which makes it impossible to classify the man as a careerist, though he never thought seriously of anything except his career.
>
> (*The Origins*, 68)

Arendt is herself more concerned with the style of Disraeli's career than with the details of his political policies. She is fascinated by his self-conscious emphasis on his own personal marginal identity and by the way he turned conventional social prejudice inside out and made it the justification for his extraordinary and original success:

> His innocence made him recognize how foolish it would be to feel *déclassé* and how much more exciting it would be for himself and for others, how much more useful for his career, to accentuate the fact that he was a Jew "by dressing differently, combing his hair oddly, and by queer manners of expression and verbiage." He cared for admission to high and highest society more passionately and shamelessly than any other Jewish intellectual did; but he was the only one of them who discovered the secret of how to preserve luck, that natural miracle of pariahdom, and who knew from the beginning that one never should bow down in order to "move up from high to higher."
>
> (*The Origins*, 68)[10]

Disraeli managed the amazing feat of combining the types of pariah and parvenu. He acted on the desires of the parvenu, while embodying the authoritative independence of the pariah; he bypassed the conformist tendencies of the assimilationists, while attaining the worldly successes they could only have envisioned in their wildest dreams. Although Arendt acknowledges Disraeli's social pretensions, she is struck by his achievement of public political power through a kind of authentic charlatanism: he alone became a powerful public figure, not despite his Jewishness, but through it.

To this extent, Arendt notes that Disraeli's political identity was inextricable from his social role. Disraeli, for Arendt, is that strangest of all creatures, a would-be hypocrite who convinces himself but also the world around him of the truth of his performance, and in so doing creates the worldly truth that transcends his own hypocrisy:

He played the game of politics like an actor in a theatrical performance, except that he played his part so well that he was convinced by his own make-believe. His life and his career read like a fairy-tale, in which he appeared as the prince—offering the blue flower of the romantics, now the primrose of imperialist England, to his princess, the Queen of England. The British colonial enterprise was the fairyland upon which the sun never set and its capital the mysterious Asiatic Delhi whence the prince wanted to escape with his princess from foggy prosaic London. This may have been foolish and childish; but when a wife writes to her husband as Lady Beaconsfield wrote to hers: "You know you married me for money, and I know that if you had to do it again you would do it for love," one is silenced before a happiness that seemed to be against all the rules. Here was one who started out to sell his soul to the devil, but the devil did not want the soul and the gods gave him all the happiness of this earth.

(*The Origins*, 68–69)[11]

Disraeli was a Jewish pagan: the closest thing Arendt can find to Greek gloriousness in the modern world.

For Arendt, what saves Disraeli from hypocrisy is his commitment to the integrity of his performance:

One of the reasons for his success was the sincerity of his play. The impression he made on his more unbiased contemporaries was a curious mixture of acting and "absolute sincerity and unreserve."

(*The Origins*, 70)[12]

Many of his contemporaries, however, were put off by the theatrical quality of his self-representation, and by his exoticism. Yet for them also, what saved Disraeli from blatant hypocrisy was his explicit personification of himself as a Jew: they recognized Disraeli's public persona as (the performance of) racial difference rather than (an essential) counterfeit.[13] Indeed, Disraeli managed to be successful, if always somewhat suspect, because he talked about what would otherwise have been his greatest secret and vulnerability: his Jewishness. He not only gave voice to his Jewish identity, he performed as a self-styled Jew in an outrageously flamboyant manner. If Arendt called antisemitism "an outrage to common sense," then Disraeli was an outrage to the antisemites, but not necessarily to the imperialists.

By coopting the characterizations of the antisemites, Disraeli managed to trump them at their own game. But he did so by playing their game. Disraeli brought the Orient home to England by embodying it there in himself, staging his own performance against a backdrop of European imperialist expansion. Without this dramatic context, Disraeli's own personification of Oriental exoticism could not have occurred. He could play the outrageous (Jewish) prince only within the fairy-tale ideology of British imperialism. His own Orientalism, to be made locally acceptable as such, required a distant backdrop of stranger wonders, wonders he presented himself as being specially privileged to understand and to master.

He could play the part of the Oriental Jew because he also acted the role of the British imperialist.

Disraeli's genius was in combining British and Jewish nationalisms under a perfectly contemporary ideology of European imperialism: he embodied Jewish otherness in British society, and British imperialism outside of England. This dual representation emphasized his Oriental exoticism within the context of British national expansion. Although his persona as the British statesman was very much that of the Oriental Jew, no one seems to have seriously doubted his primary identification with the British imperial state. His personal idealization of the Jewish race and nation may have allowed his contemporaries to doubt his credentials as an Englishman, but no one ever doubted his identity as an imperialist.

Obviously, Disraeli was an imperialist because the British were imperialists and not necessarily because he was a Jew. Arendt does bring out the degree to which he played the part of an imperialist because he believed in racial superiority and national prerogative. Nonetheless, she does not explore the deep implications of this relationship in Disraeli's life or in her own writing of it. The ideology of antisemitism encouraged imperialism, but did the Jew who successfully evaded antisemitism necessarily have to be an imperialist?[14]

Arendt avoids this question, in that she presents Disraeli as a lucky exception. For her, his significance lay in his ability to capitalize on and co-opt the dynamic of antisemitism for his own purposes, and that dynamic remains her foremost concern in *Antisemitism*. Disraeli constructed himself as a Jew, an Oriental, and a British imperialist, an identity that worked precisely because it was composed of shifting and apparently contradictory facets. The role of the Oriental became his masquerade: his Jewishness was not a religious faith but a racial performance, while his politics made him the guardian of the British imperial state. He was an Oriental at home and an imperialist abroad, an identity whose contradictions allowed him room for effective political maneuvering, even if the skill exhibited in these maneuvers was precisely what inspired suspicion in many of those around him. While the British suspected him of being essentially a Jew and an Oriental, those outside Britain suspected him of being a British imperialist statesman, despite his protestations of racial loyalty. In each case he was suspected of a hidden essentialism that was undercut by his own commitment to a truth of dramatic self-representation. Within the arena of British politics and society, Disraeli was a dramatically successful pariah; he brilliantly upstaged the antisemites by flaunting his role as a Jew. But as a politician, and especially with regard to questions concerning the empire and the East, Disraeli fully identified himself as British; being a Jewish pariah at home did not lead him into solidarity with the Oriental subjects of British imperial power abroad.

Disraeli could exoticize himself because he was already well assimilated. Although his Jewishness was supposedly essential to him, the shifting definitions of any given identity depend on the cultural and political narratives in which that identity is deployed. Disraeli was too assimilated to be able to confront society with a traditional and conventional Jewish identity, so he made one up, as much if not more out of anti-Jewish prejudice as out of any historical Jewish experience. Arendt notes Disraeli's own statement that "I was not bred among my race and was nourished in great prejudice against them" (*The Origins*, 70), yet she also shows how this very estrangement from Jewish realities provided his imagination with the freedom to create himself as a Jew. If he had not emphasized his Jewishness, Disraeli would have remained as tainted as any parvenu. As it was, the secret to his success was his imaginative publicizing of the very thing others sought to hide or at least not to speak about:

> Disraeli, who never denied that "the fundamental fact about (him) was that he was a Jew," had an admiration for all things Jewish that was matched only by his ignorance of them. The mixture of pride and ignorance in these matters, however, was characteristic of all the newly assimilated Jews. The great difference is that Disraeli knew even less of Jewish past and present and therefore dared to speak out openly what others betrayed in the half-conscious twilight of behavior patterns dictated by fear and arrogance.
> (*The Origins*, 70–71)[15]

He may have been a charlatan, but he was no hypocrite. Other assimilated Jews faced the same ambiguities of identity with shame and silence; only Disraeli reappropriated these ambiguities and affirmed them in his creation of his own distinctively Jewish role and voice.

In particular, Disraeli's independence allowed him to define himself not just as a social being but as a political actor. His Jewishness was a style he created for himself, a social and political masquerade that had less to do with any religious faith or embodied racial identity than with one individual's negotiations with disparate centers of power: "As a baptized Jew, he was of course never an official spokesman for any Jewish community, but it remains true that he was the only Jew of his kind and his century who tried as well as he knew to represent the Jewish people politically" (*The Origins*, 70).[16]

In Disraeli Arendt recognizes a self-conscious political actor who is not bound by the obligations of social identity, although he does not deny his difference. To the extent that Disraeli defines himself as a Jew, he is an Arendtian model of individual agency, a sincere pretender to the role of Jewish pariah Arendt would have given to Rahel. Despite himself, and even because of his charlatan's commitment to a Jewish masquerade, Disraeli becomes the hero of Arendt's text.

SOCIAL HYPOCRISY AND "VICE"

Arendt condemns the alternative of shamed parvenu social ingratiation. Jews with no political consciousness who kept silent about their Jewishness, while exploiting it only as an exotic means of social entry, were the worst form of parvenus. It is the quiet hypocrisy of this social maneuver that makes Jewishness into a vice, and the vice of hypocrisy is what makes parvenu Jewishness, in a corrupt society, something that is "rotten to the core" (*OR*, 103).

The last section of chapter 3 is titled "Between Vice and Crime," and in it Arendt discusses the corruption of a society so hypocritical that it makes Jewishness and homosexuality the delicious and forbidden secrets of social acceptance. In Marcel Proust's *Remembrance of Things Past* Arendt finds a description of a world in which identity is essentialized and never acted upon. Jewishness and homosexuality become acceptable in a corrupt society because they are no longer political or personal realities but essentialized secrets that can be neither escaped nor represented. In the writings of Proust, Arendt discovers decadence, and it disgusts her.[17]

To the extent that Jews and homosexuals become parvenus, their experience of their social role becomes equivalent. In Proust's writing Arendt discovers a description of a society in which embodied social identity, marked by race and / or sexuality, becomes an object of fascination rather than the subject of (self-) representation. In this context, the theatrical metaphor of free action has been repressed and perverted:

> Each society demands of its members a certain amount of acting, the ability to present, represent, and act what one actually is. When society disintegrates into cliques such demands are no longer made of the individual but of members of cliques. Behavior then is controlled by silent demands and not by individual capacities, exactly as an actor's performance must fit into the ensemble of all the other roles in the play. (*The Origins*, 84–85)

In such a contrived social setting, social artifice precludes, rather than enables, individual possibility. There is no freedom to speak and thus no truth or politics, because these social theatrics are all unspoken and self-referential; the actor discloses nothing but rather seeks to imply what is already known yet never referred to. Instead of the outrageous Jewish flamboyance of Disraeli, there is only incestuous intimacy and scandal; Arendt throughout refers to parvenu homosexuals as "inverts."[18]

The parvenu treats identity as essentialist rather than performative, given rather than created. In Proust's descriptions, Jewishness has become a public secret and a private passport to society:

> Although these cliques had no consistency in themselves, and dissolved as soon as no members of other cliques were around, their members used mysterious sign-language as though they needed something strange by which to recognize each other. Proust reports at length the importance of such signs, especially for newcomers. While, however, the inverts, masters of sign-language, had at least a real secret, the Jews used this language only to create the expected atmosphere of mystery. Their signs mysteriously and ridiculously indicated something universally known: that in the corner of the salon of the Princess So-and-So sat another Jew who was not allowed openly to admit his identity

but who without this meaningless quality would never have been able
to climb into that corner.
(*The Origins*, 85)
Here Arendt sounds as exasperated by the fact that Jews had become
dedicated parvenus only to aim for a seat in the corner as she is by the
muteness of this social drama. Not only is speech silenced; even action
is immobilized. Arendt finds that compared to Billy Budd's wild violence or Disraeli's verbal and physical posturing, Proust's social scene
entails no clear self-representation, only the production of an emotional
atmosphere.

For Arendt, it is all too much like being back with Rahel. The personal,
social salon world of Proust's novel is like the one Rahel inhabited; its fascination with personal relations is familiar from her experience. But
Arendt has found this perspective too feminine and too confining, and
she seems oblivious of Proust's humor or his deeper inquiry into the log-
ics of (social and personal) desire. What Arendt notes is that a society of
social parvenus imposes its standards of muted restraint on overtly political issues and drains the vestiges of political consciousness from the
assimilated Jewish community. Near the end of chapter 3, Arendt notes
that "wherever Jews were educated, secularized, and assimilated under
the ambiguous conditions of society and state in Western and Central
Europe, they lost that measure of political responsibility which their
origin implied and which the Jewish notables had still felt, albeit in the
form of privilege and rulership" (*The Origins*, 83).[19] This respectable and
unpolitical social assimilation negates the Jewish capacity for political
identity and action. For Arendt, it even depoliticizes the Dreyfus affair.

DREYFUS (AND LAZARE)
Although "The Dreyfus Affair" is the fourth and last chapter of *Antisemitism*, it is a comedown rather than a climax to Arendt's discussion of the
possibilities for Jewish political agency. The Dreyfus affair is disappoint-
ing, in terms of Arendt's discussion of antisemitism, because by the time
it occurs, the European Jewish community is mostly both assimilated and
depoliticized, and there is nothing particularly admirable in its response
to the incident. Arendt only brings this out in the last section of the chapter, titled "The Jews and the Dreyfusards," but the sad triumph of parvenu over pariah consciousness that the section describes works its way
through the rest of the chapter as a tone of slightly ironic cynicism.

Arendt begins the very first sentence of the initial section on "The
Facts of the Case" as though in the middle of a familiar story, specifying
only the time and place of the dramatic setting: "It happened in France
at the end of the year 1894" (*The Origins*, 89). After describing the essential facts of the affair, she introduces the participants by explicitly point-
ing to their rather absurdly dramatic and literary characters: "The *dramatis personae* of the case might have stepped out of the pages of Balzac"

(*The Origins*, 91). For Arendt, the Dreyfus affair is not so much a tragedy as a melodrama, except that nowhere can she find a hero for it.[20]

No other figure in *Antisemitism* can match Arendt's portrayal of Disraeli. Despite her succinctly witty descriptions of them, she does not develop the personalities of the players in the Dreyfus affair:

... the class-conscious generals frantically covering up for the members of their own clique and ... Picquart, with his calm, clear-eyed and slightly ironical honesty. Beside them stand the nondescript crowd of the men in Parliament, each terrified of what his neighbor might know; the President of the Republic, notorious patron of the Paris brothels, and the examining magistrates, living solely for the sake of social contacts. Then there is Dreyfus himself, actually a parvenu, continually boasting to his colleagues of his family fortune which he spent on women; his brothers, pathetically offering their entire fortune, and then reducing the offer to 150,000 francs for the release of their kinsman ... and the lawyer Demange, really convinced of his client's innocence but basing the defense on an issue of doubt so as to save himself from attacks and injury to his personal interests. Lastly, there is the adventurer Esterhazy, he of the ancient escutcheon, so utterly bored by this bourgeois world as to seek relief equally in heroism and knavery. An erstwhile second lieutenant in the Foreign Legion, he impressed his colleagues greatly by his superior boldness and impudence. Always in trouble, he lived by serving as duelist's second to Jewish officers and by blackmailing their wealthy coreligionists. Indeed, he would avail himself of the good offices of the chief rabbi himself in order to obtain the requisite introductions. ... And what shall we say of Zola, with his impassioned moral fervor, his somewhat empty pathos, and his melodramatic declaration, on the eve of his flight to London, that he had heard the voice of Dreyfus begging him to bring this sacrifice?

(*The Origins*, 91–92)

Two things stand out in this long paragraph of short descriptions. One is that the longest and most impressive description is of Major Walsin-Esterhazy, the real traitor and supposed villain in the Dreyfus case. The other noticeable thing is an absence: nowhere does Arendt mention the one (Jewish) participant one might expect her to respect—Bernard Lazare.

While Picquart is "clear-eyed," Dreyfus a parvenu, and even Zola "melodramatic," Esterhazy is a hero and a knave, impressively superior. His is the only description that has some of the aura with which Arendt invested Disraeli; in his history perhaps she recognized some of the same absolute moral ambiguity that is finally the only heroic response to bourgeois respectability. Otherwise, however, the Dreyfusards she validates are the respectable Gentiles—Clemenceau and Picquart—and the absent figure in her text is the Jew, Lazare.

Arendt barely describes Lazare as a participant, despite the fact that he was one of the earliest and most active crusaders for Dreyfus's innocence.[21] This is especially puzzling because of course Lazare is elsewhere, in earlier texts, Arendt's model of the Jew as pariah, even though he is barely mentioned in that discussion in *The Origins*.[22] Although Lazare would seem to be the perfect textual hero for Arendt—the pariah Jew with a fully developed political consciousness and a determined commitment to political action—she ignores him and hardly mentions him throughout the entire chapter.

In *Antisemitism*, Arendt tries to keep Lazare as hidden as the Dreyfus family did; for them he was an overly, overtly political presence.[23] The family went out of their way not to make the case a political incident, and although Dreyfus was the obvious victim he remained a compliant parvenu. Not only did the Dreyfus family reject for themselves the political implications of their own position; they discouraged anyone else from political analysis or action:

> The skepticism of the radical and socialist press . . . was strengthened by the bizarre tactics of the Dreyfus family in its attempt to secure a retrial. In trying to save an innocent man they employed the very methods usually adopted in the case of a guilty one. They stood in mortal terror of publicity and relied exclusively on back-door maneuvers. They were lavish with their cash and treated Lazare, one of their most valuable helpers and one of the greatest figures in the case, as if he were their paid agent. Clemenceau, Zola, Picquart, and Labori—to name but the more active of the Dreyfusards—could in the end only save their good names by dissociating their efforts, with greater or less fuss and publicity, from the more concrete aspects of the issue.
>
> (*The Origins*, 105–6)

Even if Lazare was a Jew with a political consciousness, he could even less than Disraeli represent himself as an emblematic Jewish figure. Arendt respects Lazare, and she even calls him great, but his isolation too closely resembles her own for him to provide her with a way of re-imagining her own expatriate Jewish circumstances:

> "It isn't enough for them," wrote Bernard Lazare [of the French Jewish community], "to reject any solidarity with their foreign-born brethren; they have also to go charging them with all the evils which their own cowardice engenders. They are not content with being more jingoist than the native Frenchmen; like all emancipated Jews everywhere, they have also of their own volition broken all ties of solidarity. Indeed, they go so far that for the three dozen or so men in France who are ready to defend one of their martyred brethren you can find some thousands ready to stand guard over Devil's Island, alongside the most rabid patriots of the country."
>
> (*The Origins*, 117)[24]

This frustrated sense of isolation, combined with a keen awareness of his historical and political circumstance, makes Lazare an alter ego for

Arendt but not an alternative textual model. As in her discussion of *Billy Budd*, where she overtly rejects the model of the stammering victim for the articulate voice of objective justice, Arendt in "The Dreyfus Affair" ignores the Jew Lazare while halfheartedly celebrating the Gentiles Picquart and Clemenceau. Lazare is in fact in exactly the position Arendt wants to write herself out of: the lone Jewish intellectual, stranded by antisemitism and history on a vantage point of loss, whether in the nineteenth or the twentieth century.

Arendt concludes her chapter on "The Dreyfus Affair," and the volume on *Antisemitism*, by emphasizing the depoliticized parvenu consciousness of most European Jews:

> When the Dreyfus Affair broke out to warn them that their security was menaced, they were deep in the process of a disintegrating assimilation, through which their lack of political wisdom was intensified rather than otherwise. They were rapidly assimilating themselves to those elements of society in which all political passions are smothered beneath the dead weight of social snobbery, big business, and hitherto unknown opportunities for profit. They hoped to get rid of the antipathy which this tendency had called forth by diverting it against their poor and as yet unassimilated brethren. Using the same tactics as Gentile society had employed against them they took pains to dissociate themselves from the so-called *Ostjuden*. Political antisemitism, as it had manifested itself in the pogroms of Russia and Rumania, they dismissed airily as a survival from the Middle Ages, scarcely a reality of modern politics. They could never understand that more was at stake in the Dreyfus Affair than mere social status, if only because more than mere social antisemitism had been brought to bear.
>
> These then are the reasons why so few wholehearted supporters of Dreyfus were to be found in the ranks of French Jewry. The Jews, including the very family of the accused, shrank from starting a political fight.

(*The Origins*, 117–18)

Arendt's frustration with the Dreyfus affair is a frustration with the Jewish community's determined refusal of political consciousness. From her own later historical vantage point, it becomes for her a preview of worse things to come.

Yet here, at the very end of the volume on *Antisemitism*, Arendt apparently unwittingly falls right across her own textual borders and into volume 2, *Imperialism*:

> Thus closes the only episode in which the subterranean forces of the nineteenth century enter the full light of recorded history. The visible result was that it gave birth to the Zionist movement—the only political answer Jews have ever found to antisemitism and the only ideology in which they have ever taken seriously a hostility that would place them in the center of world events.

(*The Origins*, 120)

By referring to Zionism at the very last moment of her discussion of anti-semitism, Arendt complicates and validates the structure of her own text. Within the context of the European nation-states, Zionism was a consistent political response to antisemitism: the ideology of a Jewish nation-state. But outside of Europe, Zionism breaks the Jewish identity as the European other down into its two component identities: the European and the other. Zionism becomes the Jewish version of a colonial adventure, and implicates Jews beyond Disraeli in the European imperialist project. Arendt here seems to validate Zionism as a political response; but, like Disraeli, in doing so she consolidates the Jews' European identity while jeopardizing any possible solidarity with the so-called Orient. Zionism is the underlying link between *Antisemitism* and *Imperialism*, but Zionism also, through the figure of Disraeli, serves to fold the text back in upon itself.

DISRAELI: ZIONISM AS THE (JEWISH) MASK FOR (BRITISH) IMPERIALISM

As a successful British statesman, Disraeli was a careful shepherd of British interests in the international arena; as a self-identified Jew, even one with minimal ties to his community, he was understood to be sympathetic to the general situation of his coreligionists. Although Arendt herself was most likely unaware of it and does not discuss it, there is evidence that Disraeli combined his roles as British imperialist and Jewish representative in a supposed early plan for a Jewish state in Palestine. Disraeli's project was a brilliant exhibition of his own reconciliation of his apparently contradictory double identity as British leader and Jew; it is also a reminder of the possible contradiction between masquerade and nationalism.

Disraeli's Zionist project is not mentioned in the standard biographical sources and is documented only in a strange little pamphlet published concurrently in the United States and (then) Palestine in 1947. Titled *Unknown Documents on the Jewish Question: Disraeli's Plan for a Jewish State (1877)*, the pamphlet purports to document Disraeli's secret diplomatic effort to float the question of a Jewish homeland in Palestine, organized as part of the British empire, at the 1878 Berlin Congress.[25] The veracity of this pamphlet as a historical document is not here our concern.[26] Rather, as Arendt pointed out in her discussion of the "Protocols of the Elders of Zion," its significance within the context of this discussion is that it consolidates elements of an available discourse. Whether or not the pamphlet actually describes an aspect of Disraeli's nineteenth-century diplomacy, it certainly establishes, in mid-twentieth century, that someone was carefully correlating Jewish national and British imperial interests.

The pamphlet supposedly reprints a proposal, sponsored by Disraeli, that was printed anonymously in Vienna in 1877 and suppressed before public distribution. Titled "The Jewish Question in the Oriental Question,"[27] the proposal announces the author's intention to treat the problem of the Jews' alien presence in Europe within the context of the problem of the Orient and of the specific question of European redistribution of parts of the Ottoman Empire after the Russian-Turkish War. The proposal, written in German, was intended to be circulated before the 1878 Berlin Congress in order to build support among the various European participants for a British-controlled Jewish colony in Palestine (then still part of the Ottoman Empire).[28]

The proposal itself outlines the advantages of establishing a Jewish homeland in Palestine under contemporary conditions. Noting the apparently imminent crisis of the Ottoman Empire, and the "number of new, more or less independent multi-national states" recently brought into being, "where the major powers have no contradictory designs," the author reminds the readers that the exceptions to this trend are the Jews and proceeds to argue that present circumstances are ideal for changing this situation (Disraeli in Frankel, *Unknown Documents*, 31–33). The Jews remain a question because they are, all over Europe, a nation without a homeland. They have retained their separate identity for fifteen hundred years without, the author emphasizes, that identity being only a religious one:

> Those who identify the nationality of the Jews with their religion are as gravely in error as they who would attribute the national consciousness of this scattered and dispersed people, their sense of belonging together as a nation, to their religious ideology or to their social and political situation. The incorrectness of this approach is obvious to any honest observer, and demands no elaboration.

(Disraeli in Frankel, *Unknown Documents*, 33)

Such factors are, however, given consideration in the plan. The author admits that an autonomous Jewish homeland would be a political and cultural problem:

> Consider what a mixum-gatherum of languages, costumes, dialects, customs, usages, mores and religious attitudes you would get. What power on earth could bring order out of this chaos or resolve these divers fragments into a single consistent unity? What power could hold this "Babel on Zion" together even for one day? Who could lead or govern it?

(34)

The answer to these questions is of course implicit:

> Let us assume that, under the terms of this proposed solution to the Oriental question, the Jewish homeland were to be placed under the domination of one of the European powers. . . . Is it not probable that within, say, half a century, there would be developed in that land a compact Jewish people, one million strong, speaking one language (i.e. that of the protecting power) and animated by one spirit . . . ?

(35)

Although the author argues for a Jewish homeland, that argument is embedded in assumptions of imperial and European domination.[29] The

Jewish nation can be resolved into a state only under the auspices of a European power, and only if that state is no longer religiously or linguistically Jewish. Yet the question of which European power remains.

Like Disraeli himself, this Jewish entity is to be historically or essentially (racially) Jewish while being for all practical purposes British. It will be a Jewish body governed by British interests:

> The answer is simple. If Palestine is to be served [*sic*] from the Ottoman Empire, there is only one power to whom it can logically fall, and that power is England. One has only to consider the location of the Suez Canal on the one hand and India on the other to realize that the whole Mediterranean from the Euphrates and Lebanon to the Red Sea is of the highest importance to England, whereas to the other powers it is of no significance. And, indeed, what power would be more favorable or beneficent to the realization of this project? Under whose protection could a Jewish colony stand rather than that of England?
> (36)

The Jews are to settle a homeland as British subjects. Only the state upon whose empire the sun never set could be worthy, in the author's eyes, of the full allegiance of the Jewish nation. The project is in the obvious interests of Britain and in the supposed interests of only those Jews willing to colonize a secular state under British (and Christian) authority: those Jews who would follow the example of Disraeli's own political allegiance to imperial Britain and cultural allegiance to (a masquerade) of Jewish identity.

The 1947 pamphlet also includes the printed memorandums of Leon Ritter von Bilinski, the contemporary nineteenth-century Austrian Finance Minister, among whose papers the Viennese version was supposedly found:

> I have read the pamphlet in question. Its argument is consistent and, in many respects, convincing. It is easy to grasp and easy to appreciate. Sometimes, to be sure, the author displays a certain irritation against the great powers, but even this cannot conceal the fact that the work was written not in the interest of the Jews, but of England. When the author speaks of "Jewish nationality" he is merely using the destiny of the Jews as a pawn. What he really wants to serve are the ambitions of England.
> (Bilinski in Frankel, *Unknown Documents*, 21)

Disraeli, who is here regarded as the author of the proposal, is seen to identify the Jews with the Oriental question only insofar as that identification will help advance British imperial interests, which he understands as also being in the Jewish interest (which, after all, they were for him).

Disraeli's Orientalism, his virtuosic representation of himself as a Jew, was always achieved within the parameters of British imperial power. His two roles, that of Oriental Jew and that of British imperial statesman, did not have to be in contradiction with each other, since the one was enacted entirely within the framework of the other. Disraeli's Jewishness, his role as an Oriental, could be emphasized only in a context of Orientalism, itself an elaboration of imperial power.[30]

The problematic nature of Disraeli's Jewish identity was played out in this proposal for a Jewish national homeland constructed as a British state, in which the Jewish question was embedded in the Oriental question, which was itself embedded in explicit assumptions of European cultural and British imperial dominance. That this is acknowledged even within the pamphlet is shown by the comment made by Frau Bilinski, in response to assertions of Theodore Herzl's enthusiastic reaction to the Disraeli proposal: "Yes, but don't forget that Disraeli was a Christian and an out-and-out Englishman to boot. The fact that he tosses compliments to the Jews doesn't mean that he himself felt like a Jew. If you stick to your idea of separating religion and state, what's left of Judaism—of real Judaism, I mean?" (Frau Bilinski in Frankel, *Unknown Documents*, 22).[31] The argument of the pamphlet turns in on itself; if the proposal is taken seriously, then "what's left of Judaism—of real Judaism" but the masquerade of performed Jewish identity that is Disraeli himself? The implicit alternative is an essentialized religious and national/racial ascription. But the pamphlet, whether or not it is a masquerade of another kind, presumes that the Jewish nation can be best secured within an imperial political structure.

Disraeli's early Zionism is not the movement Arendt had in mind, but his proposal focuses attention precisely on the relationship between Zionism as a political response to (European) antisemitism and imperialism as the ideological framework in which Ashkenazi settlement of Palestine occurred. In *The Origins*, Zionism provides the point of convergence between *Antisemitism* and *Imperialism*, but it also problematizes the location of Jewish identity and perspective. If Zionism provided the European Jews with a nationalist response to the problem of Jewish integration in the European nation-states, it did so by refiguring the possible pluralities of Jewish identity as a nationality, and by consolidating that nationality as European rather than Oriental. In *Antisemitism*, the Jews are the Orientals in Europe, individuals whose minority social identity problematically defines their political and cultural experience. In *Imperialism*, the Jews are simply Europeans, and general participants in the expansion of European political, economic, and cultural domination at the expense of those further from the center of a Eurocentric narrative vision.

Seven.
Race and
Economics

Now and then a boat from the shore gave one a momentary contact
with reality. It was paddled by black fellows. You could see from afar
the white of their eyeballs glistening. They shouted, sang; their
bodies streamed with perspiration; they had faces like grotesque
masks—these chaps; but they had bone, muscle, a wild vitality, an
intense energy of movement, that was as natural and true as the surf
along the coast. They wanted no excuse for being there. They were
a great comfort to look at. For a time I would feel I belonged still to
a world of straightforward facts; but the feeling would not last long.
Something would turn up to scare it away. Once, I remember, we
came upon a man-of-war anchored off the coast. There wasn't even
a shed there, and she was shelling the bush. It appears the French had
one of their wars going on thereabouts. Her ensign dropped limp like
a rag; the muzzles of the long six-inch guns stuck out all over the low
hull; the greasy, slimy swell swung her up lazily and let her down
swaying her thin masts. In the empty immensity of earth, sky, and
water, there she was, incomprehensible, firing into a continent.

JOSEPH CONRAD, *Heart of Darkness* (New York: Penguin Books,
    1994), 19–20

This chapter is primarily an examination of *Imperialism*, the second volume of *The Origins of Totalitarianism*. *Imperialism* is the volume that makes
The Origins such an original and provocative book. It is the volume in
which Arendt links the history of Jewish antisemitism with its recent culmination in totalitarian genocide through the modern experience of
European imperialism and race consciousness. Through the discussion
in *Imperialism*, a discussion in which the Jews are actually quite minor figures, Arendt establishes that their twentieth-century fate will be more
than just a singular tragedy, not because it is particularly horrific
(although it is that), but because it is particularly emblematic. Her great
insight is that the twentieth-century destruction of the European Jews
has its origins not only in their own history but also in a larger history of
European economic and political expansion, and in the dynamic of abjection that goes with that expansion. (The continuation of this dynamic

being one of the reasons that contemporary antisemitism is as often directed at Arabs as it is at Jews.) European imperialism involves the transformation of subjugated peoples into racialized units within an over-riding schema of production—a fusion of economic imperatives and racial contempt that corrupts the European political project of citizenship. Imperialism, as an ideology and a practice, establishes the dynamic of racialized abjection and depoliticized instrumental (economic) rationality that will eventually lead to the Jewish holocaust.

Even more important, establishing the connection between the dynamics of imperialist abjection and the destruction of the European Jews places Jewish specificity firmly within the context of a larger political account. The Jewish holocaust is not just one community's tragedy, a claim that asserts a form of depoliticized identity politics Arendt always held suspect. The tragedy of the Jews becomes an emblematic, human tragedy when the Jews are seen not simply as a chosen people, with a unique history, but as one people among many, whose history, specific though it may be, reflects a larger dynamic of political failure, the lesson of which is available, and relevant, to any people living in the late modern world.

In *Antisemitism* Arendt positioned European Jewish experience as a fundamental aspect of European social and political history, and she delineated various Jewish responses to the opportunity and threat of Jewish integration into European national polities and assimilation into bourgeois identity. In *Totalitarianism* she explores the disastrous collapse of the European ideal of political citizenship into genocidal self-destruction. In *Imperialism* she forges a link between her analyses of the incorporation and then the destruction of the Jews in Europe, by detouring through the degeneration of European political identity outside the European context. Through this conjoint analysis, Arendt makes clear that European Jewish history cannot be separated from the history of the peoples outside Europe, whose subjugation and abjection under the European imperial project sets the precedent for the subjugation and abjection of the Jewish people at home.

Imperialism examines the intersection of race consciousness and economic imperative that constituted the ideology of European imperial expansion. Arendt deplores this combination: race consciousness reduces social identity to a fact rather than a performance; economic calculations crowd out the possibility for political agency and action. *Imperialism* chronicles this decline of European political identity, and the narrowing of European political possibility, during the expansion of European military and economic dominion. It gives an account of how the nation became the race and how the world became the market. It also gives an account of the individuals who exemplify the contradictions inherent in this process: Cecil Rhodes and the Boers in South Africa,[1] T. E. Lawrence's masquerade for Arab nationalism in the Middle East. These exemplary figures (and groups) serve to bring Arendt's argument into focus. Willing participants in the European imperial project, they themselves become abject the more they seek, like the Boers, to abject others or, like Lawrence, to ignore the larger dynamic of abjection that encompasses the Great Game in which they play. Even Lawrence, the masquerading political agent par excellence, must in the end acknowledge the futility of a political identity performed against the backdrop of fixed racial categories and strict imperial control. Corrupted by their own privilege, the imperialists set the stage, albeit unwillingly, for the horrors of totalitarianism that will eventually be experienced back home.

Imperialism is a messy volume, a somewhat arbitrary collection of examples held together by an analysis of the combined politics of economics and race. Arendt discusses the role of the bourgeoisie, the scramble for Africa, and the European pan-movements (pan-Slavism and pan-Germanism). Less systematic in its focus than either *Antisemitism* or *Totalitarianism*, *Imperialism* is more diffuse, less coherently shaped by the trajectory of its own inquiry. My own analysis of the volume focuses on Arendt's description of how imperialism brought about the abjection of European political identity, a process she traces by constructing her discourse on the roles of apparently somewhat marginal figures. Within her discussion of imperialism, these figures—Cecil Rhodes, Count Arthur de Gobineau, Joseph Conrad, the South African Boers, Rudyard Kipling, and T. E. Lawrence—witness and participate in specific stages of a process of decline. Whether by essentializing the racial aspect of their own identity (the Boers) or through their response to the realization that their political masquerade had all along been stage-managed for imperial purposes (Lawrence), the main characters in Arendt's study of imperialism become abject. For Arendt, this is the great danger of the imperialist project: the dynamic of abjection that threatens to destroy political possibility, not because the abject are excluded from the political process, but because they no longer recognize that political agency can exist.

IMPERIALISM AND ORIENTALISM

Arendt's perspective on imperialism is resolutely critical, but it is also resolutely Eurocentric. Her lesson is precisely that the international expansion of capitalism and race ideology in the imperialist adventure did violence to the margin but also destroyed the core. She is critical of imperialism's effect on the metropole but is not necessarily concerned with its effect on the subject peoples, and her exemplary figures are the European imperialists whose stories display the transformations of (a hegemonic) European identity extended beyond the European context. Her treatment of imperialism as a European problem is not unique; lifted out of the context of her larger discussion of European political decline, Arendt's perspective in *Imperialism* can seem classically Orientalist.

In his own magisterial study of *Orientalism*, Edward Said demonstrated the extent to which the Orient was not a place but an (intellectual) attitude, determined by European political, cultural, economic, and military

domination, superimposed on existing places, peoples, and cultures.[2]
Said describes the Orient as being the dream-field of the Europeans, their
own creation, known best to themselves:

> Our initial description of Orientalism as a learned field now acquires a
> new concreteness. A field is often an enclosed space. The idea of rep-
> resentation is a theatrical one: the Orient is the stage on which the
> whole East is confined. On this stage will appear figures whose role it
> is to represent the larger whole from which they emanate. The Orient
> then seems to be, not an unlimited extension beyond the familiar
> European world, but rather a closed field, a theatrical stage affixed to
> Europe. An Orientalist is but the particular specialist in knowledge for
> which Europe at large is responsible, in the way that an audience is his-
> torically and culturally responsible for (and responsive to) dramas
> technically put together by the dramatist.

(Said, *Orientalism*, 63)

The Orient is constructed by the West as a stage on which certain truths
of cultural identity can be performed, but these performative truths origi-
nate in the cultural and political milieu of the West even if they are apparently enacted in the East. The performers themselves are representative
figures of either domain, but the meaning of their performance is determined by their audience in the West. The most privileged performers are
those who can, intuitively or consciously, comprehend the narrative and
performative strategies that construct the Oriental space of appearance
and then manipulate them successfully.

Often enough, these most privileged of performers are Westerners
who can enact the East as the West understands it: men such as Benjamin
Disraeli and T. E. Lawrence, simultaneously Western political actors and
masquerading Oriental(ist)s. Said explicitly connects the imperialist and
Orientalist, even if the active combination is not ordinarily found in one
man: "An unbroken arc of knowledge and power connects the European
or Western statesman and the Western Orientalists; it forms the rim of
the stage containing the Orient" (104). These most successful and ambivalent performers style themselves as the embodiment of the Oriental,
which they also seek, as imperialists, to create and subdue. Deeply
divided, their shifting identities as Europeans and/or Orientals are constantly constructed and effaced on the same imperial stage. But their performance is completely structured by the tenets of imperialism, and those
tenets increasingly narrowed the space of performance, inside and outside Europe, while undermining the conventions of political and cultural
representation for the sake of economic, racial, or military goals.

According to Said, the analyses of the Orientalists are more useful for
what they tell us about the West than for what they may propose about
the East. Significantly, Arendt is herself remarkably self-conscious about
this point: *The Origins* is an inquiry into modern European politics and
history, with a central detour through the imperial expansion outside
Europe. This is its strength and also its failing. *Imperialism* opens on a

note of regret, emphasizing the European perspective of the coming analysis:

> But we must admit to a certain nostalgia for what can still be called a "golden age of security," for an age, that is, when even horrors were still marked by a certain moderation and controlled by respectability, and therefore could be related to the general appearance of sanity. In other words, no matter how close to us this past is, we are perfectly aware that our experience of concentration camps and death factories is as remote from its general atmosphere as it is from any other period in Western history.
>
> (*The Origins*, 123)

One is struck both by the presumptiveness of "our experience" and by the emphasis on Western history. The "horrors" of imperialism were apparently not too horrific for the West and their effect on others is evidently not of concern here. Yet there is already an uneasiness, betrayed by the reference to "respectability," a word that in most of Arendt's work is used to indicate a craven conformism to bourgeois social values. Here, however, she uses it to effect a moment of nostalgia for a remembered world: an indulgence of regret for a past that seemed secure but was already rotting at the core.

THE TRIUMPH OF ECONOMICS OVER POLITICS: CECIL RHODES

This moment of indulgence is brief. The first chapter of *Imperialism* is "The Political Emancipation of the Bourgeoisie," and Arendt plunges directly into an argument that continually skirts around any serious consideration of political economy. She describes the bourgeoisie as "the first class in history to achieve economic pre-eminence without aspiring to political rule" (*The Origins*, 123), and what bothers her is that when the bourgeoisie do achieve political power, they are preoccupied with economic interests to the exclusion of political principles:

> The bourgeoisie had developed within, and together with, the nation-state, which almost by definition ruled over and beyond a class-divided society. Even when the bourgeoisie had already established itself as the ruling class, it had left all political decisions to the state. Only when the nation-state proved unfit to be the framework for the further growth of capitalist economy did the latent fight between state and society become openly a struggle for power.
>
> (*The Origins*, 123)

The problem with Arendt's whole consideration of imperialism emerges here, at the beginning of her discussion. Arendt ignores the extent to which liberalism was always the political as well as the economic ideology of the bourgeoisie. It developed with them and did indeed encompass their political aspirations: that those aspirations were laissez-faire (with state intervention when necessary) was precisely the point. Although her commitment to political thinking leads her to link the politics of modern antisemitism with the politics of imperialist racism, her resolute aversion to any serious consideration of the interrelationships between politics and economics (i.e., with the discipline of political economy) leads her to characterize imperialism as fundamentally an economic rather than a political project:

> Expansion as a permanent and supreme aim of politics is the central political idea of imperialism. Since it implies neither temporary looting nor the more lasting assimilation of conquest, it is an entirely new concept in the long history of political thought and action. The reason for this surprising originality—surprising because entirely new concepts are very rare in politics—is simply that this concept is not really political at all, but has its origin in the realm of business speculation, where expansion meant the permanent broadening of industrial production and economic transactions characteristic of the nineteenth century.
> (*The Origins*, 125)

In this analysis, imperialism is the final annexation of the political realm by economics, rather than a new version of the relationship between the economic and the political.[3]

Arendt's resistance to theorizing the political economy of empire weakens her analysis, but it also provides her with her greatest insight: the political significance of the modern concept of essentialized race. Imperialist expansion extends outward from the nation-state, but its principles corrupt the vestiges of public, political life that remain within. Although the political structures of the European nation-states for the most part survived the age of imperialism, their political vitality did not. The political emancipation of the bourgeoisie allowed economic reasoning to dominate political practice, and the political expansion of imperialist policies was dictated by economic interests. But this political and economic expansion then strained the created identity of the nation-state; the state became a tool for economic interests, while the nation was redefined and reemphasized.[4] National interests that spanned the globe placed in question the locus of national identity. The nation as geographical home became the nation as blood origin. Once state authority had been extended, for economic reasons, beyond a recognized national location, national identity could readily be redefined as race.

The personality who haunts Arendt's discussion of imperialism, who combines economic imperatives with racialized politics, is Cecil Rhodes. Rhodes is for Arendt the embodiment of the political emancipation of the bourgeoisie: an international political state-maker whose politics were all dedicated to economic profit and the foundation of a racist state. His is the true voice of imperialism, the unabashed combination of racial ideology and economic expansion that Disraeli was too imaginative, and too carefully self-conscious, to pursue so bluntly:

> "Expansion is everything," said Cecil Rhodes, and fell into despair, for every night he saw overhead "these stars . . . these vast worlds which we

can never reach. I would annex the planets if I could." He had discovered the moving principle of the new, imperialist era . . . and yet in a flash of wisdom Rhodes recognized at the same moment its inherent insanity and its contradiction to the human condition. Naturally, neither insight nor sadness changed his policies. He had no use for the flashes of wisdom that led him so far beyond the normal capacities of an ambitious businessman with a marked tendency toward megalomania. (*The Origins*, 124)[5]

As Arendt sees it, Rhodes's desire to carry the imperialist project to the ultimate degree of universal annexation betrays the concurrent wish to escape the human condition of rootedness and embodiment. Rhodes seeks to transcend worldly limits, to flee the inescapable abjection of his own experience. Even in *The Origins*, a text written several years before she developed this metaphor of celestial escape in the Prologue to *The Human Condition*, Arendt recognizes the overwhelming hubris of Rhodes's desire and its essential threat to political life and human experience. In *The Human Condition*, however, the desire to attain the heavens is situated in the present and prompts an analysis of the past. In *The Origins* this desire is situated in the recent past but carries with it ominous portents of the present.[6]

For Arendt, Rhodes is the epitome of the imperialist system, and she uses him emblematically throughout her discussion. But she does not discuss him in detail. Rhodes may embody the spirit of imperialism, but this spirit, with its single-minded dedication to the annexation of possibility, is antithetical to those ambiguous representations of political identity in which she is so interested. Rhodes is articulate, but he is too bluntly overwhelming; he does not encounter the other, he colonizes it and reorganizes it for commercial profit. He is the triumph of imperialism revealed as international capitalist expansion and manipulation, devoid of Arendtian politics, and therefore dangerous, fascinating, forcefully unambiguous, and also, for Arendt, fundamentally uninteresting.

(CLASS,) RACE, AND RACISM: ARTHUR DE GOBINEAU

Even Arendt must accommodate some economic analysis in her discussion of the forces that shaped the imperial scramble, and, in doing so, she provides one of her few explicit discussions of class. As in the later *On Revolution*, this is not a sympathetic focus: Arendt argues that years of capitalist economic cycles in the crowded industrial nations had created an underclass of human debris. Class stratification, even more than expansionist yearnings, had fractured the political body of the nation-state.

This deterioration in the European body politic was reflected in the concurrent rise of the mob. Abjected from bourgeois society, the mob was both outside that society and its recognized product.[7] In its late nineteenth- and early twentieth-century manifestation, however, the mob was not simply composed of the most miserable poor but was made up of the superfluous aspects of all classes. Idleness, whether among the wealthy or the poor, in a society that had adopted material standards of exchange and production as its arbiter of values, was worse than pur-poselessness or meaninglessness. Arendt connects this human superflu-ousness and the rise of race thinking through her discussion of Count Arthur de Gobineau, a disillusioned, idled aristocrat and the author of one of the earliest and most classic accounts of race as social theory.[8]

Those who had nothing to do risked becoming a commentary on the entire system of capitalist production, unless an occupation and a place could be found for them. Imperialist expansion was a means of dispers-ing this mob while maintaining a claim on its possible productions (*The Origins*, 150). Sent abroad, superfluous capital and superfluous labor clung to their tenuous shared identity: race. Not only did imperialist expansion provide a dumping ground for surplus European capital and labor; it also provided a national purpose that could transcend class divi-sions and reassert national identity as racial origin:

> The truth was that only far from home could a citizen of England, Ger-many, or France be nothing but an Englishman or German or French-man. In his own country he was so entangled in economic interests or social loyalties that he felt closer to a member of his class in a foreign country than to a man of another class in his own. Expansion gave nationalism a new lease on life and therefore was accepted as an instru-ment of national politics.
>
> (*The Origins*, 154)

Arendt does not really engage the contradiction she has herself implied: if the bourgeoisie had sought political power only in order to guarantee extranational capitalist expansion, what was it within the national politi-cal context that had led to such internal alienation and divisions of the national political identity in the first place? But Arendt does not want to confront the problem of class politics. She understands imperialist expansion to be the safety valve for the European political system, but she is not really interested in examining the class pressures it regulated. She is interested not in class per se, but in the sublimation of class into race.

Chapter 6, the second chapter in *Imperialism*, is titled "Race-Thinking before Racism" (*The Origins*, 159–84), and in it Arendt outlines an intel-lectual history of modern race ideologies. Arendt uses this chapter to point out that race thinking was by no means an exclusively German phenome-non, and also to establish the historical connection between racial theories and the nation-state system. Despite her own cultural Eurocentrism, Arendt identifies racism and race thinking as the original (although latent) and eventually fatal flaw in and among the nation-states. Economic values and bourgeois society were bad enough, but race thinking, itself a diverse collection of influences and trends, lies at the origin of totalitarianism:

> For the truth is that race-thinking entered the scene of active politics the moment the European peoples had prepared, and to a certain extent realized, the new body politic of the nation. From the very beginning, racism deliberately cut across all national boundaries, whether defined by geographical, linguistic, traditional, or any other standards, and

denied national-political existence as such. Race-thinking, rather than class-thinking, was the ever-present shadow accompanying the development of the comity of European nations, until it finally grew to be the powerful weapon for the destruction of those nations.
(*The Origins,* 161)

Race thinking is the original and opposite accompaniment to the neat distinctions among the nation-states. Whereas nationalism developed as a growing political specificity, race became an essentializing concept that could cut across national boundaries and encompass a multitude of otherwise disparate identities. But contrarily, it could also be used to justify divisions worked within state boundaries among people who had considered themselves fellow nationals.

Yet as Arendt sees it, racism and nationalism form not so much a binary opposition as a three-pointed system, in combination with humanism. The same political and intellectual ideas that began, in the eighteenth century, to nurture a belief in humanity and a commitment to nation-building also fostered a reactive interest in blood and lineage. Especially in nations like Germany that had great difficulty in achieving the political unity assumed necessary for a nation-state, shared experiences of language and culture could be roused into a kind of modern tribalism in which race substituted for a shared political identity (*The Origins,* 166). Race, as much as it was associated with the scientific and secular theories of Charles Darwin, was also the ideological weapon of aristocratic and mob reaction.[9]

Arendt distinguishes between the social theories of race thinking and the violence of racism. Racism will only come into its own as a justification for brutality when it has been fully combined with (and later separated from) economic purpose. But race thinking originates with caste and class prejudice, and Arendt credits Count Arthur de Gobineau's *Essai sur l'inégalité des races humaines* with establishing race thinking (as opposed to racism) as a legitimate subject for intellectual inquiry and social theory.[10] Gobineau, a minor aristocrat, Bourbonist, and cultural pessimist, developed a theory of racial degeneration to help him account for the obvious failure of the nineteenth-century European nobility—supposedly the old racial elite—to maintain or exert any influence. Gobineau recognized that he himself, as a member of the aristocracy, had been relegated to a marginal position in French political life. This was due not so much to his own minor rank or achievements, but because his caste, and the feudal values of land and family they represented, had been relegated to the margins, replaced by class values:

Our poor country lies in Roman decadence. Where there is no longer an aristocracy worthy of itself a nation dies. Our Nobles are conceited fools and cowards. I no longer believe in anything nor have any views. From Louis-Philippe we shall proceed to the first trimmer who will take us up, but only in order to pass us on to another. For we are without fibre and moral energy. Money *has killed everything.*[11]

Gobineau's social and racial theories were unrelievedly pessimistic, because they were prompted by his own frustrations with the changes of the modern world, and his caste's degenerate response to their own obsolescence. But Arendt makes very clear that Gobineau's race thinking, like Disraeli's, was not the same as racism. For both, the race and the nation were still separate entities; neither conceived of the nation as the race, wholly determined by blood origin rather than cultural and political affiliation. Both authors were fascinated with the Orient, and both spun their racial theories as cultural descriptions, yet neither made the direct connection between race, money, and imperial power.[12]

Even Disraeli, who was fascinated by imperialism, was unconcerned with money, and Gobineau, despite his cranky pessimism, is so utterly opposed to modern socioeconomic infringements on traditional political relations that Arendt is almost protective of him and his peculiar doctrines. Insofar as she understands imperialism to be a combination of blunt racial justification and economic and military expansion, she seeks to distinguish the intellectual eccentrics, like Gobineau and Disraeli (despite the latter's own political involvement), from the practitioners, such as Rhodes:

> Racism sprang from experiences and political constellations which were still unknown and would have been utterly strange even to such devoted defenders of "race" as Gobineau or Disraeli. There is an abyss between the men of brilliant and facile conceptions and men of brutal deeds and active bestiality which no intellectual explanation is able to bridge. It is highly probable that the thinking in terms of race would have disappeared in due time together with other irresponsible opinions of the nineteenth century, if the "scramble for Africa" and the new era of imperialism had not exposed Western humanity to new and shocking experiences. Imperialism would have necessitated the invention of racism as the only possible "explanation" and excuse for its deed, even if no race-thinking had ever existed in the civilized world. (*The Origins*, 183–84)

This distinction between innocent men of ideas and guilty men of action may be rather specious, but it is not as startling as the other idea lodged in the middle of this paragraph. When Arendt indicates that race thinking would probably not have become racism without the " 'scramble for Africa' " (itself a dubious point), she hints that imperialism, particularly in Africa, was accomplished through actions so traumatic to European sensibilities (she is not particularly interested in the trauma it imposed on local peoples) that only a completely essentialized, dehumanizing racism could make those actions acceptable. Race thinking, she seems to be saying, was still an essentially innocuous intellectual phenomenon. Racism, however, was the response not to race thinking but to the atrocities committed as Europeans implemented their (economic) imperial interests.

RACE AND BUREAUCRACY: JOSEPH CONRAD

"Race and Bureaucracy" is the third chapter of *Imperialism*, and the chapter in which Arendt explores the implications of her statement about race, the " 'scramble for Africa,' " and European identity. It is in this chapter that much of Arendt's most blatantly Eurocentric writing occurs, but it is also here that she most carefully explores the defining edge of European identity and experience. As in so many of her other books, it is at this point not surprising to discover that some of Arendt's most interesting conceptualizations are located in her discussion of the supposedly nonpolitical aspect of a political problem. In this case, she allows herself the intellectual space to explore the margins of her own theory, in a chapter on bureaucracy. If the social question replaces properly political revolutionary concerns, bureaucracy is the entity that replaces government. It is here, on the edge of known history and identity, where the political practice of self-representation is confronted by administrative fiat and fixed racial categories, that the most dramatic truths of European identity represent themselves and are represented.

Arendt opens her discussion of imperialist race politics by emphasizing the decisive role race thinking played in imperial domination, and the violence that domination entailed. Initially, she introduces race and bureaucracy as the two-pronged approach to nineteenth-century imperialism:

Two new devices for political organization and rule over foreign peoples were discovered during the first decades of imperialism. One was race as a principle of the body politic, and the other bureaucracy as a principle of foreign domination. Without race as a substitute for the nation, the scramble for Africa and the investment fever might well have remained the purposeless "dance of death and trade" (Joseph Conrad) of all gold rushes. Without bureaucracy as a substitute for government, the British possession of India might well have been left to the recklessness of the "breakers of law in India" (Burke) without changing the political climate of an entire era.

(*The Origins*, 185)

In this first paragraph, Arendt links race and bureaucracy together as the essential and two-sided device of imperialist administration: the combination that will produce political racism. But she also indicates by her choice of quotations, as she did in the previous chapters of her volume, who the determiner of her textual landscape will be. In the earlier chapters, the shadow figures were Rhodes and Gobineau; in this one it is Joseph Conrad.

Arendt relies on Conrad's descriptions of Africa, especially *Heart of Darkness*, to provide her with what she takes to be the fundamental European experience of imperialism: the encounter and confrontation with the abject other. In this chapter of her text Arendt's writing most closely approaches a discourse of Orientalism. Although she deplores the violence imperialist race thinking legitimized, she is deeply sympathetic to the Europeans' fearfulness.[13] Challenged by the foreignness of the cultures and peoples of black Africa, the European imperialists in Arendt's narrative understandably retreated into defensiveness from an encounter with the abject that was unimaginably frightening. Yet this encounter occurred, after all, on European initiative, and the description Arendt gives of it, while repudiating brutal excess, is structured by her empathic participation in a descriptive discourse that is fundamentally Eurocentric and emotionally charged. Continuing her discussion of race and bureaucracy from the first paragraph, she writes:

> Both discoveries were actually made on the Dark Continent. Race was the emergency explanation of human beings whom no European or civilized man could understand and whose humanity so frightened and humiliated the immigrants that they no longer cared to belong to the same human species. Race was the Boers' answer to the overwhelming monstrosity of Africa—a whole continent populated and overpopulated by savages—an explanation of the madness which grasped and illuminated them like "a flash of lightning in a serene sky: 'Exterminate all the brutes.' "

(*The Origins*, 185)[14]

This paragraph is quite remarkable, both for its apparently unproblematic adoption of quasi-mythical and racist rhetoric (Africa as the "Dark Continent," "European or civilized man" as interchangeable, indigenous populations as "savages") as for its use of that rhetoric in a description that predetermines the narrative terms of the encounter from the start. Given the situation Arendt describes—civilization's darkly monstrous encounter with savagery—it is no wonder that civilization responded with the order, "Exterminate all the brutes." The reasonableness of the order depends on the reasonableness of the description. Since Arendt finds the order both reasonable and unacceptable, it may be possible to read back through her text to the contingent elements of the description that are also unacceptable.

Arendt's narrative carefully incorporates those metaphors of the encounters between white and black bodies that are so powerful in *Heart of Darkness:* both texts use race and place as signs of decadent or primal modes of human existence, and both are indictments of European corruption. But in both texts, black bodies are constructed in the narrative as so unnervingly other and abject that an encounter with them, at the margins of empire, can draw white/Western civilization right over the edge and into the dark abyss beyond that, like the heart, is impossible to know.

The imperialists' encounter with the black Africans Arendt calls savages was not simply an encounter with the abject. More significantly, it was the abject's encounter with itself: the European mob's encounter with its own fearful self-conception. The blacks were superfluous brutes who could be exterminated because that is what the displaced whites feared themselves to be, relative to their own culture. Yet Arendt, who despises the degenerate racism of the imperialists, nonetheless condemns them through a narrative structure that replicates many of the most unfortunate of their assumptions. She is not necessarily a racist, but all too often race becomes for her a metaphor for possible levels of civilization, and the African blacks are described as the savages the imperialists understood them to be.

Section 1 of "Race and Bureaucracy" is "The Phantom World of the Dark Continent," a title that immediately conjures vague images of mystery and threat. In a few short paragraphs of remarkable inaccuracy, Arendt slides over the European history of colonization of Australia and North America,[15] completely ignores Latin America,[16] dismisses Asia,[17] and simply assimilates North Africa and the Middle East into the traditional sphere of European influence.[18] Their accuracy aside, these remarks very neatly dismiss the issue of European settlement elsewhere than in Africa.

Arendt's focus is on South Africa, because this is her most fully developed historical illustration of the imperialist solution to the problem of superfluous labor and superfluous wealth. In South Africa, more than anywhere else, European identity degenerated in the encounter with the racial other and in the process of an economic expansion that depended on wealth and excess rather than production. This economic boom, which, combined with a racist ideology, makes South Africa the Arendtian imperialist exemplar, is based on those most fabulous of luxury materials: diamonds and gold.

The South African gold rush was the abjecting of the surplus of an entire system—gold, labor, capital:

It was significant that a society about to part with all traditional absolute values began to look for an absolute value in the world of economics where, indeed, such a thing does not and cannot exist, since everything is functional by definition. This delusion of an absolute value has made the production of gold since ancient times the business of adventurers, gamblers, criminals, of elements outside the pale of normal, sane society. The new turn in the South African gold rush was that here the luck-hunters were not distinctly outside civilized society but, on the contrary, very clearly a by-product of this society, an inevitable residue of the capitalist system and even the representatives of an economy that relentlessly produced a superfluity of men and capital.

(*The Origins*, 188–89)[19]

Arendt characterizes the men involved in the gold rush as themselves abject: not miserable or invisible like the French pre-Revolutionary poor, but those who had been spat out by society. They were the superfluous product of a social and economic system, gone to seek superfluous wealth not because they were entrepreneurs but because they were victims with nothing better to do. Arendt emphasizes that they are not to be identified as workers. They do not share the honorable identity of *homo faber* because they had in fact rejected the European workers' movements Arendt respected for a passive role in international finance and speculation. Not quite invisible, they were nonetheless bodies without identity, the "shadows of events with which they had nothing to do" (*The Origins*, 189).

The unreality of European existence in the empty space of the Dark Continent led to a renewed value on convention and superficial similarities. These were the only bonds that identified Europeans as such and held them together—their skin and their manners—and the very tenuousness of this connection, especially in a world whose otherness seemed overwhelming, could mask a reality in which other differences disintegrated:

> Outside all social restraint and hypocrisy, against the backdrop of native life, the gentleman and the criminal felt not only the closeness of men who share the same color of skin, but the impact of a world of infinite possibilities for crimes committed in the spirit of play, for the combination of horror and laughter, that is for the full realization of their own phantom-like existence. Native life lent these ghostlike events a seeming guarantee against all consequences because anyhow it looked to these men like a "mere play of shadows. A play of shadows, the dominant race could walk through unaffected and disregarded in the pursuit of its incomprehensible aims and needs."
> (*The Origins*, 190)[20]

These adventurers—superfluous, vicious, anonymous—still claimed a European identity that apparently entitled them, in Africa, to any behavior and a sense of importance. Kurtz, and the men like him, including "Carl Peters (possibly the model for Kurtz), who openly admitted that he 'was fed up with being counted among the pariahs and wanted to belong to a master race'" (*The Origins*, 189),[21] could with impunity enact the most vicious possibilities of European political decadence. Arendt, whose understanding of civilization involves the making and knowing of a shared world, understands these men to be lost in a landscape that is entirely unmade and unknown. With no public world that was any longer able to include them, and on the margins of social acceptability, they retained their own individual strength, backed up by imperialist ideology and force.[22] On the Dark Continent, they are so far from the light of a public world that they seem to be shadow figures in a murky twilight, but as Europeans and white men they are still, to themselves and to Arendt, more visible than the anonymous blackness that surrounds them.

As depraved as she may find the European intruders to be, Arendt nonetheless finds them humanly sympathetic. She describes them as familiar figures who found themselves in a context without recognizable marks or limits. But she further emphasizes that within this context they encountered versions of themselves who were essentially unworldly rather than otherworldly. For Arendt, the black Africans in Africa are frighteningly primal. The Europeans, no matter how unrestrained, had known civilization; the Africans, in Arendt's description, exist in some horrifyingly unchanged version of the (abject) state of nature.[23]

Arendt so directly participates in the tradition of European narratives of Africa as abject that, rather than providing her own description, she simply quotes at length from Conrad's *Heart of Darkness*. In allowing Conrad's narrative to function as her own, she speaks through him, endorsing his description of the European experience of Africa. In that description, Africa is so profoundly disconcerting of any European sense of identity or self that almost any European response to the encounter, no matter how morally reprehensible, is understandable. This is an abridged quotation from Arendt's own quote from Conrad:

"The prehistoric man was cursing us, praying to us, welcoming us— who could tell? We were cut off from the comprehension of our surroundings; we glided past like phantoms, wondering and secretly appalled, as sane men would be, before an enthusiastic outbreak in a madhouse. We could not understand because we were too far and could not remember, because we were travelling in the night of the first ages, of those ages that are gone leaving hardly a sign—and no memories. The earth seemed unearthly, . . . and the men. . . . No, they were not inhuman. Well, you know, that was the worst of it—this suspicion of their not being inhuman. It would come slowly to one. They howled and leaped, and spun, and made horrid faces; but what thrilled you was just the thought of their humanity—like yours—the thought of your remote kinship with this wild and passionate uproar."

(*The Origins*, 190)[24]

What is remarkable about this passage is its recognition of racism's fragility; the racist can't help but suspect that the dehumanized objects of his scrutiny really might be human. Even for the racist, racism as a construct is always unstable. Lost in a landscape so strange it is "unearthly," the Europeans confront in those they meet a version of themselves they can neither accept nor deny. The Africans are perceived as meaningless black bodies, but they are unquestionably alive, and in their incomprehensibility and lack of recognizable language they are nonetheless more vital than the pallid Europeans. The Europeans are the ones who recognize, in their incomprehension of the other, their own alienation from any reliable sense of themselves.

In *The Heart of Darkness* Africa functions as a metaphor for the black hearts of white men, and everything encountered there is horrifying to the degree that it is recognized as a familiar, hidden secret of the soul. These encounters are with bodies that are not felt to be unknown, but rather, in their uncontrolled physicality and incomprehensible gibbering, are fearfully familiar. The white Europeans, in contact with black Africans they cannot think of as anything but savagely primitive versions of themselves, abandon what Arendt understands to be their European heritage and become all too much like their own conceptions of the Africans, except that they are white. They become abject.

RACISM AND ABJECTION: THE BOERS

The group in which this European decline is most evident are the South African Boers. In them Arendt observes a descent into tribal savagery in which only the color of their skin identifies the settlers as degenerate rather than primeval. In her narrative, the Boers' crime is not that they enslave their fellow (black) humans, but that the Boers become like (their own understanding of) them in everything but skin color. Race thus becomes their talisman, the only vestige of European identity the settlers have left.

Arendt reserves for the Boers her most appalled description of nineteenth-century degeneration. The descendants of Dutch peasants and French Huguenots who had settled on the Cape of Good Hope in order to supply a provisioning station for ships on the voyage to and from India, the settlers did not re-create in Africa the small-scale agricultural communities they knew from home. Instead, they spread out over an arid landscape, raising cattle and living on family ranches, linked together mostly by their shared fear of the indigenous population. The Boers' response to their situation was race slavery (*The Origins*, 191–92).[25]

Here again, however, Arendt's problematic Eurocentrism is all too apparent. She emphasizes the Africans' lack of civilization rather than their racial difference, but since her conception of appropriate social and material organization is so exclusively European, she essentially reinscribes a racial hierarchy within her own writing. In their native state, the Africans are anathema to her. She keeps referring to the encounter between (white) civilization and (black) savagery as horrible:

> First of all, slavery, though it domesticated a certain part of the savage population, never got hold of all of them, so the Boers were never able to forget their horrible fright before a species of men whom human pride and the sense of human dignity could not allow them to accept as fellow-men. This fright of something like oneself that still under no circumstances ought to be like oneself remained at the basis of slavery and became the basis for a race society.
>
> (*The Origins*, 192)

Arendt here conflates the European conception of what it is to be human (including the mastery of nature) with a universalizing definition of humanity, so that the Boers' rejection of the Africans' humanity becomes for her the pitiful but appropriate response of Europeans who themselves feel that they may have lost all claim to that identity, except skin color. The Boers rejected the Africans because the Africans were not like Europeans, and the Boers, who were not very much like (Arendt's understanding of) Europeans any more either, saw in the Africans an all too familiar version of themselves.

This is precisely the dynamic of abjection, intersected by race and the Protestant work ethic. The Boers see in the Africans their own fantasized escape from the constraints of their economic and religious culture, and the violence of their reaction is in proportion to the fear they have of acknowledging this possibility. Or at least this is the dynamic Arendt describes and to some extent sympathizes with. By having accepted the terms of a discourse in which the African indigenous peoples are "savages," Arendt implies that the rejection of those peoples, in this situation, was an indication of the Boers' desperate attempt to cling to civilized standards of humanity. Note how slavery is said to domesticate savagery and how the settlers' fright at encountering human beings other than themselves and their rejection of those others' humanity is accorded the status of having been motivated by a pride and dignity that is labeled "human."

The problem is that Arendt has assigned to the black Africans the same role she assigned to the poor women marching on Versailles: the role of the natural, undisciplined body whose assertive presence is by definition threatening to achieved political identity. Given this understanding, the only appropriate political response to an encounter with this abject body is to discipline it through a repression that will either hide it or transform it into a respectably civilized representation of itself. Yet even if women and blacks are disciplined to a proper civility, the marker of their social identity will always keep them suspect in an evaluation in which the standard is supposedly neutral but is by convention white and male.

Even when the Africans do organize themselves, as Arendt acknowledges the Zulus united under King Tchlaka at the beginning of the nineteenth century, she denies that the organization constitutes either a nation or a people (*The Origins*, 192–93).[26] Indeed, no matter what they might have done, short of establishing urban social organizations and regimented work schedules—short, in fact, of assimilating to a European model of national development—one suspects that Arendt would not have found their achievements sufficient to allow them the full status of "human." These passages may be some of the most disturbing in all of *The Origins of Totalitarianism*:

> What made them different from other human beings was not at all the color of their skin but the fact that they behaved like a part of nature, that they treated nature as their undisputed master, that they had not created a human world, a human reality, and that therefore nature had remained, in all its majesty, the only overwhelming reality—compared to which they appeared to be phantoms, unreal and ghostlike. They were, as it were, "natural" human beings who lacked the specifically human character, the specifically human reality, so that when European men massacred them they somehow were not aware that they had committed murder.
>
> (*The Origins*, 192)[27]

According to her own description, genocide outside of Europe may not really be genocide at all.

In fact, one fears that Arendt might have found nothing particularly wrong with the Boers' institution of a slave society if they had not abandoned the pride of their European heritage for a racial pride Arendt finds entirely specious. Black Africans, as the Boers (claimed to have) found them, were not human, and among the Boers the sign of being human was to recognize that the Africans were not. Arendt's problem with the Boers is not that they have abjected the Africans, but that they then themselves also became abject. For her, the true horror of South Africa is that everybody degenerates to the level of *animal laborans*, the human being for whom the body and its necessities are the dominant reality:

> The Boers were the first European group to become completely alienated from the pride which Western man felt in living in a world created and fabricated by himself. . . . Lazy and unproductive, they agreed to vegetate on essentially the same level as the black tribes had vegetated for thousands of years. The great horror which had seized European men at their first confrontation with native life was stimulated by precisely this touch of inhumanity among human beings who apparently were as much a part of nature as wild animals. The Boers lived on their slaves exactly the way natives had lived on an unprepared and unchanged nature. When the Boers, in their fright and misery, decided to use these savages as though they were just another form of animal life, they embarked upon a process which could only end with their own degeneration into a white race living beside and together with black races from whom in the end they would differ only in the color of their skin.

(*The Origins*, 194)

The ideal of equality—no difference but color—is for Arendt a degeneration—no difference but color—into the repetitive, necessary life of the body. Like the Boers, she essentializes race. Since the blacks lived off the land, the fact that the Boers lived off the bodily labor of the blacks was nothing more than a variation in the endless cycle of physical life at its most basic. What was a deviation and a degeneration was that the Boers did not, in living off (black) bodies, create what Arendt would recognize as an identifiably human world for themselves. Instead, they were drawn into the patterns of a life in which immediate needs were the only needs. The Boers wandered to the edge of the European world in wandering on the edge of Africa, and, in doing so, Arendt seems to be saying, they might as well have simply fallen off.

The Boers, marginal and degenerate but eerily representative Europeans, betray their future and their past for an urgent immediacy, and transform themselves into a race. In doing so, they also change themselves into a chosen people. The Boers' tribalism, which Arendt deplores, is more like that of the biblical Jewish tribes than of the black Africans. They were a white-skinned race who behaved like their conceptions of a black-skinned race, while claiming the racial prerogatives of the Jewish story. Arendt's description of the Boers makes them like Conrad's description of Kurtz: dangerous and fascinating in their ruthlessness and degeneracy but with an uncanny ability to enact the most insidious possibilities of European identity. She criticizes the Boers' tailoring of standard Christian doctrine and morality to their own convenience, and she is even more appalled by their repeated treks into Africa and away from the ever-encroaching presence of state authority and civilization. Yet Arendt accords the Boers a kind of grudging, uneasy awe. While their black former slaves are "well on the way to becoming workers, a normal part of human civilization" (*The Origins,* 195), the whites have kept apart from this normal (to Arendt) human community of those who are identified by what they produce and do. The Boers, on the contrary, identify themselves as a chosen community simply based on what they are: white.

The South African blacks are redeemed in Arendt's eyes once they have been changed from savages into workers, although she does not mention that their work is more or less forced.[28] The whites, on the contrary, refuse to work at all and so abandon the world, while the blacks are well on their way, as workers, to forming a workers' movement and learning politics. Work, although it is not the highest value in Arendt's general theory, is the basis for those higher values: action and worldliness. The significance of the South African gold rush, for her, is that it created a version of European society from which work was absent and so, necessarily, action and worldliness were absent also.

THE JEWS IN AFRICA: GOOD (BOURGEOIS) EUROPEANS

The Boers' race society developed on the back of black labor but was maintained by a rentier economy based on gold and diamonds; it could not have been maintained under ordinary conditions of production. But the South African gold rush, in which European superfluous labor and capital came seeking underground but superfluous wealth, allowed for the continuation and expansion of a race society. For those who arrived to participate in the delirium, there was little or no risk and little or no labor but plenty of profit. The gold rush brought economic activity, and it expanded and institutionalized South African race society, but it also added another, familiar gradation to the black/white distinction of race as a social issue: the fact that many of the gold rush financiers were Jews.

The second section of Arendt's chapter on "Race and Bureaucracy" is "Gold and Race," but it is really an analysis of the Jewish presence in South Africa. She describes South Africa as the first context in which the Jews were singled out not just as a separate nation but as a separate race:

> Here, for the first time Jews were driven into the world of a race society and almost automatically singled out by the Boers from all other "white" people for special hatred, not only as the representatives of the whole enterprise, but as a different "race," the embodiment of a devilish principle introduced into the normal world of "blacks" and "whites." This hatred was all the more violent as it was partly caused by the suspicion that the Jews with their own older and more authentic claim would be harder than anyone else to convince of the Boers' claim to chosenness. While Christianity simply denied the principle as such, Judaism seemed a direct challenge and rival.
> (*The Origins,* 202)

Jews confused the clear definitions of the race issue: they were white, but not quite.[29] Further, their traditional identity as a chosen people with their own historical, religious, and racial narrative put the Boers' own claim to chosenness in doubt.

But the Jews remain marginal figures in Arendt's narrative of *Imperialism*. Their financial influence having been easily usurped by the imperialist manipulations of Cecil Rhodes (who reemerges at this point in Arendt's text), the Jewish financiers found themselves left out of the wilder economic and military transactions of a society built on gold and race and began to do the one thing Arendt would, in this context, find most admirable: they began to work and to go into the professions. They began to build a normal (bourgeois) world.

It is ironic that Arendt finds this so commendable. Since the whole first chapter of *Imperialism* is about the corrupting effect bourgeois values have on European political identity, it is odd that she is so approving when Jews finally become upstanding members of the bourgeoisie. But within the context of race society, an earlier, simpler version of bourgeois identity that still prefers respectability to expansionist grandeur can almost seem exemplary.[30] For Arendt, ordinary bourgeois values finally bring to the phantom world of Africa a relieving and solidifying normalcy:

> This change in the economic function, the transformation of South African Jewry from representing the most shocking characters in the shadow world of gold and race into the only productive part of the population, came like an oddly belated confirmation of the original fears of the Boers. They had hated the Jews not so much as the middlemen of superfluous wealth or the representatives of the world of gold; they had feared and despised them as the very image of the *uitlanders* who would try to change the country into a normal producing part of western civilization, whose profit motives, at least, would mortally endanger the phantom world of race. And when the Jews were finally cut off from the golden lifeblood of the *uitlanders* and could not leave the country as all other foreigners would have done in similar circumstances, developing "secondary" industries instead, the Boers turned out to be right. The Jews, entirely by themselves and without being the image of anything or anybody, had become a real menace to race society.
> (*The Origins*, 205)

Ironically, the Jews, in prosaically going about the business of production, turn out to be better (bourgeois) Europeans than everybody else.

But what exactly does this mean in the context of Arendt's argument about the interrelation between race thinking and the profit motive within the imperialist project? Her whole critique of bourgeois identity is that it substitutes economic considerations (the profit motive) for political ones; once this has happened, race becomes a convenient way of justifying unspeakable means to expansionist ends. Arendt describes the Jews as "a real menace to race society," but they are not a political threat, bourgeois identity being by (Arendt's) definition antipolitical. Rather than an active "menace," the Jews are merely a destabilizing element within the binary of race society. As whites whose own racial alterity keeps them from being fully accommodated to the ideology of race society, the South African Jews would only have been a real menace to South African race society if they had politicized the issue of race in common with black Africans:

> Yet they cannot and will not make common cause with the only other group which slowly and gradually is being won away from race society: the black workers who are becoming more and more aware of their humanity under the impact of regular labor and urban life.
> (*The Origins*, 205)

It is not exactly clear why the Jews "cannot" make this political connection, even if they "will not," except that Arendt herself cannot conceive of a political movement that is organized around antiracism instead of a politics that is supposedly unconscious of race.[31]

At the end of her discussion of the Dark Continent, Arendt's identification of indigenous African identity as abject precludes her from acknowledging that (nonwhite) racial identity could be mobilized into a political consciousness. For Arendt, race consciousness means the racism of the Boers. Her insistence that the social must be repressed or transcended by the political blinds her to any realization that blacks and Jews could join in antiracist political solidarity. Without this political possibility, Arendt is left with a contradictory affirmation of the apolitical bourgeois identity of the South African Jews and a vague assertion that those most oppressed by a racist polity can only achieve political agency once they leave behind (materially? ideologically?) the racial identity that marks their oppression.

THE GLAMOR OF BUREAUCRACY: RUDYARD KIPLING

The last section of "Race and Bureaucracy" is on "The Imperialist Character." Surprisingly, Arendt asserts that this character is fundamentally bureaucratic, rather than economic or racist. But what she seems to have in mind is the intersection between imperialism and a vestige of political agency: the masked agency of those involved in what Arendt calls, after Kipling, the Great Game.[32]

To the extent that imperialism produced individuals who behaved as self-conscious actors rather than as essentialized white bodies, those individuals were involved not with the blunt distinctions of race, but with the complexities of imperial bureaucracy.[33] In particular, they were involved with that part of the bureaucracy that was concerned with the tricky maneuvers that could shift or maintain the international balance of power. British imperialism in Asia and North Africa (and it is only British imperialism that Arendt discusses in detail) cultivated a national ideal of bureaucratic devotion: the "white man's burden" would not have been so readily assumed if he had not been able to carry it with such a conventional dignity. The values that the British empire mythologized were those associated with the task at hand: the ability to discipline oneself to an elaborate system of organization and the intentional alienation of oneself from one's local environment.[34]

"The East is a career," said Benjamin Disraeli,[35] and Arendt notes that the bureaucratic administration of the East often became the career of England's most idealistic young men:

> The fact that the "white man's burden" is either hypocrisy or racism has not prevented a few of the best Englishmen from shouldering the burden in earnest and making themselves the tragic and quixotic fools of imperialism. As real in England as the tradition of hypocrisy is another less obvious one which one is tempted to call a tradition of dragon-slayers who went enthusiastically into far and curious lands to strange and naïve peoples to slay the numerous dragons that had plagued them for centuries.
>
> (*The Origins*, 209–10)

The best and worst of the young men who subscribed to this vision of themselves were more than mere bureaucrats—they were dragon-slayers and secret agents. They were men for whom the dull restrictions of England were exchanged for the endless possibilities of an empire on which the sun never set, and they were the dupes of a system in which race and bureaucracy could give the illusion, to those looking for it, of nobility and power.

This version of British imperialism has an ambiguous appeal for Arendt. Service in the bureaucracy allowed for a commitment to ideals of devotion and honor in a cause larger than any individual or separate purpose. These civil and military servants of empire found themselves placed upon the stage (of orientalism) in order to play out the part of dramas implicitly more significant than any they could hope to see at home. The open space for political self-disclosure and representation was now behind the scenes of bureaucratic administration, protected by that administration from the tawdry intrusions of modern society. For those who longed for the dramatic possibilities of a public world, that world was now strangely re-created out in the empire but was only approachable through the close ranks of the bureaucracy. Only those who could prove themselves devoted public servants could pass through the bureaucracy into the world of ideals and adventure.

Arendt makes much of Rudyard Kipling's fable "The First Sailor," which she understands as a foundation legend for the British Empire.[36] Although she acknowledges that it does not have the authority of the ancient foundation legends, she finds it significant for its presentation of the English as a political nation in an international context.[37] But she is actually much more intrigued by another Kipling story, "The Tomb of His Ancestor," in which generations of a particular British family consecutively serve in India, nearly anonymous within the British imperial administration but made a native legend by the local tribe.[38] These men lead double lives: as near mythic figures and heroes of their own story among the Indians and as normal servants of the Crown among the British:

> No doubt, the British government pays them for their services, but it is not at all clear in whose service they eventually land. . . . He is simply

at home in two worlds, separated by water- and gossip-tight walls. Born in "the heart of the scrubby tigerish country", and educated among his own people in peaceful, well-balanced, ill-informed England, he is ready to live permanently with two peoples and is rooted in and well acquainted with the tradition, language, superstition, and prejudice of both. At a moment's notice he can change from the obedient underling of one of His Majesty's soldiers into an exciting and noble figure in the natives' world, a well-beloved protector of the weak, the dragon-slayer of old tales.

(*The Origins*, 210)[39]

The hero of Kipling's story is also a hero of Arendt's, a figure who can move with self-conscious appropriateness between two worlds. Living up to the requirements of "foggy prosaic London," he can also clothe himself in the glamor of his inheritance, acting the part of the hero in exotic places, all the more nobly in that the role is understood as a responsibility rather than a privilege.[40]

In a modern world in which Europe had filled its public life with economic preoccupations, those who longed for a life of action devoted to public ideals had only the imperialist services on which to fall back. Those who entered most fully into the hidden drama of self-representation were the secret agents, for whom duplicity and self-display were inextricably combined. Their masquerade was self-conscious, in that they understood themselves as taking on a role, but could do so only in a bureaucratic context in which individual agency was subsumed within the economic directives and racial machinations of the imperial project. Under other circumstances their falsity might have earned Arendt's disdain; in this context she finds their political masquerade authentic enough to credit a foundation legend.

That Arendt refers to Kipling's *Kim* as a foundation legend for the secret agents of the British empire is indicative of the strange respect she accords them.[41] Only something of great and enduring significance may be accorded a foundation legend, and for Arendt the significance of the Great Game of imperial espionage is its imitation of worldliness:

Since life itself ultimately has to be lived and loved for its own sake, adventure and love of the game for its own sake easily appear to be a most intensely human symbol of life. It is this underlying passionate humanity that makes *Kim* the only novel of the imperialist era in which a genuine brotherhood links together the "higher and lower breeds," in which Kim, "a Sahib and the son of a Sahib," can rightly talk of "us" when he talks of the "chain-men," "all on one lead-rope." . . . What makes them comrades is the common experience of being—through danger, fear, constant surprise, utter lack of habits, constant preparedness to change their identities—symbols of life itself . . . and therefore no longer . . . trapped, as it were, by the limitations of one's own individuality or nationality. Playing the Great Game, a man may feel he lives the only life worth while because he has been stripped of everything which may still be considered to be accessory. Life itself seems to be left, in a fantastically intensified purity, when man has cut himself off from all ordinary social ties, family, regular occupation, a definite goal, ambitions, and the guarded place in a community to which he belongs by birth. "When everyone is dead the Great Game is finished. Not before." When one is dead, life is finished, not before, not when one happens to achieve whatever he may have wanted. That the game has no ultimate purpose makes it so dangerously similar to life itself. (*The Origins*, 217)[42]

The Great Game is played by those who themselves adopt the homelessness and rootlessness that will become the common lot of modern humanity. Although they were used by men like Cromer and Rhodes in their endless strategies of imperialist expansion, Arendt finds a remnant of authenticity in the secret agents themselves. Their Great Game was not only for the sake of expansion but also for the sake of the play, and as players they could become caught up in their roles, as much as if not more than they became caught up in the web of their bureaucratic identities. The spy or the secret agent, who lives one identity while he supposedly is another, is the epitome of the contradiction between essence and appearance. To Arendt, for whom truth is that which appears in the world, the performative reality of the agent's identity may just as well be found in his worldly appearance as in his supposedly essential loyalties.

THE GREAT GAME AS FAILED MASQUERADE: T. E. LAWRENCE

The Great Game provides a last, problematic possibility for performative political action. On the stage of the Orient, the imperial bureaucrat as secret agent could play out a masquerade of political identity. To the extent that the agent successfully committed himself to the game, his representation of an identity became as authentic as any representation in the world of appearance can be. But to the extent that he remained caught in the scheme of imperialist purpose, the agent was trapped by the racial and economic considerations that contradicted not only his individual representation but the whole notion of political representation itself. The secret agent is an emblematic political actor. But he is an actor whose role is to undermine the integrity of his own performance; an agent caught inextricably in the contradiction between being and appearance.

At the end of her chapter "Race and Bureaucracy," Arendt considers the sad career of T. E. Lawrence—Lawrence of Arabia. He is for her the most exemplary imperialist agent, one who combined the contradictory elements of secrecy and representation so well that they nearly pulled him apart. He was one of the last of those who sought in the empire what Europe had lost and who avoided, to an almost ridiculous extreme, both fame and normalcy when he returned from the noble and mythic life of his adventures:

Lawrence was seduced into becoming a secret agent in Arabia because of his strong desire to leave the world of dull respectability whose continuity had become simply meaningless, because of his disgust with the world as well as with himself. What attracted him most in Arab civilization was its "gospel of bareness . . . [which] involves apparently a sort of moral bareness too," which "has refined itself clear of household gods." What he tried to avoid most of all after he had returned to English civilization was living a life of his own, so that he ended with an apparently incomprehensible enlistment as a private in the British army, which obviously was the only institution in which a man's honor could be identified with the loss of his individual personality.
(*The Origins*, 218)[43]

By becoming part of something else, Lawrence had become something greater than he alone could ever have been. In the same way that Disraeli assumed the role of the Jew, Lawrence assumed the role of the Arab. The difference was that Disraeli, with almost no contact with the Jewish community, could construct his own version of a Jewish identity without worrying about the contradictions. He was free to fit the role as it suited him, but he was also recognizably Jewish according to the Jewish community's own laws of lineage, despite his childhood baptism. Lawrence, who lived among Arabs, knew he was not an Arab. He played the part of an Arab, but he knew he was a dragon-slayer, and he had to give up his masquerade when the official role for dragon-slayers was finished. Stripped of those garments, he was reduced to the singular Englishman he was, instead of the single most dramatic European representation of an entire foreign national movement. Disraeli could convincingly narrate himself as a Jew, because he himself was convinced. Lawrence, however, was painfully aware that he had lost himself in his role, but then lost the role, and was left with a hypocritical and anonymous sense of self.[44]

Lawrence was himself fully aware of the attributes and contradictions of his role as sincere secret agent. In a letter written in 1918, he exactly expresses the sensibility Arendt described: the intense immediacy and the dreamlike vagueness; the humility of the man doing his job and the drama of the masquerade; the significance of the Arab Revolt and the anonymity that Lawrence himself would desperately seek. This is the same letter from which Arendt draws her quote about the Arab civilization's "gospel of bareness":

For myself. I have been so violently uprooted and plunged so deeply into a job too big for me, that everything feels unreal. I have dropped all I ever did, and live only as a thief of opportunity, snatching chances of the moment when and where I see them. My people have probably told you that the job is to foment an Arab rebellion against Turkey, and for that I have to try and hide my frankish exterior, and be as little out of the Arab picture as I can. So it's a kind of foreign stage, on which one plays day and night, in fancy dress, in a strange language with the price of failure on one's head if the part is not well filled. . . . When they untie my bonds I will not find in me any spur to action. Though actually one never thinks of afterwards: the time from the beginning is like one of those dreams, seeming to last for aeons, out of which you wake up with a start, and find that it has left nothing in the mind. Only the different thing about this dream is that so many people do not wake up in life again. . . . The whole thing is such a play, and one cannot put conviction into one's day-dreams. If we succeed I will have done well with the materials given me, and that disposes of your "lime-light." If we fail and they have patience, then I suppose we will go on digging foundations. Achievement, if it comes, will be a great disillusionment, but not great enough to wake one up.[45]

Lawrence (who had discovered that his illegitimacy made even his name a masquerade) understood his role as a political performer and also understood that the role was doomed. The performance existed in the twilight of the larger hypocrisy of imperialist and bureaucratic intrigue. There was no longer any possibility of a heroic life of public action in England or Europe. But even the stage on which Lawrence had been able to act, which had been made possible by the administrative decisions of the imperialist bureaucracy, was after the war repossessed by those interests, making clear that the performance had ultimately been in their possession all along.[46] His actions, no matter how glorious, remained a tool of the bureaucracy. Politics had become a business of conferences and great-power compromises, and even the man of action who thought he had escaped that world, as Lawrence thought he was and had, found in the end that he had been used up and emptied in the effort to be.

The secret agent inevitably betrays the heroic appearance of his performance because that betrayal is the premise upon which he is provided with the stage on which to perform. The secret agent is not allowed to experience truth as that which appears in the world. Yet Lawrence, having experienced a version of that truth in his public actions, was caught between the "lime-light" he knew to be false and the unreal world of bureaucratic intrigue he had learned was a kind of deadly nothingness. Back in England, enlisted in the RAF under a different name, he deliberately sought to degrade himself from any possible further public use: "I have changed my skin, & love the new one: though the job is less good . . . if things were twenty times worse I would still do it with contentment, for the R.A.F. is a show of my own."[47] Writing from the barracks a month later, he described the personal cost of trying to reconcile his sense of self and the remnants of his having played the Game:

The trouble tonight is the reaction against yesterday, when I went mad:—rode down to London . . . and called in the morning on [King] Feisal [of Iraq], whom I found lively, happy to see me, friendly, curious. He was due for lunch at Winterton's (Winterton, with me during the war, is now Under-Secretary of State for India). We drove there together and . . . of course had to talk of old times . . . as though the R.A.F. clothes were a skin that I could slough off at any while with a laugh.

But all the while I knew I couldn't. I've changed, and the Lawrence who used to go about and be friendly and familiar with that sort of people is dead. . . . From henceforward my way will lie with these fellows here, degrading myself (for in their eyes and your eyes and Winterton's eyes I see that it is degradation) in the hope that some day I will really feel degraded, be degraded to their level.[48]

Lawrence abjected himself from the life and the world he had known. He did everything he could to make himself unacceptable to his former peers, and his insight was that only renunciation, not any new form of notoriety, would make him truly inadmissible. Usually speculation about Lawrence's self-imposed "degradation" revolves around his inability to confront his own sexuality, and specifically his homosexual impulses or experiences. But Lawrence also seems to have been appalled by the personal glamor and power that would have devolved on him as a bureaucrat once his role as an agent was finished. He had played his role (in the Game) sincerely in his championing of the cause of Arab nationalism. But once the Game moved on, and he recognized the extent to which even his role and his cause had been staged for other interests, he became disgusted by the implications of his own experience. He died futilely, under the name of T. E. Shaw, while riding his motorcycle on a quiet road in England: the Game was finished, and life was over.[49]

In transforming himself from T. E. Lawrence into Lawrence of Arabia, Lawrence had discovered the glory of a role and the meaningfulness of a public world. When the role was over and the drama was revealed to have been initiated and co-opted by those whose values were bound by race and bureaucracy, he discovered himself unfit for the life to which he was expected to return. He chose anonymity but not secrecy: the anonymity of the enlisted man, not the bureaucrat. The dramatic role, for all its glorious appearance, had been premised on bad faith. He had known himself to be an actor, but he had believed in the sincerity of the play, and when he realized the larger context, he found himself to be a hypocrite. In recognizing that, Lawrence found himself with nothing left that he, as Lawrence, could bring himself to do, except write about it, which he did. He had come to an end of himself, and he dimly but deeply understood that some way of being in the world had ended, too.

Lawrence is for Arendt a conclusion. Although she continues in her discussion of *Imperialism* with chapters on "Continental Imperialism: The Pan-Movements" and "The Decline of the Nation-State and the End of the Rights of Man," these chapters turn the text back to Europe, and *Totalitarianism*. The tribal nationalism of the pan-movements is an imperialism applied to Europe, but that degeneration is already thoroughly involved with the third volume of the entire text. Lawrence is one of the last men to experience the political possibilities of a social masquerade, and one of the last to experience even a remnant of authenticity in his experience of public appearance:

> This, then, is the end of the real pride of Western man who no longer counts as an end in himself, no longer does "a thing of himself nor a thing so clean as to be his own" by giving laws to the world, but has a chance only "if he pushes the right way," in alliance with the secret forces of history and necessity—of which he is but a function.
> (*The Origins*, 220–21)[50]

For Arendt, Lawrence of Arabia is possibly the last, ambiguous, example of public performative political agency as she understands it. Lawrence strains to achieve a masquerade in which artifice realizes performative truth. Yet when his performance is over, it is revealed to be a fraud, a mockery of the ideals he supposedly represented: a game of essentialized racial identities and bureaucratic strictures. Caught between his own glory and his own abjection, Lawrence is an authentically tragic modern figure. In Arendt's text, he is also a presentiment of tragedies to come.

Eight.
The Banality
of Evil

Hitler, as early as 1929, saw the "great thing" of the movement in the fact that sixty thousand men "have outwardly become almost a unit, that actually these members are uniform not only in ideas, but that even the facial expression is almost the same. Look at these laughing eyes, this fanatical enthusiasm and you will discover . . . how a hundred thousand men in a movement become a single type."
  ADOLF HITLER, quoted in Hannah Arendt, *The Origins of Totalitarianism*, 418

The final volume of *The Origins of Totalitarianism* is itself titled *Totalitarianism*, and is the culmination of the three-part analysis. Although it was the last volume of the larger text to be written, it deals with the most recent events, events that were considered essentially contemporary at the time the volume was written. Their immediacy had only barely subsided, leaving a kind of desolate exhaustion and the suspicion of the loss of the simple continuity of the Western tradition.

Arendt responds to this loss by writing her book, by insisting on the necessity and the possibility of reclaiming meaning from despair. This insistence confronts her with the question of agency and provokes a complex analysis of systemic responsibility and participation. But if Arendt's discussion of *Totalitarianism* is severe, it is not shocking, as some sections of *Imperialism* are. In that volume, the (different) abjection of both the Boers and T. E. Lawrence is appalling, as is even Lawrence's moving attempt to atone for his hypocrisy through a new masquerade of anonymity. In *Totalitarianism*, Arendt's refusal to be appalled leads her to struggle toward the theory of political agency she will variously enunciate in all of her subsequent work. In this section of her text, itself full of some of the most depressing accomplishments of the twentieth century, Arendt also begins to identify the necessary, minimal basis for independent political action: the inherent masquerade of self-representation that is the thinking self.

In the preface to the volume, written for a later edition, Arendt offers a certain intellectual apologia for the book's appearing in 1951, so soon after the war:

In retrospect, the years I spent writing it, from 1945 onwards, appear like the first period of relative calm after decades of turmoil, confusion, and plain horror . . . part of the story had come to an end. This seemed the first appropriate moment to look upon contemporary events with the backward-directed glance of the historian and the analytical zeal of the political scientist, the first chance to try to tell and to understand what had happened, not yet *sine ira et studio*, still in grief and sorrow and, hence, with a tendency to lament, but no longer in speechless outrage and impotent horror.

(*The Origins*, xxiii)[1]

In stating that "part of the story had come to an end," Arendt is directing the reader toward the closure of her own narrative: *Totalitarianism* is the final volume of *The Origins*. But she is also announcing her own emergence from that narrative. The events examined in *Totalitarianism* are the ones that have most directly affected her and have helped produce the voice she has struggled to achieve. This written volume is the sign that she has emerged from "speechless outrage and impotent horror"; she is herself no longer simply an objectified (innocent) victim but can lay claim to the moral complexities of a political voice.

Arendt's concern here, as it is in the prologue to *The Human Condition*, the work written immediately after *The Origins*, is "to think what we are doing" (*HC*, 5). Both texts refer to history in order to find meaning in the present, but in *The Origins* the history is much more recent, and so more overwhelming. Indeed *Totalitarianism*, as the most emotionally explosive of the three volumes of *The Origins*, is also the most insistently controlled. But this historical and philosophical project, a struggle "to tell and to understand," is also deeply political. The political impetus behind *The Origins* is simple: to resist the apparent necessity of being overwhelmed, by either the past or the present, through the enunciation of a possibility for political agency.

In *The Origins* Arendt traces the modern decline of political possibility. First there is the triumph of a bourgeois ideal of private life over political membership in a public world, then the subsumption even of apolitical bourgeois identity into the combined imperatives of economic expansion and racial justifications. In the last two chapters of *Imperialism*, and in *Totalitarianism*, Arendt describes the development of the imperialist dynamic of abjection inside Europe, applied to Europeans. This process transforms identity from a social construction into an all-determining category. Under a totalitarian system, all the possibilities for identity are assumed to be already inscribed on the body; the categories of social identity (whether of race, ethnicity, gender, class, or whatever) become embodied absolutes, and the fate of any individual is simply determined by the policies of the all-encompassing system in which the body is confined.[2] But Arendt is not interested only in the unfolding of a tragedy. The urgency of her entire project—the hubris, which she herself admits, in writing such a book so soon after the events it describes—bears witness to a deeper purpose.

At each stage of her narrative, Arendt's attention is caught by those individuals who maintain a possibility for individual political agency, even when public acknowledgment of such a possibility has all but disappeared. Even, and especially, under totalitarianism, Arendt looks for these exceptions and then interrogates their histories. If some few exemplary figures can retain the ability to conceptualize themselves as political beings even in the darkest of times, then the possibility also remains for more ordinary mortals in more prosaic circumstances.[3]

Arendt's inquiry into the relation between totalitarianism and agency begins in *The Origins*, but she did not finish with it there. Her intention had been to extend her analysis into a fuller discussion of Soviet totalitarianism and Marxism.[4] That project became instead a work on the *vita activa* in classical Greece; Arendt's skepticism about the role of a politics of representation in the (post)modern world sidetracked her into an analysis of a distant and possibly originary past.[5] I will consider *The Human Condition* in chapter 9. But over and over again, her later work returns to the same questions she introduced in *The Origins*, approached in each text through slightly different perspectives and methodologies. *The Origins* is historical; *Eichmann in Jerusalem* is a mix of journalism and sociology; the essays in *Men in Dark Times* are biographical; *The Life of the Mind* is a return to philosophy.[6] Although Arendt's analysis of Eichmann is distinct from her analysis of totalitarianism, and her theory of Eichmann's evil as thoughtless is distinct from her later, more philosophical project, a strong continuity exists among them.

In this chapter I consider aspects of several of these texts, including the last chapters of *Imperialism, Totalitarianism, Eichmann in Jerusalem*, and *Thinking*, the first volume of the unfinished *Life of the Mind*. Over time, as she wrestles with the problem of agency, Arendt focuses more and more closely on the problem of the internal self-representation of the thinking individual. This chapter follows her example: tracing her own shift from an analysis of totalitarian abjection, through a description of totalitarian evil and resistance, and finally through her discussion of the possibility that the political space of appearance—the grounding for agency and political self-representation—has always existed first as a possibility in the individual's own mind.

ABJECTION IN EUROPE

Just as the textual precedents for the analysis in *Eichmann* are set in *Totalitarianism*, the historical precedents for totalitarianism are set in imperialism. Eventually, the race thinking that accompanied the implementation of imperial policies abroad infected the organization of political movements at home. The cultivation of racism in Europe, between Europeans, bridges the separate discussions of *Imperialism* and *Totalitari-*

anism, and reintroduces the European Jews as a major focus of Arendt's analysis.

Arendt concludes *Imperialism* with a discussion of the pan-movements (Pan-Germanism and Pan-Slavism), which applied the concepts of race and expansion to the European world and transformed the European nations into peoples and tribes.[7] In doing so, they rejected the historical construction of citizenship on which the political organization of the European system of nation-states was based.[8] The xenophobic expansionism of the pan-movements signified the collapse of a shared, traditional European identity:

> Politically speaking, tribal nationalism always insisted that its own people is surrounded by "a world of enemies," "one against all," that a fundamental difference exists between this people and all others. It claims its people to be unique, individual, incompatible with all others, and denies theoretically the very possibility of a common mankind long before it is used to destroy the humanity of man.
> (*The Origins,* 227)[9]

In returning imperialist ideologies and practices to Europe, the pan-movements were confronted by an older tribal identity that was already established within the European nation-state system.[10] The pan-movements, whose intention was to reorganize the political landscape according to national rather than state priorities, confronted in the Jews a model and a rebuke. Just as the Boers' degeneration into tribalism was accompanied by a deepening suspicion of the Jews, whose earlier claim to chosenness as the tribe of Israel would seem to have preempted any other Western claim to tribal supremacy, the nineteenth-century pan-movements discovered in the European Jewish diaspora and assimilation an antithesis to their own ideology of xenophobic tribal nationalism.[11]

Arendt does not herself identify the European Jews as the European abject. But writing about abjection in *Powers of Horror,* Kristeva notes that the Jews—who are not only an ancient tribal people but also, and perhaps more important for the Western Judeo-Christian tradition, the People of the Law—are particularly suspect by those who would set up their own tribe and confound the present political, social, and cultural order.[12] The Jews are not only an archaic and continuous tribe; they are also the founders of the singular law of monotheism. Those who would set themselves up as tribal leaders or *volks*-prophets incessantly confront the already established identity of the Jewish other, itself an amalgamation of contradictory principles:

> The anti-Semite is not mistaken. Jewish monotheism is not only the most rigorous application of Unity of the Law and the Symbolic; it is also the one that wears with the greatest assurance, but like a lining, the mark of maternal, feminine, or pagan substance. If it *removes* itself with matchless vigor from its fierce presence, it also integrates it without complacency. And it is possibly such a presence, other but still inte-

grated, that endows the monotheistic subject with the strength of an other-directed being. *In short, when a scription on the limits of identity comes face to face with abjection, it enters into competition with biblical admonitions and even more so with prophetic discourse.*
(Kristeva, *Powers of Horror,* 186)

The rhetoric of the pan-movements, like the rhetoric of the Boers and the rhetoric and practices of the totalitarian fascists, confronts in Jewish history and presence its own alter ego. According to Kristeva, those who endeavor to remove themselves from the known community of identity, in seeking a newly supposed truth in blood and bodies, inevitably encounter a biblical origin and prohibition.

The pan-movements sought to redefine and extend national identity beyond territorial and cultural limits. To do so, however, they needed to postulate an other against which to direct and define themselves, and Kristeva helps explicate the logic by which the Chosen People became the chosen object / abject. As in the African imperialist context, in which the dislocated white Europeans encountered in the black Africans their own fearful version of the other as themselves, the continental imperialists needed to discover in the Jews their own abjected version of what they would become. The difference between the two examples is that Arendt does not present the Jews' identity as only what the dominant group describes it to be. Arendt never allows the Africans their own voice; they are always described from the European perspective. But Arendt is herself a Jew, and one of the projects of her text is the assertion of her own independent Jewish (and female) voice. She must mediate between her description of historical victimization and her own insistence on an authorial voice. In seeking a proper enunciation for this abjected Jewish self, hemmed in by bureaucracy and accident, Arendt turns to the work of Franz Kafka (*The Origins,* 245–46).

THE ABJECT AS VICTIM AND AS PARIAH

Arendt mentions Franz Kafka, briefly and graciously, in only one paragraph in *The Origins.*[13] She calls him the great modern humorist and critic of bureaucracy, and she asserts that it was a miracle that he could so well imagine the articulations of a structure that was still cloaked in respectability (*The Origins,* 245–46). But like Bernard Lazare in her discussion of the Dreyfus affair in *Antisemitism,* Kafka is too close to Arendt's own identity as a near victim and adamant pariah for her to take his persona as a mask through which to assert her own. She barely acknowledges him, and then in a footnote she identifies the Kafka story that contains a description of a character who provides a remarkable combination of specifically feminine agency and victimization.

The Kafka story Arendt refers to is not *The Trial,* which would seem, within the context of *The Origins,* the obvious choice, but *The Castle.* In both novels the protagonist is known only as K., a semi-anonymous observer rather confusedly caught up in the inscrutable workings of a bureaucratic authority that is impersonally distant but insidiously ever-present. In *The Trial* the story deals explicitly with bureaucratic justice in a recognizably modern and urban European setting. In *The Castle*, however, space and time are much more indeterminate, and the story, especially the central story described in Arendt's footnote, is about the intermingling of bureaucratic politics, victimization, and social identity—in this case, gender.

In her footnote, Arendt directs her reader to "see especially the magnificent story in *The Castle* (1930) of the Barnabases, which reads like a weird travesty of a piece of Russian literature. The family is living under a curse, treated as lepers till they feel themselves such, merely because one of their pretty daughters once dared to reject the indecent advances of an important official" (*The Origins*, 246 n. 63). The story of the Barnabases, which Arendt selects as especially indicative of the bureaucratic conditions of European degeneration, is the central story of *The Castle*. Included in the fifteenth chapter, the story is set off in the only episodes of narrative in the novel that are individually titled. Identified as "Amalia's Secret," "Amalia's Punishment," "Petitions," and "Olga's Plans,"[14] these sections are all part of an incident that does not directly involve K. The story is as Arendt describes it: a scandal that shames, incapacitates, and silences the innocent rather than the guilty. The story is told to K. by Olga, who defends her sister Amalia's actions, but also passively accepts the shame they bring. Amalia, however, not only breaks sexual convention by rejecting the sexual address of an all but unknown masculine authority; she also accepts the responsibility, instead of the shame, for her actions. Amalia, who (almost) never speaks, is the only alternative authority in the story: a silent woman who tore up the letter that defined her as a whore. Her life is as ruined as the rest of her family's; she is as much, if not more, a victim, but she evades victimization.

For Arendt, Amalia's story is a parable about the only political option left when one has been trapped, by authority and convention, into the role of victim: the self-conscious pariah. Like Billy Budd, Amalia is beautiful and good, she is punished for her rejection of an attempt to dishonor her, and she accepts that punishment in silence. Unlike Billy Budd, however, she does not resort to physical violence, although she does violence to the letter, and she rejects any opportunity to explain, justify, or defend herself. But whereas Billy Budd remained silent before the political possibility offered by Captain Vere, Amalia's silence occurs in an entirely different context. Billy Budd rejects the possibility of (political) self-representation, and in doing so condemns himself. Amalia's actions, however, occur in a context entirely lacking in possibilities of self-representation: even K. is anonymous, an observer rather than a judge like Captain Vere. But Amalia, by rejecting, alone among the girls of her village, the language of sexual objectification and the role of sexual compliance, succeeds in defining herself as a subject.

She cannot escape being regarded as an essentialized body and becoming a feminine victim, but she refuses to cooperate in her own victimization or identify with its shame.[15] By taking an action that will myste-riously mark her as the one who is both pure and defiled, Amalia posi-tions herself as a pariah on the margins of society. This self who would define herself can only do so by becoming abject; Amalia's agency puts her outside convention. Her family is shunned, but only because she self-consciously rejected what others, including her sister, would have accepted as the normal politics of (sexual) objectification. Repeatedly, Olga insists that if her family had been able to accept the blame and put it behind them, they would have been welcomed back into the com-munity. But the family cannot reconsider its position without shame, and Amalia will not accept her own objectification as the price of social acceptance.

By rejecting the language that would allow her the compromised status of the parvenu, Amalia chooses the role of the pariah. She enacts her own role, but she never gets to tell her own story. Even her rejection is done without words: she simply tears up the demanding, obscene letter. Her action has been reduced to a single act, in which she both rejects and marks herself with the role of the feminine. Refracted through her self-consciously marginal identity, much more even than through K.'s, is the knowledge that in this society no one is safe. In the most extreme cir-cumstances, the only possibility available for self-representation may be the seemingly futile rejection of an identity that is nonetheless outwardly imposed.

In the situation presented in *The Castle*, the only possible way of expressing the truth or an honorable role in the world is through silence. Language has, in a significant respect, lost its power; it only further entangles the speaker in the social guilt and confusion of an explanation. For Arendt, Amalia's silence, described as it is by another, is familiar and even heroic: the behavior of a feminine pariah. But this is a pariah who cannot enact herself, who has little possibility for agency or social mas-querade. Arendt is of course well aware of the problem of voicing a spe-cifically feminine agency, and the Kafka story (and her use of it) mimic her own earlier experiment of finding a voice through Rahel for her own feminine silence. But in this text Arendt can only gesture toward Amalia in a footnote. In the extremity of the world that Kafka describes and that Arendt refers to as best representing the claustrophobia of the last (respectable) days of bureaucratic and bourgeois Europe, "Amalia's Secret" offers only a muted and enclosed version of self-representation and agency.

BODIES, MASSES, MOBS, AND FAMILY MEN

The rest of *The Origins*, including the last chapter of *Imperialism* and the volume on *Totalitarianism*, describes the disintegration of national iden-tity into national bodies, and the reorganization of national bodies into masses, mobs, and alienated family men who would adapt themselves to any policy that would give them a remnant of security. The pan-movements reintroduced tribal nationalism into the European context, and once national affiliation was of more significance than, and in fact often precluded, state affiliation, the nation-state could not maintain itself as a unified political entity. The disintegration of the nation-states into minorities and stateless peoples strikes Arendt as almost apocalyptic. As the sovereignty of the state breaks down, so does the authority of the law, and the sheer blood-right of national interest takes over. Arendt understands the disintegration of the nation-state structure as the plunge from order into chaos.[16]

The triumph of national over state interest meant that states could no longer integrate nonnationals into national and political life, and whole populations were often expelled or supposedly repatriated to territories that refused to accept them as citizens. Arendt regards this phenomenon of statelessness not simply as a personal or a political tragedy, but as a disease that spread like an epidemic and ate away at the structures of legal identity and state authority in even previously healthy states:

> It was also most pathetic to see how helpless the European governments were, despite their consciousness of the danger of statelessness to their established legal and political institutions and despite all their efforts to stem the tide. Explosive events were no longer necessary. Once a number of stateless people were admitted to an otherwise normal country, statelessness spread like a contagious disease.
> (*The Origins*, 285)[17]

These random national bodies, injected into single states and floating loose throughout the nation-state system, reduced the organized identity of the citizen to the blood truth of national origin.

Being reduced to national bodies placed those peoples outside of their national states outside of the law.[18] Arendt argues that the breakdown of the legal authority of the nation-state was obvious once a situation had arisen in which an individual's legal status was often improved by the commission of a petty crime (*The Origins*, 286–90). The supposition that some core of justice remained intact within the internal workings of the legal systems, so that the legal identity and rights of a criminal supplanted the same individual's helplessness as a stateless person, seems a bit too much like wishful thinking.[19] But it does indicate the extent to which Arendt is willing to trust the law to impose a necessary order on the body: the law provides the body with an identity and a name.[20]

Without the legal circumscription of citizenship, these random nationalized bodies coalesced into masses and mobs. Arendt begins *Totalitarianism* with a chapter titled "A Classless Society" and a discussion of these terms. She does not exactly define either mass or mob, but she distinguishes between them as part of her own attempt to understand how the European political tradition gave rise to totalitarian terror. Both emerge after the breakdown of class distinctions and solidarities.[21] The masses are the ordinary, alienated remnants of a class society that has fallen apart, held together only by the lack of any distinct individual or group interests:

The term masses applies only where we deal with people who either because of sheer numbers, or indifference, or a combination of both, cannot be integrated into any organization based on common interest, into political parties or municipal governments or professional organizations or trade unions. Potentially, they exist in every country and form the majority of those large numbers of neutral, politically indifferent people who never join a party and hardly ever go to the polls.

(*The Origins*, 311)

The organization of the masses into a totalitarian movement is not the same as their politicization; mass movements are not social movements. Mass support of totalitarianism does not involve the broadening of political participation as representation but the reduction of political identity to a few essentialized categories. Totalitarianism does not push the masses toward the possibilities of political self-representation. Rather, it organizes the masses into a movement in which membership and opposition are defined by category rather than action, and identity is essentialized rather than achieved. Arendt understands the masses as arising out of the breakdown of a class society dominated by the values of the bourgeoisie. The masses are all that remains of the society of the nation-state once even class interests have given way to vaguely racist and expansionist passions. This is not simply the intrusion of the poor and the social question into the revolutionary concerns of the political realm. Even the abject poor understood the French Revolution (and later anticolonial revolutions) as a political project as well as an economic cause. But Arendt is describing a general popular disillusionment with the practices and analyses of politics per se. The failure of the modern political projects to provide answers to the age-old political questions led to a pervasive, volatile cynicism:

The fall of protecting class walls transformed the slumbering majorities behind all parties into one great unorganized, structureless mass of furious individuals who had nothing in common except their vague apprehension that the hopes of party members were doomed, that, consequently, the most respected, articulate and representative members of the community were fools and that all the powers that be were not so much evil as they were equally stupid and fraudulent.

(*The Origins*, 315)[22]

Alienated and frustrated, with very little sense of self, class, or group interest, the masses of ordinary people rejected the individualized burden of citizenship to coalesce around essentialized racial or religious categories.

Whereas the masses were made up of the reluctant members of ordinary society, the mob was composed of criminals, crackpots, and extremists. For Arendt, the difference between the mass and the mob is the difference between the sheep on the one hand, and an unholy alliance between the shepherd and the wolf on the other. Made up of those who were both disgusted by bourgeois ideals and attracted by violence, the mob included thugs, but it also carried along idealists who in the previous generation would have been secret agents and dragon-slayers for the imperialist bureaucracy:

> They had been more deeply touched by misery, they were more concerned with the perplexities and more deadly hurt by hypocrisy than all the apostles of good will and brotherhood had been. . . . There was no escape from the daily routine of misery, meekness, frustration, and resentment. . . . Without the possibility of a radical change of role and character, such as the identification with the Arab national movement or the rites of an Indian village, the self-willed immersion in the suprahuman forces of destruction seemed to be a salvation from the automatic identification with pre-established functions in society and their utter banality, and at the same time to help destroy the functioning itself.
>
> (*The Origins*, 331)

In the period of postwar economic dislocation and nationalist ideology, the bourgeois conventions of apolitical respectability and economic rationality were no longer credible, but neither were the conventions of duty and caste that glorified imperial service. If the masses were confused and gullible, the mob was cynical and sincere, and ready to offer a new rationality of forthright destruction.

The totalitarian movements were made up of masses of ordinary and conventionally respectable people, whose public leaders were the disciplined extremists of the dispossessed mob. In a society that had already substituted economic commitments for political ones, no one was easier to manipulate than the ordinary persons who thought themselves well disabused of political ideals[23]:

> [Himmler] proved his supreme ability for organizing the masses into total domination by assuming that most people are neither bohemians, fanatics, adventurers, sex maniacs, crackpots, nor social failures, but first and foremost job holders and good family men.
>
> The philistine's retirement into private life, his single-minded devotion to matters of family and career was the last, and already degenerated, product of the bourgeoisie's belief in the primacy of private interest. The philistine is the bourgeois isolated from his own class, the atomized individual who is produced by the breakdown of the bourgeois class itself. The mass man whom Himmler organized for the greatest crimes ever committed in history bore the features of the philistine rather than of the mob man, and was the bourgeois who in the midst of the ruins of his world worried about nothing so much as his private security, was ready to sacrifice everything—belief, honor, dignity—on the slightest provocation. Nothing proved easier to destroy than the privacy and private morality of people who thought of nothing but safeguarding their private lives.
>
> (*The Origins*, 338)

This statement, that the mass supporters of totalitarianism were respectable workers and fathers, is still shocking.[24] But its insight remains: the people who supported totalitarianism were ordinary people, exceptional only in the degree of their social and political anomie. Alienated, frustrated, and frightened, they proved unable or unwilling to oppose what seemed to be the forces of blood and history, organized into an all-encompassing ideological and practical experience.

EICHMANN: THINKING WHAT WE ARE DOING

In most of the rest of *Totalitarianism* Arendt discusses the structure of totalitarian organization. But her brief, sharp insight into the ordinariness of what in this text she is still calling "radical evil" is the direct link to *Eichmann in Jerusalem*. In *Eichmann*, Arendt will seem to contradict herself by describing "the banality of evil," but the core of the political perspective she enunciated in *Eichmann* is already present in *The Origins*.[25] The analysis in *Eichmann* will continue Arendt's preoccupation with the problem of the relationship between overwhelming evil and individual agency. On the one hand, it is precisely because Eichmann rejects all claims to individuality, even the individuality of manifest cruelty or evil, that he is for Arendt so perfectly the epitome of the mass (totalitarian) man. But on the other hand, she pays particular attention to those figures who are able to maintain an individual political identity at odds with the mass ideology around them. Even if their actions seem relatively meager, their ability to retain the capacity to think of themselves as individual members of a shared, public world becomes exemplary, and their thought process becomes the model for Arendt's own theory of thoughtful political action.

Eichmann clings to his lack of specificity, refuses to claim any special talents or to associate himself with any particular interests. With apparently baffling sincerity, he refuses his own public role. Eichmann's refusal to put on a public mask, to be anything other than a simple man who was reasonably ambitious and good at his job—a bourgeois bureaucrat—marks him as the man who refuses even to imagine the possibility of individual self-representation. Arendt emphasizes that he cannot think outside of the trite formulas of the bureaucracy, let alone recognize that bureaucracy as involving an alternate moral compass. Incapable even of imagining himself, he is likewise incapable of imagining himself as another, but perfectly capable of supervising the unthinkable.

Arendt contrasts Eichmann's inability to recognize the significance of his own story with the stories of two other specific individuals. Within a few pages, toward the end of the book, Arendt mentions Zindel Grynszpan and Anton Schmidt: two men whose very different stories nonetheless provided the only moments of tragic, transcendent clarity Arendt finds in the whole trial. Zindel Grynszpan, the very first prosecution witness, and the aged father of the unstable young man whose assassination of a German official was the excuse for *Kristallnacht*, tells the story of his 1938 expulsion from Germany, and Arendt finds herself deeply moved:

This story took no more than perhaps ten minutes to tell, and when it was over—the senseless, needless destruction of twenty-seven years in less than twenty-four hours—one thought foolishly: Everyone, everyone should have his day in court. Only to find out, in the endless sessions that followed, how difficult it was to tell the story, that—at least outside the transforming realm of poetry—it needed a purity of soul, an unmirrored, unreflected innocence of heart and mind that only the righteous possess. No one either before or after was to equal the shining honesty of Zindel Grynszpan.

(*Eichmann*, 229–30)

In this context, no apparent artifice is appropriate, but complete honesty of purpose attains the artistry of poetry. The power of Grynszpan's story is that it is completely uncluttered by sentiment: simple fact, pared down to its emotional truth. This is of course the style to which Arendt herself had aspired for *The Origins*, and it is this clarity of narrative that recommends Zindel Grynszpan to her as an individual who, without benefit of a public mask, nonetheless is able to present an individual story both unique and universal.

But Arendt is still concerned with representation. In the very next paragraph, Arendt identifies what might be the only " 'dramatic moment' " in the whole trial: the only story of an individual who was able to conceive of himself beyond the reductiveness of his supposedly defining identity:

At this slightly tense moment, a witness happened to mention the name of Anton Schmidt, a *Feldwebel*, or sergeant, in the German Army. . . . Anton Schmidt was in charge of a patrol in Poland that collected stray German soldiers who were cut off from their units. In the course of doing this, he had run into members of the Jewish underground . . . and he had helped the Jewish partisans by supplying them with forged papers and military trucks. Most important of all: "He did not do it for money." This had gone on for five months, from October, 1941, to March, 1942, when Anton Schmidt was arrested and executed.

(*Eichmann*, 230)

Arendt cites this story as uniquely compelling.[26] It haunts her not only with the question of what might have been (if there had been more Anton Schmidts), but even more significantly, with the questions of why this one apparently ordinary man did what he did. Alone, most likely aware that his actions could accomplish little and would lead to his death, what made Schmidt decide to act beyond the expectations of his role as *Feldwebel*? What made him, and the other comparable instances of modest, martyred German heroism, like the tiny White Rose resistance cell in Munich, able to act within a moral compass other than the one that surrounded them and the other ordinary people living under Nazi totalitarianism?

Arendt doesn't answer this. But at the end of this chapter in *Eichmann*, she reiterates the significance of Schmidt's example:

For the lesson of such stories is simple and within everybody's grasp. Politically speaking, it is that under conditions of terror most people

will comply but *some people will not*, just as the lesson of the countries
to which the Final Solution was proposed is that "it could happen" in
most places but *it did not happen everywhere.*
(*Eichmann*, 233)

While most people understand themselves in terms of the norms that sur-
round them, some will always comprehend that neither those norms, nor
our identities, are essential. Even under totalitarianism, some people will
be able to keep in mind another moral reality. Arendt wondered whether
this depended on thinking: Eichmann wouldn't think of what he was
doing, Schmidt did, and as she writes in *The Human Condition*, we must.
But perhaps this quality of thinking must be inflected further. Politically
speaking, the lesson may not just be that we must think but that we must
be able to think in terms of masquerade: to think ourselves as agents who
can construct an identity beyond that which is merely assigned to us.

It seems Schmidt was able to envision himself in a context beyond his
immediate one. It is not simply that he thought about what he was doing;
in the same discussion, Arendt discusses a German Army physician whose
postwar writings made clear that he knew the mass killings he observed
in Sevastopol were wrong (they occurred next to his quarters). The physician assumed that without even the possibility of a heroic death, it was
pointless to try to do anything. But Schmidt faced the same situation, and
surely he didn't help the partisans because he thought his martyrdom
would gain him postwar fame. Instead, he seems to have acted according
to what he thought was right, despite the consequences; his ability to act
depended on his ability to conceptualize himself beyond his immediate
circumstances. The physician's lack of action presumes that resistance
would have been senseless without guarantee of a compensatory, enduring heroic narrative. Schmidt's actions indicate that a moral, or political,
narrative can provide for heroic action, even if the narrative exists
(almost) only in the mind of the actor.

Schmidt was not living in a grandiose world of make-believe. But he
seems to have been able to keep in mind an alternative audience for his
actions, even if that audience was merely the observant other of his own
conscience. This split self-consciousness, the ability to envision ourselves
apart from our immediate existence, is the basis for our ability to act as
though our immediate existence were other than it is: for Schmidt's
ability to act as though his actions were meaningful rather than futile,
signs of solidarity rather than suicidal tendencies. The irony is, having
played this part for himself alone (although his actions were enacted with
others), after the war Schmidt's actions gained the public significance of
his solitary reality. Having thought as though, and acted as though, his
actions mattered, they did.

THINKING WITH OURSELVES

Arendt herself addresses this aspect of thinking as self-performance, not
in *Eichmann* but in her final project, *The Life of the Mind*. As she moves

through her investigation in the first volume, *Thinking*, she is constantly circling around, both approaching and delaying, the problem of the connection between thought and action.[27] Having conjectured in *Eichmann* that evil is connected to thoughtlessness, and therefore that refraining from evil must be connected to thought, Arendt tries to think about thinking from an inherently political perspective—i.e., from a perspective that always relates thinking back to our being together in the world.

In developing this inquiry, she considers the strange relationship between the solitude of thinking and the plurality of a single consciousness. Thinking is a solitary dialogue: one listens to oneself. Thus Arendt moves along an unexpected continuum: the plurality of individuals acting together; the singularity of the individual thinking alone; the plurality of the thought process itself. Part of the connection between thought and action is that they are remarkably parallel processes.

Toward the end of *Thinking*, Arendt bears down on the question of the possible essential morality of thinking, which has nothing to do with the moral content of the thought process. (Her model is Socrates, not Plato.) In a section called "The two-in-one" she considers a quote from the *Gorgias* (482c) in which Socrates states:

> It would be better for me that my lyre or a chorus I directed should be out of tune and loud with discord, and that multitudes of men should disagree with me rather than that I, *being one*, should be out of harmony with myself and contradict me.
>
> (*Thinking*, 181)

Within this modest statement lies a clue to the answer to her larger question, and that clue is the apparent contradiction of a self that is both unified and split. This seemingly postmodern contradiction is glossed by Arendt very simply, by understanding the thinking subject as a self unified through the achieved stability of its role with others and fragmented when alone with itself:

> Socrates talks of being one and *therefore* not being able to risk getting out of harmony with himself. But nothing that is identical with itself, truly and absolutely *One*, as A is A, can be either in or out of harmony with itself; you always need at least two tones to produce a harmonious sound. Certainly when I appear and am seen by others, I am one; otherwise I would be unrecognizable. And so long as I am together with others, barely conscious of myself, I am as I appear to others. We call *consciousness* (literally, as we have seen, "to know with myself") the curious fact that in a sense I am also for myself, though I hardly appear to me, which indicates that the Socratic "being one" is not so unproblematic as it seems; I am not only for others but for myself, and in this latter case, I clearly am not just one. A difference is inserted into my Oneness.
>
> (*Thinking*, 183)

When we appear before others as worldly beings who act and experience a shared existence, we gain the stability of a unified role that is accumulated though multiple appearances. Self-contradiction in one's public self is really a perceived difference between the public memory of past appearances and the public expectation that the present appearance should be in keeping with the past. Thus, among others, the self is singular, alone in a crowd, even if the particular singularity keeps changing. But on my own, I am literally by myself. Alone with myself, I must reconcile my own differences, or risk not being able (or willing) to live with myself.

THINKING AND MASQUERADE

This multiplicity of the thinking ego is crucial to Arendt's moral investigation, and to our own. The key to the masquerade of social identity was the ability to enact for others a social role that was not understood to be essential. The social role, itself a construction of artifice and in that sense artificial, secures a stable public identity for the fragmented, plural self. Hypocrisy arises from assuming that the social role is essential and that the deviation from it that is the multiplicity of the thinking ego is a betrayal. But very few of us are Zindel Grynszpan. Hypocrisy will seem to be inevitable, if the continual plurality of the thinking ego, manifested through the endless possibilities for self-disclosure, is mistaken for deviation from a given identity.

The concept of the masquerade authenticates the split between appearing before others and appearing before oneself; the public self, which is a role we play for others, will always be at a remove from the plural, private, thinking self, and the plurality of the private self will inevitably manifest itself in shifts in the public self. Arendt's discussion helps us see that the performative, split quality of the social masquerade is deeply related to the split identity of the thinking self:

In brief, the specifically human actualization of consciousness in the thinking dialogue between me and myself suggests that difference and otherness, which are such outstanding characteristics of the world of appearances as it is given to man for his habitat among the plurality of things, are the very conditions for the existence of man's mental ego as well, for this ego actually exists only in duality. And this ego—the I-am-I—experiences difference in identity precisely when it is not related to the things that appear but only related to itself. (This original duality, incidentally, explains the futility of the fashionable search for identity. Our modern identity crisis could be resolved only by never being alone and never trying to think.)

(*Thinking*, 187)

Plural in ourselves, we can recognize the possibilities of our own otherness only when by ourselves. With others, we may be different, but we do not experience the plurality of our own difference; we are still only one. Even when we discover others who share our difference, our discovery then is that we are one of many. Only alone, through the process of thinking, can we discover that our singular difference exists in an internal plu-

THE BANALITY OF EVIL

rality. Recognizing our own multiplicity, we can recognize the possibility of the small community within the thinking ego. Thinking for ourselves, with ourselves, we can create the basis for our acting alone.

THINKING AND PLURALITY

The solitary process of thinking is not a replacement for acting together. Indeed, our political life depends on the recognition that we exist in a shared, created world, and that the power of our actions is a function of our collectivity. But Arendt's problem here is precisely with the connection between thinking and acting, her thesis that in order to act well, or at least refrain from evil, it is necessary to think.

Thinking, like action, is premised on plurality. To the extent that we recognize that we are ourselves different from ourselves, we begin to recognize that we are ourselves both different and the same. Recognizing the difference in ourselves, it is easier to recognize the similarity in others. The two-in-one of the thinking ego must be in harmony or discord, because it is not merely identical; if I am not the same as myself, perhaps I am more like you, although you are still different from me. In itself, thinking questions any absolute singularity, involves within itself another perspective. Thinking with ourselves, we come close to thinking as another.

The Socratic two-in-one illuminates the puzzling difference between Anton Schmidt and Adolph Eichmann. What made Schmidt act differently from Eichmann or, to make an even closer comparison, differently from the German Army physician who lacked the "conviction" to make "a practically useless sacrifice for the sake of a higher moral meaning"? (*Eichmann*, 232.) Even under totalitarianism, Schmidt, on encountering the (Jewish) other, was able to retreat into the plurality of his thinking and, by himself, with himself, judge what he should do.[28] Apparently alone, Schmidt, through thinking, seems to have recognized a solidarity with the partisans and found solidarity with himself. Thinking, he was able to be as another for himself: he could put himself in another's place, and he could support his own convictions that he must, like Socrates, not "be out of harmony with myself and contradict me" (*Thinking*, 181).

That the thinking ego is indeed able to (bear) witness (for) itself is borne out by another discussion in which Arendt derives a lesson from Socrates, this one in *On Revolution*. In the context of her examination of the political functions of nature and artifice, Arendt refers to Socrates to emphasize that appearance rather than essence is the valid political value, because appearance is the essence of our experience: "Socrates, in the tradition of Greek thought, took his point of departure from an unquestioned belief in the truth of appearance, and taught: 'Be as you would wish to appear to others,' by which he means: 'Appear to yourself as you wish to appear to others'" (*OR*, 101). Arendt here links the private life of the mind with the public world of appearance, by constructing them both as self-representations. In the essential plurality of our thinking, we appear to ourselves, and that self-appearance is as authentically essential as we will ever get to be.

Although in her discussion in *On Revolution* Arendt describes the classical self-consciousness as fundamentally different from the modern, her analysis could as well be of Anton Schmidt's situation as of Socrates':

> For Socrates . . . it was an authentic problem whether something that 'appeared' to no one except the agent did exist at all. The Socratic solution consisted in the extraordinary discovery that the agent and the onlooker, the one who does and the one to whom the deed must appear in order to become real . . . were contained in the selfsame person. The identity of this person, in contrast to the identity of the modern individual, was formed not by oneness but by a constant hither-and-thither of two-and-one; and this movement found its highest form and purest actuality in the dialogue of thought which Socrates did not equate with logical operations such as induction, deduction, conclusion, for which no more than one "operator" is required, but with that form of speech which is carried out between me and myself. What concerns us here is that the Socratic agent, because he was capable of thought, carried within himself a witness from whom he could not escape; wherever he went and whatever he did, he had his audience, which, like any other audience, would automatically constitute itself into a court of justice, that is, into the tribunal which later ages have called conscience.
>
> (*OR*, 102)

In her later discussion in *Thinking*, Arendt no longer distinguishes a modern unified self from a classical plurality; she distinguishes a plural thinking ego from the selves who will not think, those whose refusal of their own plurality also isolates them from the plurality of the world. But here, writing about Socrates, she comes close to answering her own puzzle over Anton Schmidt. Through the plurality of thinking, the individual can create the small community necessary for the self-disclosure of action. Alone, but with the other of himself, Schmidt found a singular independence of mind, the result of a plural thinking ego that, as such, recognizes itself in the plurality of the world.

Neither Eichmann nor the physician could manage this. They would not think about what they knew or what they were doing, and therefore they could not encounter solidarity with themselves or others. They remained isolated, even when most in conformity. Over and over, Arendt emphasizes Eichmann's entrapment in his own bureaucratese. He could not think because he would not part company with the stock phrases and obfuscations that defined the norms of the totalitarian system. Hence his exceptional banality; in refusing to think, to engage alone with himself, he always remained, even when most segregated, a creature who was only one among many. "I am no different from anyone else" is another way of saying "I am no different from myself," and without ever being different in ourselves, we can never attain the difference of individuality among each other.

If Eichmann depended on jargon to keep him from himself, the Army physician depended on the company of his fellow officers. Knowing about the killing that was going on next door, knowing it was wrong, he nonetheless listened only for a voice from another, and hearing none, he kept silent too. Ignoring the two-in-one of his own thinking self, he ignored the possibility that the community necessary for action may begin in the actor's own mind. Since the physician valued only the approbation of others, he could not imagine acting unless assured heroic status, and he could not imagine heroic status without a recognized martyr's death. Yet Schmidt, in a similar situation, was able to be his own witness. Having thought about the circumstances, Schmidt could act for himself; he could appear before himself in his mind's eye without fearing, like the physician, that he would "disappear in silent anonymity" (*Thinking*, 232). In the fullness of time, at the Eichmann trial, others would bear witness for him, but only because he had first been able to do so for himself.

There are no absolute answers to the problem of evil in the world, whether radical or banal. And it can seem all too self-indulgent to assert that by withdrawing into our own minds we oppose it, as though quietism also guaranteed moral absolution. Our life together is a political life, and shaping that life requires action. But action is not necessarily commotion, just as thought is not the same as cognition. Meaningful action, to shape a meaningful world, requires thinking: the plurality in the mind intersecting with the plurality of the world through the singularity of the appearing, acting self.

THE DIALECTICS OF THE THINKING SELF IN THE PLURAL WORLD

Why don't we think? If all it takes is a bit of solitude for the thinking ego to engage itself and find the resources to engage the world, why didn't it, doesn't it, happen more often? But Arendt's version of thinking is not mere idealism, and it is crucial to remember that Schmidt wasn't simply thinking on his own; his thinking was prompted by his encounter with the Jewish partisans. As thinking beings, our relation with the world is always dialectical, and Schmidt thought as he did and acted as he did because he met others whose (politicized) experience was in complete contradiction to the reigning dicta.

Both Schmidt and Socrates were individuals active in the world; Arendt always emphasizes that Socrates, unlike Plato or most other philosophers, was willing to engage in the dialectic with all comers, for the sake of the meaning of the experience itself rather than for the sake of a philosophical system. Active with others, acting with others, they were also able to be active with themselves, to find within the plurality of the thinking ego the confirmation of their experience of plurality in the world. Through the singularity of the active self, they could pivot between the plurality of the world and the plurality of the mind. But perhaps it is critical that they first experienced plurality as an encounter with the other in the world. Then they thought about it. Then, having thought about it in the plurality of the mind, they encountered the other again, and recognized in the other the plurality of themselves—which they had, however, first encountered in the other in the world.

Arendt's is, after all, a political theory of thinking and action, in which the reflexivity between plural mind and world cannot be premised on a privileging of the mind. For if thought by itself were enough to guarantee a moral outcome to action, why then are those who primarily lead the life of the mind so susceptible to misjudging their role in the world? Within Arendt's own compass, the obvious example is Heidegger, and possibly also Plato. For these thinkers, the plurality of the world may be a reflection of the plurality of the mind, but only of the two-in-one; they envision the world as a reflection of their experience of themselves. And the experience of oneself, no matter how thoughtful, will always be solipsistic unless countered by an engagement with the material otherness of the world. Simply thinking about otherness through the example of oneself is not enough; a privileging of the philosophical position can lead to seeing the world as a reflection of one's own systematic endeavor. The encounter with difference in the world offers a profound disruption to the thinking self. But without this encounter, the thinking self is all too likely to understand the world as simply like itself. For such individuals the world is indeed a reflection of the mind, and the otherness of the mind will always be more available to a thinker's attempt at systemization than the otherness of the world.

Thinking plays a different role in the *vita activa* and the *vita contemplativa:* in the one an experience of alterity, in the other a confirmation of itself. Schmidt and Socrates, thinking about the world from a perspective in the world, never made the mistake of taking it for a version of the mind. Heidegger and Plato, thinking about the world from a philosophical perspective, perhaps did.

Arendt herself is a product of both traditions, a young philosopher who was forced to encounter the otherness of her own Jewishness through the history of her times. As she herself famously put it in her open letter to Gershom Scholem during the controversy over *Eichmann:*

> I came late to an understanding of Marx's importance because I was interested neither in history nor in politics when I was young. If I can be said to "have come from anywhere," it is from the tradition of German philosophy.
>
> (*Pariah*, 245–46)

Thus Arendt herself, while reaching for a synthesis of thought and action, perhaps hesitates to give up her loyalty to her first love, whether this be understood as philosophy or Heidegger. Committed to thinking about the world, she nonetheless seems to have limited her encounter with difference to her own encounter with Jewishness. Her reflections on Jewish identity, individuality, and community are indeed profound, and her theoretical insights can be applied to thinking about other identities as well.

But Arendt herself doesn't do this, and the limitations in her discussions of race, gender, and ethnicities other than Jewish reflect this lack.

Yet her own ideas on the relation between thought and action can be pulled together to offer some insight into the problem of evil. Thinking about the world is not enough; on its own it is no better than being in the world without thought. Nonetheless, thinking, when the *vita contemplativa* is understood to be a complement to, and not a substitute for, the *vita activa*, provides a way of synthesizing identity and difference. Other than ourselves, we may be like another, but only the material specificity of the others' differences can bring home to us how truly varied and yet how similar we are.

THE FACELESS, THOUGHTLESS BANALITY OF EVIL

Even in the best of times, thinking is work most of us are happy to shirk. For Arendt, what distinguishes totalitarianism is its institutionalization of the unthinkable. By the end of *The Origins*, Arendt is more and more often emphasizing specifically Nazi atrocities. The particular horror of the concentration camps, according to Arendt, was not their organized cruelty but their attempt to eliminate all distinctions and differences within any given group, and thus abolish the most basic material conditions for thought, identity, and agency.[29] This absolute homogenization, of which Hitler was so proud in the elite organizations, was attained in the camps through the organized application of arbitrary terror. Human beings were reduced to bodies: "Total domination, which strives to organize the infinite plurality and differentiation of human beings as if all of humanity were just one individual, is possible only if each and every person can be reduced to a never-changing identity of reactions, so that each of these bundles of reactions can be exchanged at random for any other" (*The Origins*, 438).[30]

The experience of total domination in the camps separated all those who participated in them, as guards or inmates, from the general world of human experience.[31] The camps produced faceless beings who could not as such be integrated into the ordinary world from which they came. Arendt includes in a footnote this self-description by an SS camp guard: "Usually I keep on hitting until I ejaculate. I have a wife and three children in Breslau. I used to be perfectly normal. That's what they've made of me. Now when they give me a pass out of here, I don't go home. I don't dare look my wife in the face" (*The Origins*, 454 n. 159).[32] This, then, is the ordinary job holder and good family man, reduced finally to a faceless phenomenon of perverse bestiality. When the good husband and father has become a man without a face, a body that shamefully marks itself as sexually perverse while it marks the body of the other with violence, the human differences between the identities of the victim and the perpetrator have indeed become confused. This is not to say that innocence and guilt have no role to play in moral and political judgment. But in such an extremity of violence and anonymity, in which individual identity has been reduced to the essentialism of the (racially determined) physical body, the self becomes the body, and the body itself becomes abject.

Yet despite the utter degradation of politics and identity she has chronicled in *Totalitarianism*, Arendt concludes her text on a note of hope. *The Origins* comes full circle; the book that began as an attempt to make sense of the present through an analysis of the recent past finishes by returning to the present as the site of new beginnings. This is, again, a sign of Arendt's political commitment: her insistence on thinking through the overwhelming weight of recent history to a renewed possibility for agency.

In the last few pages of *The Origins* Arendt points out that the great precondition for totalitarian domination is the modern condition of loneliness, which "has become an everyday experience of the evergrowing masses of our century" (*The Origins*, 478). Loneliness is not solitude, for in these last pages Arendt also explains that

> As Epictetus sees it (*Dissertationes*, Book 3, ch. 13) the lonely man (*eremos*) finds himself surrounded by others with whom he cannot establish contact or to whose hostility he is exposed. The solitary man, on the contrary, is alone and therefore "can be together with himself" since men have the capacity of "talking with themselves." In solitude, in other words, I am "by myself," together with myself, and therefore two-in-one, whereas in loneliness I am actually one, deserted by all others. All thinking, strictly speaking, is done in solitude and is a dialogue between me and myself; but this dialogue of the two-in-one does not lose contact with the world of my fellow-men because they are represented in the self with whom I lead the dialogue of thought.
>
> (*The Origins*, 476)

At its most basic, the possibility for agency begins with the possibility for thought in each individual. In the contemporary world, we are more often lonely than alone, but each mind harbors its own potential solitude, and in that solitude is the potential for thinking that is the basis for agency in our shared world.

Arendt concludes *The Origins* with the concept with which she will begin *The Human Condition:* natality. Alone we die, but alone we are born: the possibility for thinking is re-created at every individual birth. Totalitarian domination may attempt to reduce individuals to lonely, faceless bodies, but the body is also a modest, solitary place from which to begin to reconstruct the pluralities of political possibility:

> But there remains also the truth that every end in history necessarily contains a new beginning; this beginning is the promise, the only "message" which the end can ever produce. Beginning, before it becomes a historical event, is the supreme capacity of man; politically, it is identified with men's freedom. *Initium ut esset homo creatus est*— "that a beginning be made man was created" said Augustine. This beginning is guaranteed by each new birth; it is indeed every man.
>
> (*The Origins*, 478–79)

This simple message is the point at which Arendt releases her text. She has achieved her voice, and concluded her project: the writing of a narrative that, by reconsidering the recent past, releases the present from its thrall, and reconstructs the possibilities for the future.

By attending to those marginal, exemplary individuals who were able to rethink their own relationship to their political context, Arendt writes a renewed relationship to the present and to the future. Yet the past still presents a problem, whether of necessity or of nostalgia. In her next book, *The Human Condition*, Arendt turned back to classical Greece in search of the origins of the political thinking she wanted to preserve for the modern world. But origins are always tricky, as she herself demonstrated, and *The Human Condition* is a book that seems to ignore some of its author's own lessons about the possibilities for agency in a plural world.

Nine.
Politics
as Masquerade

Alcibiades resided at that time in a small village in Phrygia,
together with Timandra, a mistress of his. As he slept, he had this
dream: he thought himself attired in his mistress's habit, and that
she, holding him in her arms, dressed his head and painted his face
as if he had been a woman; others say, he dreamed that he saw
Megaeus cut off his head and burn his body; at any rate, it was but
a little while before his death that he had these visions.
  Plutarch's Lives, trans. John Dryden (New York: P. F. Collier &
  Son, 1909), 150–51

In this chapter I return to the text I considered at the beginning of this
book. My first chapter examined the prologue to *The Human Condition;*
this chapter circles back to that same text and to its arguments for a public, political life of action. Thus, this chapter concludes where the first
chapter began, except that the intermediate discussion determines a different approach. My discussion of the prologue was a straight textual
analysis of Arendt's writing on the fundamental relationship between
politics, embodiment, and natality. This close reading complicated the
assumptions of the (non)relationship between embodied identity and
political possibility that are usually made about Arendt's work, but did so
through a rereading of her own writing.

At this point in my own argument, however, more is at stake. I have
tried to provide a deconstruction of much of Arendt's thought while proposing a revised coordination of her most important insights. I have done
this by deploying a critical apparatus based in feminist psychoanalytic
theory, historical supplements, and a close reliance on Arendt's own texts,
and I have emphasized Arendt's own reliance on marginal, exemplary figures who offer models of performative political action. Often these figures perform a social masquerade, enacting an alternative, explicitly constructed identity that Arendt recognizes to be as authentic as any other.
By tracking the significance of these figures through her major political
works, we can develop a revised understanding of Arendt's thinking
on the relationships between social identity, political agency, and self-
conscious self-representation.

To this radical rereading of Arendt, which challenges her own some-times explicit hostility to any politics of social identity, *The Human Condition* would seem to stand as a rebuke. This is the text in which Arendt argues that individuals marked by their social categories (gender and class) must be excluded from public participation and political possibility if the political life is to fulfill its own potential. How can I argue that much of Arendt's writing offers profound insights into the relationship between agency and the political representation of constructed social identity without acknowledging this book?

I cannot, and this chapter is my response to that demand. But I am choosing an unusual strategy. Instead of arguing with Arendt point by point over her analysis of the Greek polis, I am going to challenge the integrity of her own argument, on her own terms. Arendt's writing is fun-damentally historical, and her political theory is rooted in context and example. In my readings I have tried to show that Arendt often presented some of her most original and provocative theorizing on the edges of her main argument when she attended to the exemplary individuals who enacted themselves as self-conscious political agents. But in *The Human Condition* she does not do this. She writes instead an almost entirely theo-retical book, abstracted from the lives and politics of its historical actors, and so she makes an argument that cannot hold its own against a histori-cal challenge. The figure I use to challenge Arendt's insistence that a gulf appropriately divided Athenian public and private life is Alcibiades.

In *The Human Condition* Arendt constructs a political narrative in which the private body and the public space are each delimited and defined by the other; this supposedly clear demarcation establishes politi-cal identity and allows for a politics of transcendent self-enactment. While this conception of politics is premised on the body's physical pres-ence, Arendt understands political life to be threatened when the physi-cal bodies of those defined by their social identities (gender, class) are either too prominent (thus disrupting political life by their presence) or wholly absent (thus disrupting political life by their absence, since the would-be political actors would have to get busy doing their own domes-tic work). Yet while the discursive space of the polis is cleared by the exclusion of women and slaves, it is reoccupied in the person of the his-torical Alcibiades, who brings with him all the problematic associations of femininity and insistent physicality.

Alcibiades is like Disraeli: a dramatically self-conscious public figure who masquerades his controversial social identity to good political effect. Alcibiades exploded the norms of identity and behavior that structured Athenian political life, but he was also the most successful political actor of his day. He combined the ideal achievements of masculine virtue with self-consciously theatrical dramatizations of the feminine, blurring the distinctions between genders under the full public gaze of the masculine political sphere itself, while similarly blurring the defining line between historical hero and traitor. Alcibiades' ambivalently gendered personality was inextricable from his role as a controversial political actor. Since there is no room for him in Arendt's text, I have made room for him in my own. Alcibiades both confounds Arendt's insistence on the clear separation of public and private and affirms her theorization of a politics of vibrant self-disclosure. In this chapter I explore the extent to which his political and personal notoriety involved his own emphatically theatricalized bodily self-representation: a politics of masquerade.

Thus this chapter is both quite Arendtian, in that it emerges from the psychoanalytically informed reading of Arendt's work I have already performed, and in contradiction to the whole conceptual arrangement of *The Human Condition* as it is explicitly laid out. But *The Human Condition* was a retreat for Arendt, an escape from the issues she had been grappling with and would inevitably return to. It is a supposedly historical analysis of a philosophical ideal, rather than a philosophical consideration of a detailed historical and political reality, and as such it is deeply nostalgic. Arendt was seeking a past example of a context in which self-conscious political participation was taken for granted, in which social and political identity could not conflict. But she invented her example; the politics of the polis turn out to be more ambivalent than Arendt would have liked. They also provide a more accessible, if less pure, potential model for political action than she would have thought possible. It is therefore in a spirit of both loyalty and challenge that I offer this chapter, an alternative discussion of the politics of social identity in the classical Athenian polis.

THE HUMAN CONDITION

Arendt's text is a philosophical analysis of the *vita activa* of Athenian life; although thought is incorporated within the political life, she does not here give it a preeminent value.[1] Instead she seeks to comprehend how the structuring of daily life allowed for an agonistic politics of self-representation and agency. For Arendt, as for Aristotle, political life is premised on speech, for "finding the right words at the right moment, quite apart from the information or communication they might convey, is action" (*HC*, 26).[2]

If classical political life was defined by and organized around a commitment to speech and action, the exclusion of the mute threat of violence was what in part defined the borders of that commitment. The internal and external limits of the strictly political life of the city are demarcated by the abrupt restrictions on the possibility of violence. The space of the political is enclosed by the violence outside the city walls; within those walls, violence is privately present but publicly mute, legitimately existing within the domestic confines of the household:

In Greek self-understanding, to force people by violence, to command rather than persuade, were prepolitical ways to deal with people characteristic of life outside the *polis*, of home and family life, where the household head ruled with uncontested, despotic powers, or of life in the barbarian empires of Asia, whose despotism was frequently likened to the organization of the household.

(*HC*, 26–27)[3]

For Arendt, the codification of violence into something other than the public—whether that other be domestic or barbarian, and either way barbarous, stammering, deprived of speech—is absolutely necessary for her theoretical schema.[4]

Within this conceptual organization, the (mute) body is displaced and replaced by the (speaking) subject. This is the silent, abject body of reproductive necessity, whether slave or freeborn, whether female or male, whose toil is endless and inevitable to the human condition. In its most laboriously functional reproductive form, the mastery of necessity involved the mastery of the body of the woman or the slave, the body whose disciplined function provided the physical circumstances out of which political freedom could emerge.

Since Arendt's conception of politics is of a mutual self-representation among equals, a putting on of a recognized public persona, she denies that political freedom can exist for either master or slave, as long as they are defined by those (household) identities. The citizen, in the Arendtian polis, shed his private life and his role in the mutual unfreedom of the master / slave dialectic when he crossed from the household into the public, participatory life of the assembly. The great value of public life was its commitment to a shared plurality of experience:

[T]he reality of the public realm relies on the simultaneous presence of innumerable perspectives and aspects in which the common world presents itself and for which no common measurement or denominator can be devised. For though the common world is the common meeting ground of all, those who are present have different locations in it, and the location of one can no more coincide with the location of another than the location of two objects. Being seen and being heard by others derive their significance from the fact that everybody sees and hears from a different position.

(*HC*, 57)

According to Arendt, the common public world respected the plural perspectives of those who participated in it, although those participants were only an elite few. "The privation of privacy lies in the absence of others" (*HC*, 58), but those others are the citizen-subjects, not the exotically foreign other of the barbarian or the more locally familiar other(s) of women, children, and slaves. It is as though, for Arendt, freedom means getting out of the house.

The common world of difference she so admires can exist only among the sameness of one's peers, not in the dark, shared necessities of the household.[5] Despite the smoothly mastered functioning of productive necessity within the household, reproduction—the mystery of birth and death—remains a sort of natural, hidden phenomenon. It cannot be mastered in discourse. Thus the household is overwhelmed by its own silence. The speaking (male) subject flees its sheltering confines; the mysteriousness of the body is left behind the household walls, silenced, frightening, but secure(d).[6]

But the dark necessity of the private is itself undermined by its transformation into the social, a transformation that Arendt seems to associate with the early rise of capitalism (*HC*, 68).[7] Arendt's understanding of the social, arising out of her work in *The Origins* and developed later in *On Revolution*, is of a realm of mass conformity and numerical statistics, its political tendency being toward despotism and bureaucracy (*HC*, 40–43).[8] Her hostility toward the social arises from her protective reverence for the conceptual space of the political, a space created through work and worldliness but cleared by the mastery of necessity and the confinement of the abject body and those associated with it.[9] Arendt presumes that this public space will provide us with a shared assurance of our own reality and sense of self. The private provides for the public realm; it is both fundamental and subordinated to the public. Because she so badly wants to secure the historical possibility of an open, stable space for the revelatory performance of speech and action, Arendt decries the degradation of two distinct and hierarchically ordered realms into the uniform amalgamation of the social.

When Arendt, near the end of the section "The Public and the Private Realm," acknowledges that the private, hidden realm of physical necessity was lost when "the modern age emancipated the working classes and the women at nearly the same historical moment" (*HC*, 73), she is identifying the private (realm of reproduction and production, of labor but only indeterminately of work) as both the backstage home of the laboring body and, somewhat ambivalently, the space in which certain groups of bodies are confined. A private sphere is absolutely necessary as a backstage area from which citizens emerge to be seen in public performance, but some of those who labor in the background never emerge at all. Arendt is left, then, rather awkwardly justifying the exclusion from the public life and light of all those whose lives were "laborious," whose hidden service to physical necessity provided the artifice for civic freedom (*HC*, 72–73).[10]

But precisely by emphasizing the fixed and stationary quality of physical identity, Arendt herself begins to place in question the clean distinctions she has taken such pains to delineate. How is it that some selves are confined to their bodies, and some selves are able temporarily to leave all concern for the necessities of physical embodiment behind? How is it that the social identities of class or gender can render one's physical identity absolute, even in a political context that supposedly predates the social?

For Arendt, the confinement of the mute and possibly violated body in the private sphere (and / or its exclusion beyond the city walls) clears the public space for speech and action, and it is this embodied identity that must be presupposed and transcended in political life. The public and the private realms must coexist for the political to be fully operative, but the two remain clearly separate; citizen-actors left the necessities of their bodies within the confines of their homes and presumably engaged in public, political behavior as free men, emancipated from drudgery and taint. In *The Human Condition* this separation is theorized as having been clearly maintained during the glory of the Athenian polis. But a more historically grounded consideration of the conditions that structured Athenian political life does not necessarily bear this out.

THE CONTINUITY OF PRIVATE AND PUBLIC IN THE POLIS
In fact Athenian political life was always very much inflected by concerns with its citizens' private lives. The strong philosophical distinction between private and public may be historically untenable, more a product of the reproductive / productive split (itself often understood as a private, domestic / public, political division) in the modern societies Arendt so decries. Classical political thinkers understood that an individual's successful public life required not just the practical mastery of private necessity but proper private behavior: sexual, sartorial, religious.[11] The great flaw in modern thinkers' reconsiderations of the conditions of classical political life may very well be the tendency to underestimate the continuity, not the gulf, classical actors recognized between their public and their private lives.

To the extent that Athenian citizens did not think that they left their private experiences of mastery or subordination behind in the household, their negotiations of identity were not so simplistic as Arendt's schema would imply. Free men had to enact themselves, in public and in private, in an appropriately masculine way, and this had less to do with the mastery of necessity than with the mastery of the feminine. Since, as we have noted before, Arendt lacked a conception of gender, she misses this dynamic and presumes that women and slaves are excluded from public life because of their essentially reproductive identities. The implication of this construction would be that if women and slaves could emancipate themselves from reproductive necessity, without lapsing into the social question, they too could enter the public sphere.[12] But the condition for entrance into Athenian public life was that the citizen be an active masculine subject, and what was adamantly excluded from the political sphere was any association with femininity.

Women and slaves could not be political subjects because they were feminized, in that they were subordinate to others' practical and sexual demands. Feminine identity meant a passive identity, and the political subject had at all costs to be understood to be active, to be the agent of his own desires rather than the object of another's. The free citizen did not transcend his household relations to enter the public realm; his identity was expected to remain consistently masterful in both, the difference being that in private he was master of others, while in public he was the master of himself among peers.[13] The vaunted equality and plurality of

Arendt's public realm is based on a norm of masculinity that precludes not reproductive physicality, but a differently gendered social identity.[14]

But it is important to note that for her the public space is defined as the space of appearance in which stories are enacted.[15] In presuming that this space is violated by the appearance of abject bodies or improper social identities, Arendt ignores the stories themselves: the accumulation of dramatic, philosophical, historical, and literary writings that document the lives of the political actors. In doing so, she ignores the possibility that the values she associates with action, storytelling, and self-enactment could be associated with the social identities she has precluded from the public realm. She has so insistently separated the realms of the public/private hierarchy that she cannot, in this text, conceive of a reconsideration of performative political experience that enacts social identity in the public realm; she will not recognize that the condition for classical political action is not the separation of public and private but its continuity. Because part of the purpose of *The Human Condition* was to explore the presocial conditions for political action, it is ironic that the structure of Arendt's own text undermines the goal of her project.

ALCIBIADES: SOCIAL IDENTITY AND POLITICAL PRACTICE

Conventional wisdom presents Alcibiades as the bad boy of the Athenian democracy, somewhat scurrilously attached to Socrates and greedy for imperial glory. But if one even desultorily investigates the various materials available that describe his presence, his habits, and his life, what is quite striking is the degree to which Alcibiades' most scandalous behavior is that which transgresses the contemporary codes and expectations of a conventionally appropriate, restrained masculinity. Given Arendt's own emphasis on the values of stories in giving meaning to public life, I here discuss the narrative of Alcibiades' life rather than the strictly historical facts of his biography. In telling the story of someone's life, what is said about him may be as significant as what he said: the mythology of a life can tell us of the meaning associated with an individual's actions. Thus I consider references to Alcibiades in contemporary plays and essays as well as the more conventionally documented historical accounts.

Alcibiades was the scion of two important Athenian families, and after his father's death in battle, he was raised in the household of Pericles, a distant uncle on his mother's (and the more prestigious) side of the family.[16] He grew up during the height of Athenian power and glory, in a privileged position to observe the building of the Parthenon, the first presentations of plays by Sophocles and Euripides, and his uncle's remarkable, and remarkably long, political success.[17] Yet if Alcibiades came of age during the Golden Age of Pericles, his adult life was lived during the most difficult years of the Peloponnesian War. After Pericles' death, the political consensus he had managed for more than twenty years devolved into factions and power struggles. As the war progressed, Athens abandoned Pericles' famous policy of not overextending herself while guarding her navy, and sought to add to the empire as well as defend it. Overcrowding, plague, civil strife, and military setbacks endangered the city's democratic tradition.

Into this context of the public life of the city steps Alcibiades, a free adult male citizen who has every right to be there, outstandingly gifted with every characteristic for remarkable political leadership: well-born, well-connected, quick-witted, handsome, and ambitious. Groomed to assume the mantle of Pericles, he displayed his precocity early, transforming even the hindrance of his lisp into a particularly personal style of speaking. He would seem to have been the exemplary Athenian. Yet while excelling at displays of conventional masculinity, he also flouted the city's masculine conventions. A virtuosic masculine actor, Alcibiades also enacted a consistent feminine masquerade. In doing so, he confounded the most entrenched norms of political identity, not because his private life became publicly notorious, but because he challenged the exclusion of the feminine from the public sphere.

Public life, organized around the political space, is, on the introduction of Alcibiades, forced to acknowledge the social (construction of a gendered) identity it has carefully managed to exclude, in the person of an individual it cannot publicly do without. Alcibiades was notorious for his luxuriating in pleasure, a luxuriance considered both slavish and feminine, and therefore revealing of something radically undisciplined in a masculine character. His political and personal flamboyance made him the Athenian popular democratic hero and the man most feared by his aristocratic peers. Plutarch, one of the best sources for the legends of Alcibiades' unconventionality, quotes Aristophanes' characterization of him in *The Frogs:*

> "Best rear no lion in your state, 'tis true;
> But treat him like a lion if you do."[18]

According to Aristophanes (the satiric playwright associated with the democratic faction in Athenian politics), Alcibiades might be difficult, even dangerous, but he was also the man upon whom the democratic city most depended.[19]

In *The Fragility of Goodness: Luck and Ethics in Greek Tragedy and Philosophy,* Martha Nussbaum presents an unusually detailed and sympathetic reading of Alcibiades' character as it is available to us in the extant texts.[20] Nussbaum particularly emphasizes Alcibiades' associations, both practical and symbolic, with the Athenian democracy and the dramatic spirit that flourished during the democracy:

> In *The Frogs,* Alcibiades is a central character long before he is mentioned by name (1422). The pivotal test for the two dead poets in Hades, to determine whose moral advice will save the city in its time of trouble, is a test concerning his return. The city "longs for him, it hates him, and it wants him back" (1425). What should it do? Euripides, using language linked with sophistic and Socratic philosophizing, gives an oligarch's answer: think of him as a self-centered and useless

individual, and hate him. Aeschylus, in obscure and noble poetic language, urges the city to take him back. This tough old democrat who fought at Marathon, not the refined comrade of allegedly anti-democratic intellectuals, proves in this way that he is the poet that the soul of Dionysus, god of tragic and comic poetry, desires (1468). He will be brought back from the dead, and, together, tragedy, comedy, and Alcibiades will save Athens from the death of freedom; also, as they see it, from Socrates.

(Nussbaum, *Fragility of Goodness*, 169–70)[21]

Alcibiades' successful enactment of a remarkable democratic political persona is achieved as much through the skillful flouting of traditional norms as through their fulfillment.

More than anything else, Alcibiades seems to display this mastery as a dramatic tension that maintains the contradictions invested in his person. He was a theatrical actor, in his private and his public life, and he did not seem to distinguish particularly between the two. He played with gender, and this dynamic identity made him dangerous. Although the citizens of the city are appalled by him, they are also fascinated, awestruck observers of a political performer who has triumphantly, openly mastered the sensual byplay of the democratic political game. In a culture in which slave and free, male and female, and thus public and private were supposedly clearly divided, Alcibiades embodied an apex of free masculinity that was also precisely the point at which the defining limits were transcended and transgressed.

In Plutarch's "Alcibiades," the anecdotes of his life, even of his childhood, display this ambiguity:

Once being hard pressed in wrestling, and fearing to be thrown, he got the hand of his antagonist to his mouth, and bit it with all his force; and when the other loosed his hold presently, and said, "You bite, Alcibiades, like a woman." "No," replied he, "like a lion."

(*Plutarch's Lives*, 111)[22]

As Alcibiades became an adult, this apparent contradiction between masculine vigor and slavish, feminine sensual indulgence was only more emphatically displayed:

But with all these words and deeds, and with all this sagacity and eloquence, he intermingled exorbitant luxury and wantonness in his eating and drinking and dissolute living; wore long purple robes like a woman, which dragged after him as he went through the market-place; caused the planks of his galley to be cut away, that so he might lie the softer, his bed not being placed on the boards, but hanging upon girths. His shield, again, which was richly gilded, had not the usual ensigns of the Athenians, but a Cupid, holding a thunderbolt in his hand, was painted upon it.

(*Plutarch's Lives*, 123)

One presumes that Alcibiades' deviance was so disturbing because it could not be dismissed as effete diffidence. Instead, his wantonly ambivalent masculinity was the most glorious and the most notorious public persona possible.

What Alcibiades seems to have represented to the Athenian populace was not, simplistically, the best and the worst of classical virtues and vices, but a dream-figure demigod, the personal configuration of all the community most formally admired, ordered, excluded, and repressed. Thucydides, describing the Athenian preparations for the Sicilian expedition, points out that it was the public mistrust of Alcibiades' private life that was his, and Athens's, political undoing:

> For he was very much in the public eye, and . . . most people became frightened of a quality in him which was beyond the normal and showed itself both in the lawlessness of his private life and habits and in the spirit in which he acted on all occasions. They thought that he was aiming at becoming a dictator, and so they turned against him. Although in a public capacity his conduct of the war was excellent, his way of life made him objectionable to everyone as a person; thus they entrusted their affairs to other hands, and before long ruined the city. (Thucydides, *Peloponnesian War*, 418–19)[23]

Alcibiades is a myth of fear and desire: the power to appear as the forbidden, as well as that which is most esteemed. The embodiment of both the feminine abject and the masculine subject, he presents the highest culmination of and the deepest challenge to the norms of Athenian political subjectivity.[24]

INDIVIDUAL AGENCY AND DEMOCRATIC POLITICS

Thucydides and Plutarch attested to Alcibiades' skills as a political speaker and actor, but Plato particularly emphasized his symbolic role in philosophical and erotic life, and provided him with a privileged characterization. Alcibiades is present in a surprising number of the dialogues, even if only as a kind of shadow-figure, as in the *Protagoras*.[25] Eloquent, seductive, disruptive, Alcibiades is particularly so in the *Symposium*, in which he is the only character to assert himself against Socrates: the protégé who talks back.[26]

When Alcibiades enters the *Symposium*, and disrupts it, he has already been crowned with a garland of ivy and violets. To quote again from Nussbaum's analysis:

> The crown of violets is, first of all, a sign of Aphrodite (cf. *H. Hom.* 5.18, Solon 11.4). This hardly surprises us, except for the strange fact . . . that this aggressively masculine figure sees himself as a female divinity. It is also, further, a crown worn by the Muses. Alcibiades, then, presents himself as a poet, and an inspiring god of poets (Plato?).
>
> But the violet crown stands for something else as well: for the city of Athens herself. In a fragment from Pindar . . . she is addressed:
>
> O glistening and violet-crowned and famous in song,
> Bulwark of Hellas, glorious Athens,
> Fortunate city.

The crown of violets is the delicate, growing sign of the flourishing of this strange and fragile democracy, now, in the time of Alcibiades, in its greatest danger. . . .

The ivy is the sign of Dionysus, god of wine, god of irrational inspiration. . . . Dionysus, male in form yet of softly female bearing, exemplifies the sexual contradictions of Alcibiades' aspirations. He embodies, too, another apparent contradiction: he is the patron god of both tragic and comic poetry. . . . Tragedy and comedy cherish the same values, value the same dangers. Both, furthermore, are linked through Dionysus to the fragile fortunes of the Athenian democracy; both are in danger at the dramatic date, dead, along with Alcibiades, soon after.

(Nussbaum, *Fragility of Goodness,* 193–94)

Masculine and feminine, comic and tragic, Alcibiades presents to the philosopher of fixed and orderly ideals, whether of cities or beauty, a vividly protean challenge. Appearing as the disorderly stand-in for the democratic spirit, he delivers his famous tribute to Socrates as his contribution to the evening's speeches on love. But whereas all the other participants speak of love as a system or a generalized experience, Alcibiades speaks of his own personal love for Socrates; he speaks of the pain, chagrin, and inspiration he has felt because of this one man. In doing so, in proposing a narrative of the difficult experience rather than the perfect idea of love, he gives the only effective counter to Socrates' lesson of Diotima. As opposed to the philosopher's cleanly hierarchical vision of an absolute ideal, Alcibiades offers the messy glory of living with specific others in a plural world.

In the *Symposium,* Alcibiades challenges Socrates and convention by being both the *eromenos* and the *erastes*—the beautiful, appropriately passive youth who is the object of desire and the active lover whose desperate desire leads him to humiliate himself.[27] But the conventional *erastes* is an older man pursuing a younger one, his desire entirely physical, his agency unquestioned. When Alcibiades, as a conventional *eromenos,* thinks to exchange his youthful beauty for mature wisdom, he is entirely within the tradition of Greek sexual norms: making himself available as a temporary sexual object in order to gain the mentoring that will assist him to a properly adult social, sexual, and political agency. But when Alcibiades begins to pursue the old man, actively putting himself into the passive role in order to force Socrates to fulfill the conventional duties (and pleasures) of the *erastes,* he is transgressing all the most inviolable rules of sexual social behavior. Yet he does so, playing two roles at once in a way that illustrates how the love of even the best of ideals can lead not necessarily to its expected transcendent goal but to its own fallible, compromised wisdom.

Properly experienced, the relationship between the *erastes* and the *eromenos* should eventually resolve into *philia,* a devoted friendship between peers. Alcibiades and Socrates, although attached to each other (recall Alcibiades' stories of Socrates' devotion on the battlefield), always seem to retain a spiky rivalry in their relationship. If they are not exactly peers, it is never quite clear who is in charge, either. This is not simply a question of personalities, but one of philosophies: Alcibiades insists on the value of a political life lived in a world of specific experience; Socrates (at least according to Plato) advocates a philosophical life removed from worldly vicissitudes. In the *Symposium*, Alcibiades is himself the symbolic representation of democracy: wayward, stubborn, insistently individual, but also tolerant and even celebratory of his own and others' inevitable self-contradictions and idiosyncrasies.

Alcibiades' tribute and challenge is specifically addressed, in the *Symposium*, to Socrates, but its significance extends to any ideal (political or philosophical) system that sets itself above the ambiguous pluralities of worldly existence. Alcibiades speaks for the ambivalent, contradictory achievements and lapses of worldly experience; he speaks his unique truth through the mask of his ambiguous, disruptive sexuality, which is also the persona of the democratic spirit. Socrates pretends to be afraid of him. How indeed should the city reconcile itself to such an individual in its midst, one who not only seems able to unleash the community's collective libidinal energy but who in himself is both the lover and the best beloved?

PRIVATE LIFE / PUBLIC SCANDAL

Alcibiades combines an ideal masculinity with a masquerade of femininity. In his own person, he confuses the codes of social identity that structure Athenian political roles. This ambiguous feminine persona, enacted by an utterly masculine man, would almost be enough to challenge Arendt's argument that political self-representation in the polis depended on the complete exclusion of private identity. But an inquiry into Alcibiades' life goes further. Alcibiades' masquerade of feminine identity performed within the public, political sphere of the polis made him notorious, and he paid the price for it. His dramatic unconventionality made him vulnerable to accusations that he would do anything, since he would do some things that others wouldn't. But he may not have done everything he was accused of, just as there were others who may have done things no one would have suspected.

Arendt is right that women were excluded from direct participation in Greek political life. That may not, however, mean that they did not participate. If Alcibiades can be recognized as smuggling the feminine into the Athenian public sphere, perhaps it is also appropriate to recognize that women may have found ways of smuggling political agency into their supposedly entirely private lives. Alcibiades himself is the link to an investigation of Athenian women's particularly feminine political agency. The site of this possibility is a scandal; the historical evidence is unclear. Yet if Alcibiades has provided us with an example of an ambiguously gendered politics of masquerade in the public sphere, he provokes our inquiry into the possibility of an agency masquerading behind the mask of femininity in the private sphere.

The public suspicion of Alcibiades' private life had its most drastic effect on his political career when it led to his being associated with the profanation of the Eleusinian Mysteries and the mutilation of the herms.[28] In 415, just before the launching of the ships of the Sicilian expedition, a great many of the herms of Athens were mutilated. The herms (*hermae*) were public statues to the god Hermes, consisting of a stone block surmounted with a carved head, and an erect phallus positioned about midway on the front of the "body." Although Thucydides refers only to the smashing of the statues' faces, most scholarship agrees that the exposed genitals were also attacked, resulting in a kind of public castration.[29] The incident had tremendous symbolic meaning, and extensive political ramifications.

Thucydides gives this account of the situation:

While these preparations were going on it was found that in one night nearly all of the stone Hermae in the city of Athens had had their faces disfigured by being cut about. These are a national institution, the well-known square-cut figures, of which there are great numbers both in the porches of private houses and in the temples. No one knew who had done this, but large rewards were offered by the state in order to find out who the criminals were, and there was also a decree passed guaranteeing immunity to anyone, citizen, alien, or slave, who knew of any other sacrilegious act that had taken place and would come forward with information about it. The whole affair, indeed, was taken very seriously, as it was regarded as an omen of the expedition, and at the same time as evidence of a revolutionary conspiracy to overthrow the democracy. . . . One of those accused was Alcibiades, and this fact was taken up by those who disliked him most because he stood in the way of their keeping a firm hold themselves of the leadership of the people, and who thought that, if they could drive him out, they would step into first place. They therefore exaggerated the whole thing and made all the noise they could about it, saying that the affair of the mysteries and the defacement of the Hermae were all part of a plot to overthrow the democracy, and that in all this Alcibiades had had a hand; evidence for which they found in the unconventional and undemocratic character of his life in general.

(Thucydides, *Peloponnesian War*, 426–27)

At the time, the desecration of the herms (the charge of profanation of the Mysteries was separate, although included in the general inquiry) was thought to be a bad omen for the Sicilian expedition, and a possible act of protest against it and against the undertakings of the democracy. The act was assumed to have been done by a person or persons with an improper respect for conventional religious piety and, by extension, an improper respect for the democratic constitution.[30]

Although there was no evidence against him regarding the herms, Alcibiades was denounced, as were a number of others.[31] Insisting on his innocence, he argued that he should be investigated immediately, and cleared or put to death, "and he pointed out how unwise it would be to send him out in command of such a large army with such serious accusations still hanging over his head" (Thucydides, *Peloponnesian War*, 427). Nonetheless, the expedition set sail, with Alcibiades and Nicias in joint command while the inquiry into the desecrations of the herms and the Mysteries proceeded in Athens. Over the course of several months various men were denounced or arrested; a prisoner confessed, causing the release of some and the execution of others; and the main informer in the original denunciations was found to have made false accusations and was put to death.[32] In the midst of this, a ship was sent out to bring Alcibiades back from Sicily, but he escaped. Since all those then implicated who had not fled were being executed, Alcibiades' flight seems more like a prudent search for asylum than the treachery for which he is so often vilified. After his escape, he was tried in absentia and sentenced to death, and he went over to Sparta.

WOMEN'S (POLITICAL) AGENCY

If he didn't do it, who did? Who would have had the nerve to perform a private act (or acts—the herms were damaged in the same evening, all around the city) that challenged the conventional balance of religious and political power on the eve of an enormous military expedition?

In *The Reign of the Phallus: Sexual Politics in Ancient Athens*, Eva Keuls hypothesizes that the women of Athens were responsible for the mutilation (castration) of the herms.[33] Keuls sees the desecration as the possible political statement of women without any recognized form of access to the public world. She notes that one of the women's festivals (the Adonia) had been celebrated just before the incident, giving the women the chance to meet together in a context that commemorated death and sexuality.[34] Keuls further notes that when the Adonia is described by a magistrate in Aristophanes' *Lysistrata*, "This character, quite rightly, considers the Adonia a ritual of rebellion against the social order" (Keuls, *Reign of the Phallus*, 23–30).[35] She also conjectures about the emotional effect the arrival in Athens of the enslaved Melian women and children might have had on the women of Athens, who were watching their men prepare for a huge and risky campaign.[36] Furthermore, Euripides' *The Trojan Women*, a play about the tragic enslavement of noble women from a heroic (if enemy) city, was performed after the captives' arrival and shortly before the Adonia and the desecration of the herms. Shaken by the arrival of the Melian women, many of whom must have entered private homes as domestic slaves in the women's quarters; made thoughtful by rumors of *The Trojan Women*, which the women would have heard of even if they hadn't seen it; and provided the opportunity to meet together in the rebellious atmosphere of the Adonia, the women of Athens, theorizes Keuls, lashed out at a familiar and available symbol of male power and authority: the erect phalluses on the statues of the herms.[37]

Examining the cultural and political context in which the herms were desecrated (the celebration of a women's festival and the imminent departure of a controversial military expedition), delving into the possibilities of collective feminine emotions and power, Keuls postulates that those Athenian women most unseen and unheard (which is Pericles' exhortation and commendation to them in the Funeral Oration), respectable women cloistered in the private home, collectively slipped out of doors one night to act in defiance of masculine norms and authority. No one suspected them: the association with femininity that made the man Alcibiades a suspect kept the women completely outside suspicion.[38]

It is impossible to determine just who mutilated the herms, but Keuls's theory allows us to associate a different element of covert femininity with the actions with which Alcibiades was most scandalously associated. The castration of the statues was an act that aggressively questioned the conventional representations of masculinity. Alcibiades flaunted those conventions openly; he could appropriate convention into his own self-consciously dramatic self-representation. The Athenian women, as we know of them, were almost entirely subject to convention; even to suspect or accuse a woman of having violated the local symbols of masculine power would have been itself a violation of the conventions of gender-specific identity and action. Alcibiades is definitely suspected of the desecration of the herms, and the Athenian women are unquestionably innocent, only so long as those gender-specific identifications are presumed to be firmly in place.

A POLITICS OF SOCIAL IDENTITY

But we have already seen that they are not. Alcibiades' feminine masquerade daunted his fellow citizens, whereas the Athenian women's feminine masquerade may have functioned just as it did for Riviere's analysand: to hold off masculine retribution for women's having (in this case literally) seized the phallus. Just as Keuls argues that the women, hidden in the domestic sphere, may nonetheless have been capable of stepping outside the household and accomplishing an act of public, political significance, it is possible to see how, in the person of Alcibiades, public conventions of sexual and social order were personally disrupted within the public frame.

Alcibiades rewrote the social identity of gendered femininity back into the narrative of Athenian political life. Dominating the public sphere as the most capable and charismatic man in Athens, if not in the entire Greek world, Alcibiades also brought with him into the public arena those embodied feminine attributes that the division between public and private that Arendt elaborates was designed to keep out: physicality, indulgence, charm, passion. If the women's actions were covert, Alcibiades' actions were not. But in a political context premised on the exclusion of certain social identities, their possible agency becomes a radical argument for pluralism. This threat to the conventionally constituted political identity provokes a response: the abjection of that intimate particular whose exclusion is presumed to guarantee the integrity of the purified self.

The Athenians ascribed to Alcibiades the thirst for autocratic power that his political enemies in the oligarchic faction in fact had and acted upon; his assassination while in exile was most likely arranged by them in order to prevent the return of democracy to the city (Ellis, *Alcibiades*, 95–97). He was killed at night, ambushed in the house in which he was staying, by men who were afraid to engage with him face to face and shortly after the dream in which he saw himself as a woman:

> Alcibiades resided at that time in a small village in Phrygia, together with Timandra, a mistress of his. As he slept, he had this dream: he thought himself attired in his mistress's habit, and that she, holding him in her arms, dressed his head and painted his face as if he had been a woman; others say, he dreamed that he saw Megaeus cut off his head and burn his body; at any rate, it was but a little while before his death that he had these visions.
>
> (*Plutarch's Lives*, 150–51)

Plutarch says that he was buried by his mistress Timandra, in her own clothes.

The gendered ambiguity that Alcibiades personified even in exile and death was at the heart of Athenian polis identity. Even (if not especially) in the context of political life in the Athenian polis, the gender distinctions of the public and private realm were not as absolute as Arendt's discussion would have us believe. Alcibiades' conscious redefinition of his own identity within the conventional narratives of Athenian public and private life allowed him to dominate that life, much as Disraeli, in a later age, did with his social identity as a Jew. Disraeli's masquerade enabled him to live to a successful, controversial, venerated old age; although convention would not allow Queen Victoria to attend his funeral, she paid him the extraordinary personal compliment of traveling herself to sit in mourning in his home a few days later. Alcibiades died alone and far from home, but his masquerade of social identity was also inextricable from his political success, which was itself dependent on the commanding dynamism of his public persona.

The personification of disorder and the embodiment of transgression, gendered and otherwise, Alcibiades achieved a recognized level of political excellence that transcended ordinary political or cultural codes; his flamboyant womanliness was inseparable from his undisciplined manliness. Plutarch comments on this ambiguity in the following, in which the epitome of symbolic masculinity (Achilles) is revealed to be the epitome of human masculinity (Alcibiades), is revealed to be the feminine (Alcibiades still):

> " 'Tis not Achilles's son, but he himself, the very man" that Lycurgus designed to form; while his real feelings and acts would have rather provoked the exclamation, " 'Tis the same woman still."
>
> (*Plutarch's Lives*, 132)

Alcibiades rewrote the gendered identity of the Athenian political narrative by emphasizing his identification with the feminine and by emphasizing the theatricality and artifice of that identification. In reworking social identity Alcibiades did not merely feminize himself; rather, his self-representation politicized the feminine.

ARENDTIAN AGENCY IN A POLITICS
OF ENACTED SOCIAL IDENTITY

In her discussion of the ideal politics of the Athenian *polis*, Arendt does not mention Alcibiades, the historical figure who disrupts the schematic construction of her political model. Yet Alcibiades is otherwise an exemplary Arendtian political actor: a man of speech as well as action; a man whose actions are themselves dramatic stories; above all a man who understands politics as the self-conscious representation of himself among others, who in turn must represent themselves to him. Although Alcibiades disrupts Athenian political conventions, and Arendt's description of them, by re-presenting social identity back within the political realm, his performance qualifies as excellent Arendtian politics. He breaks down the (gendered) divisions between public and private that Arendt understands as allowing for political life, but by doing so, he achieves an astonishing political career.

The moment of social transgression is also the moment of political realization; the social masquerade, occurring within the political realm, achieves an extraordinary political presence. Alcibiades performs his social identity, but he does not reduce politics to a question of social identities. Rather, he politicizes social identity itself; he dramatizes it; he allows a vividly made relationship of representation between the social and the political.

Nonetheless, as far as Arendt's text is concerned, Alcibiades is an outsider. In searching for a model context for political action, agency, and identity, she turned back to the Athenian polis, the conventional origin for the Western democratic political tradition. She tried to secure this model by attending to its definitions, the categories of identity that supposedly enabled Athenian political practice. She then presumed that the historical fragility of democratic politics was a result of not attending to the appropriate categories: the wrong people dominating the political sphere with the wrong questions. This may have been the right interpretation, with the wrong application. Arendt was right to realize that people obsessed with categories of race or ethnicity (or any other social identity), like the Nazis or the Boers, can transform political practice into a deadly or degenerate application of essentialized identity politics. But she was wrong to then assume that the way to prevent this transformation is to ban questions of social identity entirely.

Arendt's full-scale inquiry into the long process through which modern social identity becomes essentialized, and then genocidal, is contained in the three volumes of *The Origins of Totalitarianism*. After that extensive project, she turned her attention to the idealized democratic politics of *The Human Condition* and eventually to the inauguration of modern republican politics in *On Revolution*. But *On Revolution* is the text in which her thesis on social identity shows its cracks. In her chapter on "The Social Question," Arendt acknowledges that the fact of race slavery undermines the political premise of the new U.S. republic, and she characterizes the political participation of the feminine poor as a threat by the abject. Her own argument pulls against itself, as she not only attempts to limit the political legitimacy of essentialized identity questions but also ambivalently endorses the political exclusion of those who are themselves essentialized.

I have tried to show that Arendt's enunciated hostility to questions of social identity is actually contradicted by her own preoccupation with individuals who enact social identity as a politicized masquerade. Even in *The Human Condition*, the text from which Arendt banished any consideration of individual historical figures, she describes a politics of agency as self-representation that in fact does not depend on the rigid identity categories she presents. Drawing on a Socratic model of a plural, protean self in continual dialectic with the world (itself utterly different from a Platonic model of metaphysical truths), she presumed that this self could best represent itself when most free of the fixed (essential) determinations of social identity. This may be true, but that does not necessarily mean that the self who is most free is the one who is free by definition. Arendt's other writings show us that freedom must also exist in the mind, and that those individuals who most forcefully seize the possibility of defining their own actions may actually be those who recognize the possibility of shifting the definitions of who they are supposed to be rather than those who depend on general convention to tell them who they are.

Arendt's political ideal is actually a politicized self free to put on and off the personas of public life, to construct a public role apart from questions of essential authenticity. This is indeed an admirable goal, and one of terrible significance to contemporary social theory. If we recognize that social identity (be it of gender, class, ethnicity, race, sexuality, or whatever) is constructed but also enforced, not only by obviously harsh punitive measures but even more emphatically by the subtle regimes and disciplines of the ordinary habitus, then how are we, individually or collectively, to break forth in any form of agency? How are free will or action to be rescued from the insidiously subtle determinations of the social field?[39]

Despite herself, Arendt gives us an answer to this. Or perhaps it is more appropriate to say that I have tried, through Arendt, to formulate an answer. By focusing on her discussions of exemplary figures engaging in politically relevant masquerades of social identity, I have drawn from her work a theory of agency as strategic performance. This theory is fundamentally Arendtian, in that it is based on her writing, but I have taken liberties with it, in that I have traced a different thematic than she herself might have emphasized. Yet I do not believe she would necessarily oppose this. I have tried, in this book, to reappropriate and reactivate the theory of political agency that was at the core of all of Arendt's political thinking. This was always what was most important to her, and what she most regretted in her understanding of the limits of modern politics. She feared the dangers of modern racism and the thoughtlessness of individuals reduced to an apparent singularity. She feared that essentialized social identities spelled the end of political possibility. She may very well have been right. But although we live in what we now recognize to be an inevitably social world, social identity is not necessarily essential. It can be understood to be constructed and strategically performed. It can be politicized without being essentialized.

If I have been able, through this writing, to readjust the relationship between social identity and politicized Arendtian agency, then this project has succeeded both because of and in spite of itself. The key theoretical formulation that has made this readjustment possible is the theory of agency as masquerade, a theory itself premised on the link between the plurality of the self alone and the plurality of the self with others. Masquerade is enacted self-representation, qualified by the awareness of its own contingency. Thought is not action, but the dynamic of plurality experienced by the thinking self is an initial practical model for agency among others: for the realization that no one is ever entirely singular or static and that no one among many (no plurality) is ever completely fixed. Masquerade is the self-consciously plural self acting in an affirmedly plural world. Integral to this theory of agency through masquerade is the notion of legitimated artifice, a recognition that playing a recognizable, self-conscious role within a larger circumstance is as authentic a form of being as any other. Arendt's exemplary political actors are the self-conscious pariahs who assert a problematic social identity even while they negotiate its meaning, and in doing so help shape the ensuing possibilities for action for the rest of us. Their masquerade unsettles our expectations and challenges us to reconsider the presumed politics of any social identity. As a theoretical model rather than a merely anecdotal one, masquerade is the leverage by which we can enact ourselves as political beings in an inevitably social world.

In contemporary society, we are all disciplined by the very institutions that enable us: statistical probabilities in a volatile, predictably ordered field. Agency can seem like a luxury or a frivolous exercise in self-discovery. Certainly, almost all of Arendt's social actors seem rather ridiculous: Rahel's exquisite sensitivity; Disraeli the Oriental dandy; Lawrence playing the Great Game. None of them are very conventionally heroic, and Alcibiades is simply a scandal, while Anton Schmidt's integrity is tempered by its own practical limits. But that is precisely the point: even in ancient Greece the heroes weren't necessarily what they should have been, and in our own dark times a political theory of agency as self-conscious masquerade can begin to loosen the strictures on political possibility. In the end, the necessarily plural politics of enacted social identity, the politics of masquerade, is indeed only a place to begin: a strategy for opening up the room for political maneuvering in a strictly ordered but nonetheless permeable social field.

Notes

ONE. THE HUMAN CONDITION AS EMBODIED

1. Hannah Arendt, *On Revolution* (New York: Penguin Books, 1986), hereafter cited as *OR*.

2. I used the following editions of Hannah Arendt's writings: *Rahel Varnhagen: The Life of a Jewish Woman*, trans. Richard Winston and Clara Winston (New York: Harcourt Brace Jovanovich, 1974), hereafter cited as *Rahel*; *The Jew as Pariah: Jewish Identity and Politics in the Modern Age*, ed. Ron H. Feldman (New York: Grove Press, 1978), hereafter cited as *Pariah*; *The Origins of Totalitarianism* (New York: Harcourt Brace Jovanovich, 1973), hereafter cited as *The Origins*; *Eichmann in Jerusalem: A Report on the Banality of Evil* (New York: Penguin, 1977), hereafter cited as *Eichmann*; *The Life of the Mind* (New York: Harcourt Brace Jovanovich, 1978), hereafter cited as *Thinking*; *The Human Condition* (Chicago: University of Chicago Press, 1958), hereafter cited as *HC*.

3. In *The Human Condition*, Arendt declares that the classical world was divided into the public and the private, the social being an emphatically modern, hybrid phenomenon. But gender and class are social categories; women and slaves may have been identified with the private realm, but the identities that placed them there are social identities, not merely a function of private selves. It is precisely because she does not recognize gender (or class) as a social category, rather than a private fact, that Arendt cannot recognize a politics based on social identity as anything other than a politics of *ressentiment*. Yet social categories inevitably insert themselves into even her distinction between private and public lives, and I will use the tern "social identity" to evaluate the realities of that distinction.

4. From the service for Holy Eucharist, Rite Two, in *The Book of Common Prayer* (New York: Seabury Press, 1977), 370. Although Arendt does not herself use this exact phrase, it conveys the almost religious reverence with which she treats the given, physical realities of our human life in the earthly world.

5. Others have pointed out how significant natality as founding is to her as a political concept. See, for instance, André Enegrén, *La pensée politique de Hannah Arendt* (Paris: Presses Universitaires de France, 1984); Patricia Bowen-Moore, *Hannah Arendt's Philosophy of Natality* (New York: St. Martin's Press, 1989); Seyla Benhabib, *The Reluctant Modernism of Hannah Arendt* (Thousand Oaks, Calif.: Sage Publications, 1996); and Nancy Hartsock, *Money, Sex, and Power: Toward a Feminist Historical Materialism* (Boston: Northeastern University Press, 1985). Some of these theorists emphasize that for Arendt natality is a purely political and existential concept, while others rehabilitate it as a more specifically maternal and biological fact of human existence. See Mary G. Dietz, "Feminist Receptions of Hannah Arendt," in *Feminist Interpretations of Hannah Arendt*, ed. Bonnie Honig (University Park: Pennsylvania State University Press, 1995), 17–50, for an overview of this split among the English-language critics.

6. For Arendt, birth technologies are on a par with the satellite, in that both present the political problem of technological threats to bodily existence, and therefore threaten political meaning (see *HC*, 2). This emphasis on our earthly, physical embodiment would also seem to indicate that political natality (as conceptual beginning) does presume maternal natality (as physical birth); natality as founding can only be a meaningful practice to the natal beings who inhabit this earth.

7. The tension in Arendt's conception of natality reflects the diverse influence of both Aristotle and Heidegger in her thinking. From Aristotle she takes the notion that the defining human capacity of speech can only be realized in a political context; from Heidegger the insight that even the most abstractly poetic of human creations function as such only because they distill into metaphor the banal literality of our necessary physicality.

8. As a comparison, note how Heidegger contrasts the different river landscapes evoked by the images of a hydroelectric plant, a bridge, and Hölderlin's poem "The Rhine." See Martin Heidegger's "The Question Concerning Technology," in *Basic Writings*, ed. David Farrell Krell (New York: Harper & Row, 1977), 297. An early version of this essay was first delivered as a lecture in 1953.

9. Compare Arendt's brief description of the satellite with the monster in Mary Shelley's *Frankenstein*, the creature that is an abomination precisely because it is created by (a) man out of a violated (dead) nature, without natality.

10. See Martin Heidegger's "The Origin of the Work of Art," in *Poetry, Language, Thought*, trans. Albert Hofstadter (New York: Harper & Row, 1975), 149–87. In this essay Heidegger describes how our understanding of our world is most clearly presented to us in particularly evocative works of art that both reveal and conceal the reality that prompts them. He discusses the earthly world that is evoked and contained in a Van Gogh painting of a pair of peasant shoes, and then describes a Greek temple as firmly attached to the earth (its bulk, location, and context), but revelatory of a made, and transcendent, human world. An early version of the essay was first presented as a lecture in 1935.

11. She writes, "[I]t was not pride or awe at the tremendousness of human power and mastery which filled the hearts of men, who now, when they looked up from the earth toward the skies, could behold there a thing of their own making" (*HC*, 1). Note that here she uses "power" as "mastery," in relation to a masculine *techne*, and in direct contradiction to her own otherwise explicitly elaborated definition. For a discussion of Arendt's notion of power, see chapter 9, "An Alternative Tradition: Women on Power," in Hartsock, *Money, Sex, and Power*, 210–30.

12. Compare the Platonic notion of escape from the cave (of the world) to an extraworldly realm of Truth with Arendt's political notion that truth is here in our inhabited world of shadow and appearance.

13. Not only this prologue, but especially the much more controversial *Eichmann in Jerusalem*, originally published in 1963, seem to be Arendt's attempts to think and speak about that which seems to be unspeakable.

14. Arendt's prescience on this issue is validated in the court cases over surrogate motherhood, in which rulings have been made on the conceptual basis that no child can have two (biological) mothers, when the problem is that the technology of donor eggs means that, in fact, these children do.

15. This can be read simplistically as a wish to have the working class kept busy at their labors, or it can be read as an acknowledgment of Marx's apprecia-

tion of work: if all work is reduced to labor, and even that is taken away from us, how will we make the world, how will we make ourselves in it?

16. For Arendt's discussion of the origination of the distinction between private, public, and / or social, see for instance *HC*, 23-29.

17. To quote Enegrén: "on peut dire qu'il constitue une dimension 'transcendentale' qui fixe l'assise et trace les limites de l'interaction politique; cette dimension est celle du 'par où' en vertu de laquelle quelque chose est rendu libre à l'intérieur de limites" (Enegrén, *Pensée politique*, 50). ("We can say that it constitutes a 'transcendental' dimension that sets the foundation and traces the boundaries of political interaction; this dimension is the one of 'finding a way' in accordance with which something is rendered free within set boundaries." Translation my own.)

TWO. THE SOCIAL QUESTION

1. Here again she seems to be following Aristotle, who, despite his celebration of political practice, simply defines women and slaves as being inherently outside the scope of political life.

2. Julia Kristeva, *Powers of Horror: An Essay on Abjection*, trans. Leon S. Roudiez (New York: Columbia University Press, 1982), originally published as *Pouvoirs de l'horreur* (Paris: Éditions du Seuil, 1980).

3. As a historically accurate study of the French and American revolutions, *On Revolution* has been criticized from a variety of perspectives. E. J. Hobsbawm, for instance, in "Hannah Arendt on Revolution," in *Revolutionaries* (New York: Meridian Books, 1973), 201-8, dismisses *On Revolution* as entirely useless for the serious student of revolution—the historian or the sociologist. He finds Arendt too metaphysical, and too little concerned with fact. Norman Jacobson, on the other hand, in "Parable and Paradox: In Response to Hannah Arendt's *On Revolution*," *Salmagundi* 60 (spring–summer 1983): 123–39, gives a thoughtful analysis of Arendt's thesis of the "lost treasure" within the context of American revolutionary history. Jacobson describes the controversy between the Federalists and those who favored the system in place under the Articles of Confederation as being the defeat of precisely the kind of participatory democracy Arendt had in mind.

For a perceptive discussion of *On Revolution* as a text on revolution and political possibility in the modern era, see James Miller, "The Pathos of Novelty: Hannah Arendt's Image of Freedom in the Modern World," in *Hannah Arendt: The Recovery of the Public World*, ed. Melvyn Hill (New York: St. Martin's Press, 1979), 177–208. Miller is particularly attentive to Arendt's strange antipathy to Rousseau, and he is careful to evaluate that hostility as resulting from her very modern commitment to freedom and participatory political action. See also the brief discussion of *On Revolution* in Margaret Canovan's *The Political Thought of Hannah Arendt* (London: Methuen, 1977), 92–100. Canovan, emphasizing Arendt's similarity to Rosa Luxemburg, notes Arendt's understanding of revolution as human beginning, and her disappointment that neither the American Revolution nor any other has succeeded in preserving the manifestation of that beginning: the popular organs of self-government that emerge spontaneously in any revolutionary situation.

I am less concerned with Arendt's general political argument than with a reconsideration of her conceptions of embodied identity, political agency, and representation.

4. This last statement, that violence and speech confront each other across an
    abyss of meaninglessness, will have a different resonance when Arendt
    reworks it in her discussion of Herman Melville's *Billy Budd*, which I will
    discuss in the next chapter.

5. Note that whereas in *The Human Condition* the metaphor for beginning is
    maternal, and in *On Revolution* it is that of (fraternal) siblings, neither
    text particularly emphasizes a paternal role or metaphor.

6. Arendt's brief remarks here, at the conclusion of her Introduction, are remark-
    ably evocative of Freud's own theories that civilization arises from patri-
    cide. For a later reworking of similar ideas, see the discussion of social,
    political, and narrative origin in violence and fratricide in René Girard,
    Violence and the Sacred, trans. Patrick Gregory (Baltimore: Johns Hop-
    kins University Press, 1977).

7. Even after the precedent of the French Revolution, peasant revolts and urban
    food riots were not necessarily interpreted by either state officials or his-
    torians as political actions; often they were understood as mass outbursts
    of unrest that simply needed to be controlled and suppressed. Much of
    the work of the Subaltern Studies group over the last two decades has
    been to document the political significance of these local events. See, for
    instance, Ranajit Guha, "The Prose of Counter-Insurgency," 45–86;
    Gyan Pandey, "Peasant Revolt and Indian Nationalism: The Peasant
    Movement in Awadh, 1919–22," 233–87; Partha Chatterjee, "More on
    Modes of Power and the Peasantry," 351–90; all in *Selected Subaltern
    Studies*, ed. Ranajit Guha and Gayatri Chakravorty Spivak (New York:
    Oxford University Press, 1988).

8. The modern transformation of statecraft into policy, with its strange combi-
    nation of disciplinary/police functions and welfare obligations, is
    investigated, from a very different perspective, in Michel Foucault's late
    essays on governmentality. Foucault is not mourning a lost political
    past, but seeking to make sense out of a mixed category (the social-
    welfare state) of the present, especially since that category is now itself so
    threatened. See especially his "Governmentality," in *The Foucault Effect:
    Studies in Governmentality*, ed. Graham Burchell, Colin Gordon, and
    Peter Miller (Chicago: University of Chicago Press, 1991), 87–104.

9. Arendt's references to "poverty" imply a material state of economic want com-
    bined with economic integration. In that sense "poverty" is distinct
    from "pauperism," a condition in which the poor, rather than laboring
    under the necessities of their bodies, seem to revel in their immediate
    bodily pleasures, rejecting their own abjection by rejecting their incor-
    poration into modern systems of economic production and political
    organization. See Giovanna Procacci, "Social Economy and the Gov-
    ernment of Poverty," in *The Foucault Effect*, ed. Burchell et al., 151–68.

10. One of the most forthright critical evaluations of Arendt's problem with the
    social is presented by Hanna Pitkin in "Conformism, Housekeeping,
    and the Attack of the Blob: The Origin of Hannah Arendt's Concept of
    the Social," in *Feminist Interpretations of Hannah Arendt*, ed. Bonnie
    Honig (University Park: Pennsylvania State University Press, 1995).
    Pitkin's title is to be appreciated; Arendt's concept of the social does
    indeed seem to combine the shapeless horror and modern, doomsday
    threat of the inhuman protagonist from a bad black-and-white science
    fiction movie. Pitkin makes explicit, at the end of her essay, that "the
    Blob is a fantasy of regression, of losing one's separate self and being
    once more dissolved in—swallowed up by—an engulfing mother" (Pit-

kin, "Conformism," 79). But Pitkin looks only at Arendt's definition of the social in *The Human Condition*, and at an alternate description of society in *Rahel Varnhagen*. Although she uses a discussion of Arendt's life to discredit her definition, Pitkin does not deconstruct it. She does not involve *On Revolution* at all, and her comments on a psychoanalytic interpretation come only as concluding remarks to her discussion. Pitkin treats Arendt's discussion of the social as a mistake; I treat it as a key element of a revived politics of action.

11. Judith Butler also notes the political applications of a psychoanalytic threat in her own discussion of Kristeva's work on abjection. When, while writing my dissertation, I was already working on Kristeva and Riviere in relation to Arendt, Butler was kind enough to give me manuscript copies of relevant sections of *Gender Trouble* (New York: Routledge, 1990), which was then not yet published. I found these sections to be very useful in my own considerations. But Butler's project is different, and her analysis of abjection focuses on the either/or aspect of the internal/external boundary and the disgust associated with anything ejected out. I am emphasizing the impossibility of that boundary and therefore the concurrent impossibility of the ejection, not just of desire, but of the (physical) premise of the self.

12. The epigraph to Georges Bataille's novel *My Mother* functions as a remarkable description of the threatened return to and of the abject, a return that impossibly confounds both natality and mortality: "Terror unendingly renews with advancing age. Without end, it returns us to the beginning. The beginning that I glimpsed on the edge of the grave is the *pig* in me which neither death nor insult can kill. Terror on the edge of the grave is divine and I sink into the terror whose child I am" (Georges Bataille, *My Mother*, in *My Mother/Madame Edwarda/The Dead Man*, trans. Austryn Wainhouse [New York: Marion Boyers, 1989], 25).

13. It should be noted here that the maternal is not the same as the individual mother, just as no woman can hold the position of the phallic woman; the psychoanalytic constructs are not identities. For Lacan's own denial of this specification, see for instance Jacques Lacan, "God and the *Jouissance* of ~~The~~ Woman," in *Feminine Sexuality: Jacques Lacan and the École Freudienne*, ed. Juliet Mitchell and Jacqueline Rose (New York: Norton, 1982), 137-48.

14. See Jacques Lacan, "The Mirror Stage as Formative of the Function of the I as Revealed in Psychoanalytic Experience," in Lacan, *Ecrits: A Selection*, trans. Alan Sheridan (New York: Norton, 1977), 1-7.

15. The most telling myth concerning the self's reencounter with the abject is that of Oedipus, who in sleeping with his mother and fathering children by her confounds his filial, paternal, and fraternal roles. His transgression of the conventions of productive and reproductive function initially damns his kingdom to the plague and then himself and his family to wasteful death and tragedy. Once he knows of his own deep implication with the abject, he can sustain neither his kingly power nor his generative contribution, and both present and future (as well as, retroactively, the past) are lost. For a discussion of Oedipus and abjection, see Kristeva, "From Filth to Defilement," in *Powers of Horror*, 83-89.

16. Kristeva herself addresses this problem in the later *Strangers to Ourselves*, trans. Leon S. Roudiez (New York: Columbia University Press, 1991), originally published as *Étrangers à nous-mêmes* (Paris: Fayard, 1989).

This book, which deals with the psychoanalytic construction of an ethnic or national other, seems to strain for optimism when compared with *Powers of Horror*. For a critical comparison of the two works, see my "National Abjects: Julia Kristeva on the Process of Political Self-Identification," in *Ethics, Politics, and Difference in Julia Kristeva's Writings: A Collection of Essays*, ed. Kelly Oliver (New York: Routledge, 1993), 135–49.

17. In Arendt's writing, America functions very much as the symbol of exceptionalism Louis Hartz described in *The Liberal Tradition in America: An Interpretation of American Political Thought since the Revolution* (New York: Harcourt, Brace & World, 1955). America's symbolic function as a supplement to Europe is well known, but Arendt's America is, despite its exceptionalism, oddly reminiscent of European history and identity. What seems to be an escape from history in a new land bears an uncanny resemblance to the familiar history of the old world. In this, Arendt's America resembles Franz Kafka's *Amerika*, his supposedly optimistic tale, in which the happy ending of the final chapter describes what could almost be a totalitarian concentration camp. See Franz Kafka, *Amerika*, trans. Willa and Edwin Muir (New York: Schocken Books, 1969). Kafka apparently conceived the idea for *Amerika* around 1913.

18. Race has been a peculiarly haunting aspect of American political identity, and the historical narrative of American exceptionalism has been constructed upon a willed obliviousness. For an interesting mention of the invisibility of nonwhites to American whites (and thus the absence of a "social question"), see the description of the well-known Americanist Perry Miller's moment of continental inspiration in Africa, when he saw an "empty" landscape rather than the black workers he was supervising. Miller transposed the experience of "emptiness" to the American continent before the arrival of European colonial settlers, thereby totally ignoring the presence of the American indigenous population. See Jane Tompkins, " 'Indians': Textualism, Morality, and the Problem of History," in *"Race," Writing, and Difference*, ed. Henry Louis Gates (Chicago: University of Chicago Press, 1986), 59–78.

19. Historically, the political voice of the American slave was not so effectively silenced as that of the Athenian. See David Brion Davis, *The Problem of Slavery in the Age of Revolution: 1770–1823* (Ithaca: Cornell University Press, 1975), 276, for a description of slaves in colonial America arguing for their freedom in the language of natural rights. Davis describes as a "typical plea" a quite remarkable quote, framed in explicitly political language: "We have in common with all other men a naturel right to our freedoms without Being depriv'd of them by our fellow men as we are a freeborn Pepel and have never forfeited this Blessing by aney compact or agreement whatever" (*Collections* of the Massachusetts Historical Society, 5th ser., 3 [Boston, 1877], 432–36).

THREE. THE MASK AND MASQUERADE

1. Joan Riviere, "Womanliness as a Masquerade," in *Formations of Fantasy*, ed. Victor Burgin, James Donald, and Cora Kaplan (New York: Methuen, 1986), 35–44; first published in *International Journal of Psychoanalysis* 10 (1929): 303–13.

2. It should be noted here that my use of the term "representation" is predominantly theatrical rather than strictly political. When Arendt writes about self-representation she is referring to individual public political

participation; my use of the term deliberately blurs the distinction between presentation of self and political participation. By emphasizing the quality of controlled dramatic appearance in representation, I hope to indicate the degree of theatricality that inheres in Arendt's own conceptualization of political practice.

3. Herman Melville, *Selected Writings of Herman Melville: Complete Short Stories; Typee; Billy Budd, Foretopman* (New York: Modern Library, 1952). The manuscript for *Billy Budd* was found in draft form on Melville's death in 1891 and was published posthumously. An earlier work was *The Confidence-Man: His Masquerade*, published in 1857. Although Arendt proceeds, after her discussion of compassion and *Billy Budd*, to discuss hypocrisy and the role of the mask, she never mentions this other work of Melville's, in which one actor plays a variety of roles in quick succession. Melville's masquerade is not Riviere's, but the overlapping relations between power, truth, and appearance remain.

4. The argument that narrative (oral or written) stabilizes violence is not the same as the argument that writing provokes violence. For a story that seeks to illustrate the latter point, see Claude Lévi-Strauss, "A Writing Lesson," the account of the confrontation between Europeans and Nambikwara tribesmen, in which writing is used to broker power, and its use provokes violence. According to Lévi-Strauss, a native guide's (illegitimate) usurpation of the power of writing provokes a violent reaction among his peers, which the narrator characterizes as appropriate to the guide's fraudulent attempt to claim the power of writing. What Lévi-Strauss's narrative evades is the possibility that the violence is provoked, not so much by the guide's pretense to literacy, but by his close association with the European anthropologist. In that case, then, the guide's "writing" would not have provoked violence, but Lévi-Strauss's narrative would have consolidated the violence and shifted responsibility for it onto those who are otherwise "speechless," as in Arendt's example (Claude Lévi-Strauss, *Tristes Tropiques*, trans. John Weightman and Doreen Weightman [New York: Atheneum, 1975], 294–304). In *Of Grammatology*, Jacques Derrida provides a scrupulously close reading of "A Writing Lesson." Derrida carefully elaborates the way that Lévi-Strauss follows Rousseau in treating cultures as pure and savage until they are corrupted by civilization, which they encounter through writing. But Derrida's focus is also on the cultural role of writing itself, rather than on the way writing can consolidate relationships that have other than purely grammatological histories. See the section "Writing and Man's Exploitation by Man" in Jacques Derrida, *Of Grammatology*, trans. Gayatri Chakravorty Spivak (Baltimore: Johns Hopkins University Press, 1984), 118–40.

5. In chapter 1, "The Meaning of Revolution," Arendt carefully reviews the old idea that any revolution was a restoration rather than a novelty, a fresh return rather than an absolute break. See especially section three, 35–47 in that chapter.

6. Note Arendt's characterization of this story as being about that which is, not beyond good and evil (to use Nietzsche's terms), but beyond virtue and vice, a distinction that places in question the supposedly clearly divided morality of good and evil.

7. Billy Budd's violence, although honorable, cannot be recognized as political because it is so absolutely and seemingly unreasonably mute; and as such Arendt refuses to consider it to be any form of (political) action.

Her demand here seems to be that a just cause, to be politically recognized as such, must speak up for itself. Unfortunately, she does not really consider the probable outcome of a just but inarticulate and underprivileged cause in confrontation with a less virtuous but more polished, better endowed one. Her model would seem to presuppose a wise, disinterested magistrate the likes of Captain Vere, or a perfect world of clear communication, rather like that Habermas proposed in his works on communicative ethics.

8. Note that on the same page Arendt also writes that compassion is like love in respect to the abolishing of worldly distance.

9. Unfortunately, Arendt completely excludes from this discussion the problem of the legitimacy of state-sponsored violence. This is especially troubling since she often seems ready enough to deny political recognition to whole sectors of the population; if these people are defined as outside the political, then the state will not attend to them politically, and may only recognize their self-presentations as violent disruptions. Since her argument is not against the sentimental futility of charity but against compassion as fellow-feeling, and since this fellow-feeling is itself to be excluded as a political motive, then how are these others ever to gain political recognition? Is self-interest the only legitimate political passion among the powerful?

10. In her discussion of the Grand Inquisitor section of *The Brothers Karamazov*, Arendt considers the interaction between Christ and the Inquisitor quite similar to that between Billy Budd and Captain Vere. The roles are more emphatically defined, however: Christ is more fully compassionate and silent, the Inquisitor more articulate and worldly. Also, Christ himself is of course not violent; rather, he is associated with the undisciplined emotional energy (compassion) that is all too close, for the political actor, to irrational violence. Precisely because the Billy Budd episode is more morally ambivalent, it is more apt as a political metaphor (see *OR*, 85–86). Arendt is always careful to distinguish the historical strength and political power of the Catholic Church and Christianity from early church Christianity and Christ's message as an individual (see *OR*, 25–27; *HC*, 53–54).

11. I use the term "proper appearance" as an intentional play on contemporary discussions of the *propre* (feminine) body: a body that is contained and released by its relation to (private) property and the proprieties. See, for instance, Luce Irigaray: "Woman would always remain multiple, but she would be protected from dispersion because the other is a part of her, and is autoerotically familiar to her. That does not mean that she would appropriate the other for herself, that she would make it her property. Property and propriety are undoubtedly rather foreign to all that is female. At least sexually. *Nearness*, however, is not foreign to woman, a nearness so close that any identification of one or the other, and therefore any form of property, is impossible." Luce Irigaray, *This Sex Which Is Not One*, trans. Catherine Porter (Ithaca: Cornell University Press, 1985), 104–5.

12. Arendt will return to these quotes much later, in the discussion of *Thinking* in her final philosophical project, *The Life of the Mind*. In chapter 8, my own discussion of evil and agency in the third volume of *The Origins of Totalitarianism* and *Eichmann in Jerusalem*, I will also return to this later consideration and will address the extent to which the plurality of the

private self can become, in times of crisis, a substitute for the plurality of the public world of appearance.

13. For a fine discussion of Arendt's thesis that political action is revelatory of the real and worldly self, a self made coherent through action and narrative, see George Kateb, *Hannah Arendt: Politics, Conscience, Evil* (Totowa, N.J.: Rowman & Allenheld, 1984), 8–10.

14. The notion of "performativity" has become fashionable in contemporary discussions of identity. Language theorists such as J. L. Austin had used the term to categorize types of speech, but Judith Butler's extremely influential *Gender Trouble: Feminism and the Subversion of Identity* (New York: Routledge, 1989) focused attention on the performativity of gender, sexuality, and, by extension, other forms of social identity. Butler pulled together close readings of (mostly French) social and psychoanalytic theorists to elaborate for an American audience a theory of constructed gender and sexuality grounded in practice, discourse, and social perception rather than any supposedly objective physiology. The term has now come to be associated with her work, but her texts, themselves careful engagements with a variety of other writers, are the best evidence for the wider currency of the basic concept.

Arendt herself does not use the term, but others have aptly characterized her politics as performative, as a way of describing the quality of public self-disclosure Arendt particularly associates with political action. See for instance Bonnie Honig, "Toward an Agonistic Feminism: Hannah Arendt and the Politics of Identity," in *Feminist Interpretations of Hannah Arendt*, ed. Bonnie Honig (University Park: Pennsylvania State University Press, 1995), 135–66. My own use of the term emphasizes the worldly quality of Arendt's own writing, drawing as much from a Shakespearean notion of (tragic) theatricality as from the more contemporary social and psychoanalytic theorists.

15. This concern resonates with Arendt's discussion in the earlier *Origins of Totalitarianism* of the problem of the secret agent or the spy, a problem I address in the chapter on *Imperialism*. The performative truth of the secret agent's public role is undercut by its hidden purposes. In the case of T. E. Lawrence, Arendt notes that the man's commitment to a performative standard of truth is precisely what made him tragically hypocritical: he believed in the truth of a role he knew to be impossibly compromised.

16. Arendt further explores the problem of self-deception and hypocrisy in relation to lying in her 1971 essay, "Lying and Politics: Reflections on the Pentagon Papers," *New York Review of Books* 17 / 18 (18 November 1971), reprinted in *Crises of the Republic* (New York: Harcourt Brace Jovanovich, 1972), 1–47.

17. The hypocrite's self-conviction is also dangerously seductive, and it is hard not to wonder if some of the animus Arendt directs here toward the figure of the hypocrite is not a veiled, displaced criticism of Heidegger. Arendt may have been captivated all her life by Heidegger's intellect, but she was no fool, and his rather forced political naïveté is in direct contradiction to her own emphasis on the connection between politics and thinking. If she was able to come to terms, in their personal relationship, with Heidegger's political past, she may nonetheless have passed implicit judgment on it in her theoretical writing. I deal more fully with Arendt's use of displacement and a mask or persona when

writing about issues of personal relevance to her, especially her early involvement with Heidegger, in my chapter on *Rahel Varnhagen.*

18. While here comparing hypocrisy to "radical evil," Arendt emphasizes the further rottenness of the hypocrite. Arendt's own investigation of radical evil and hypocrisy was *Eichmann in Jerusalem: A Report on the Banality of Evil,* published in New York by Viking Press in 1963. *On Revolution* was published by the same press in the same year, and both books were revised and republished in 1965. Arendt was finishing work on the manuscript of *On Revolution* when the Eichmann trial began, and the two texts, with their two distinct discussions of evil, illuminate each other: Eichmann's evil is radical, criminal, but also self-deceiving and banal; hypocrisy may be only a vice, but it is nonetheless vicious.

   Arendt emphasizes Eichmann's hypocrisy: he is a man who accomplished extraordinary evil but remained convinced of his own very ordinary lack of moral culpability. Indeed, what was shocking in Arendt's account was the thesis that Eichmann was, despite his crimes, quite an ordinary individual with no self-consciousness that he was also a criminal. The wording of Arendt's passage on hypocrisy—which is described as not necessarily radical but nonetheless rotten—indicates that she had not yet written or at least not yet fully considered her analysis of the "banality" of evil when she wrote this part of "The Social Question," even though she allowed the phrasing to remain in later editions. Although essays that would be incorporated into the text of *On Revolution* had appeared in various publications as early as 1960, none of these directly addressed the social question: "Revolution and Public Happiness" appeared in *Commentary* 30 (November 1960): 413–22; "Action and the Pursuit of Happiness" appeared in *Politische Ordnung und Menschliche Existenz: Festgabe für Eric Voegelin* (Munich: Beck, 1962); and "Revolution and Freedom: A Lecture" appeared in *Zwei Welten: Siegfried Moses zum Fünfundsiebzigsten Geburtstag* (Tel Aviv: Bitaon, 1962). The Eichmann work appeared first as articles entitled "A Reporter at Large: Eichmann in Jerusalem," *New Yorker,* 16 February 1963, 40–113; 23 February 1963, 40–111; 2 March 1963, 40–91; 9 March 1963, 48–131; and 16 March 1963, 58–134.

19. Arendt's condemnation of hypocrisy as the vice that, in institutional practice in totalitarian regimes, most effectively destroys all valid political possibility by destroying the self-conscious basis for agency will be further examined in my discussion of *The Origins of Totalitarianism,* especially the chapter on *Totalitarianism.*

20. Arendt rejects the organic metaphors for revolution (Marx's "birth-pangs") in favor of those of the theater (*OR,* 106). This apparent contradiction between a natural, organic body, the associated metaphor of natality, and theatricality will be addressed more explicitly in the conclusion to this chapter.

21. For an extremely perceptive discussion of the significance of the mask within Arendt's political philosophy, see the section titled "What Is the Existential Achievement of Political Action?" in Kateb, *Hannah Arendt,* 8–14.

22. I return to this issue of the relationship between evil, self-consciousness, appearance, and action in my discussion of *Eichmann* and *Thinking* in chapter 8.

23. Arendt is quoting Robespierre, in his speech to the National Convention on 17 November 1793, in *Œuvres de Maximilien Robespierre,* ed. Laponneraye (Paris: Chez l'editeur, 1840), 3.336.

24. Arendt is quoting Lord Acton, *Lectures on the French Revolution* (New York: Noonday Paperbacks, 1959), originally published in 1910. Arendt quotes Acton that the women "played the *genuine* part" (emphasis added): they were essentially, even mindlessly, themselves, rather than consciously enacting a political role.

25. By *jouissance* I refer to the concept of a radically posed construction of feminine sexual and physical pleasure, a self-fulfillment that breaks the conventions of gendered subjectivity and self-restraint. For an extremely perceptive discussion of the particular threat embodied in a theatrically flaunted feminine sexuality as the enacted metaphor for a radical assault on political order, see Neil Hertz, "Medusa's Head: Male Hysteria under Political Pressure," in *The End of the Line: Essays on Psychoanalysis and the Sublime* (New York: Columbia University Press, 1985), 100–215.

26. Arendt's assumption that the abject, identified as the poor, feminine body, cannot represent itself is a reflection of her own difficulty in finding a way to speak as a woman. Her struggle to find a voice that combines a specifically feminine identity with an empowered political analysis will be traced in chapter 4.

27. See *OR*, 114. Arendt totally elides the question of the (political) control of technology under the assertion that technological progress will make the abject free, emancipating them from the tyranny of their bodies and of necessity. Since she has already given a much more thoughtful analysis of precisely this attitude in the Preface to *The Human Condition*, this simplistic statement seems justifiably suspect.

28. "Film and Masquerade: Theorising the Female Spectator" was first published in *Screen* 233–34 (1982); "Masquerade Reconsidered: Further Thoughts on the Female Spectator" was first published in *Discourse* 11, no. 1 (1988–89). Both articles were reprinted in Mary Ann Doane, *Femmes Fatales: Feminism, Film Theory, Psychoanalysis* (New York: Routledge, 1991), 17–32 and 33–43.

29. Most recent attention to Riviere's essay has been from a feminist perspective and has focused on the extent to which the essay provides a model for thinking of (feminine) gender as a performance. This is certainly true of Doane's approach, as well as Butler's in *Gender Trouble*, 43–57; Stephen Heath, "Joan Riviere and the Masquerade," in *Formations of Fantasy*, 45–61; and Efrat Tseëlon, *The Masque of Femininity* (Thousand Oaks, Calif.: Sage Publication, 1995), 37–40. But this isn't the only interpretation of Riviere; some psychoanalytic approaches to her article read it only for its description of the analysand's early compulsive behavior, without any of the sense of masquerade as strategy that Riviere herself theorizes later in the article and that the feminist theorists find so crucial. See, for instance, M. Athol Hughes, "Personal Experiences—Professional Interests: Joan Riviere and Femininity," *International Journal of Psychoanalysis* 78 (1997): 899–911. Hughes's article gives no indication in the discussion or the notes that the author is at all aware of this other, feminist perspective on Riviere. It is interesting to note that this quite traditional analysis, which discounts Riviere's analytic contribution in order to emphasize the determinant role of (her own) mother/child experience, was published in the same journal in which Riviere's article first appeared.

30. Doane goes on to connect Riviere's definition of femininity as "the play of masks" with a Lacanian understanding that "the assumption of a mask

NOTES TO PAGES 41-45

conveys more of the 'truth' of sexuality ... than any recourse to 'being' or 'essence' " (Doane, "Masquerade Reconsidered," 37). Note the surprising similarity between the characterization of a Lacanian psychoanalytic theory in which (sexual) "truth" is conveyed through masks and Arendt's political theory in which worldly "truth" is conveyed through them. Though dissimilar in many ways, both theorists are radical in their emphasis on the performed rather than natural or essential quality of their subject of study, and, in doing so, both break ranks with much of the assumed truth in their field of study.

31. The omitted section deals with the woman's dreams, especially those involving black men, in which she asserts the femininity of her own body as a way of mastering (the) forbidden masculinity (of the black body). Note also that the analysand's assertion of her feminine sexuality is precisely what makes her "guiltless and innocent." Doane, who is concerned with the details of feminine sexual representation, is critical that theorists so often overlook precisely this section of the analysis, including Riviere's relative lack of theoretical concern with intersecting representations of race, sexuality, and power (see Doane, "Masquerade Reconsidered," 38). I deal more fully with representations of race in the following chapters on *The Origins of Totalitarianism;* at this point my concern is to establish an argument about masquerade and the social identity of femininity. The argument will then be extended to consider masquerade and ethnicity, including race.

32. Doane links the image of the thief turning out his pockets, empty of the stolen goods, with the image of the woman who plays innocent to the accusation of castration because she doesn't have the phallus. This is the classic image of the feminine woman who recognizes her essential lack of the fundamental signifier of agency and masculinity (see Doane, "Masquerade Reconsidered," 34). However, Riviere's profoundly original early essay, with its careful hedges against assimilation to the then contemporary psychoanalytic discourse and its own masquerade of deference to Freudian authority, can just as easily be assimilated to more recent post-Lacanian feminist psychoanalytic theories like Luce Irigaray's, in which femininity is both embodied and performed, lacking the phallus but inhabiting the performance of itself.

33. Riviere's retreat, whether staged or not, from the apparent conclusions of her own observations and psychoanalytic logic is remarkably evocative of Freud's own anxiety about the practical implications of the seduction theory. For an extraordinarily subtle interpretation of Freud's own possible reasons for anxiety, see Marie Balmary's wonderful, under-read *Psychoanalyzing Psychoanalysis: Freud and the Hidden Fault of the Father,* trans. Ned Lukacher (Baltimore: Johns Hopkins University Press, 1982).

34. In *Behind the Mask: On Sexual Demons, Sacred Mothers, Transvestites, Gangsters, and Other Japanese Cultural Heroes* (New York: Pantheon Books, 1984), Ian Buruma analyzes the high degree of artifice invested in the construction of sexual personas in Japan. According to Buruma, the Japanese are expert at the representation and codification of sexual roles, a mask that hides the vulnerability and tension of the private self: "Baudelaire's maxim, 'la femme est naturelle, c'est à dire abominable,' echoes traditional Japanese sentiments exactly. People, especially women, have to be redecorated as it were, ritualized and as far as humanly possible, turned into works of art" (65).

35. Arendt does figure the body as essential to the human condition and therefore to all that we create in our world; Riviere does not address the question of the body specifically, but her own work on masquerade places in doubt any notion of an essential feminine nature.

36. Riviere's avoidance of the question of private masquerade thus segues neatly into Arendt's own distinction between private and public roles.

37. Arendt herself develops this notion of the political dramatization of oneself as the social other in her discussion of Benjamin Disraeli in *Antisemitism*, vol. 1 of *The Origins of Totalitarianism*.

38. For a discussion of artifice and the presentation of a dramatically sexual female body, see Deborah Drier, "The Defiant Ones," *Art in America* (September 1987): 47–51. Although it describes clothing, a social issue particularly associated with women, Drier's article is interesting in that it emphasizes a fashion "silhouette which . . . is highly abstract, highly narrative, and highly fetishized" (47) and designers who "flagrantly embrace the artificial, that is, an understanding of the sexualized body as a construction, even as a distortion" (49). Further, Drier addresses much of her essay to the possibility that explicitly and aggressively sexual clothing does provide (working) women, like Riviere's analysand, who speak and write in public relations of power with men (and women), with a greater sense of control.

FOUR. SPEAKING AS RAHEL

1. Hannah Arendt, *Rahel Varnhagen: The Life of a Jewess*, trans. Richard and Clara Winston (London: East and West Library, 1957).

2. The revelation of the affair burst like a bombshell on the scholarly community with the publication of Elisabeth Young-Bruehl's biography, *Hannah Arendt: For Love of the World* (New Haven, Conn.: Yale University Press, 1982). It had been such a closely kept secret that there hadn't even been speculation about such a possibility, and Young-Bruehl was the first scholar to have access to the papers that document the affair, which were extremely restricted until only very recently. Young-Bruehl herself emphasizes the parallel between the two women's lives in her chapter on the period when Arendt was working on the Rahel project; the chapter itself is titled "The Life of a Jewess (1929–1933)" (77–110).

3. In a 1952 letter to Karl Jaspers, Arendt explicitly credited Blücher and Benjamin with having prodded her to finish the last few chapters of the book, and Kurt Blumenfeld with having made her aware of the political problem of antisemitism. As quoted in Young-Bruehl, *Hannah Arendt*, 91.

4. This distance from Rahel Varnhagen's experience as a *woman* was compounded when the original title of the English edition, *Rahel Varnhagen: The Life of a Jewess* (London: East and West Library, 1957), was changed slightly for the first American edition, to *Rahel Varnhagen: The Life of a Jewish Woman* (New York: Harcourt Brace Jovanovich, 1974), when it was published more than ten years later. The German editions all avoid the problem for simple grammatical reasons: *Rahel Varnhagen: Lebensgeschichte einer deutschen Jüdin aus der Romantik* (Munich: Piper, 1959; Frankfurt am Main: Ullstein Verlag, 1975; Munich: Piper Verlag, 1981). Liliane Weissberg's fully annotated scholarly English edition returns to the original English title; see Hannah Arendt, *Rahel Varnhagen: The Life of a Jewess*, ed. Liliane Weissberg, trans. Richard and Clara Winston (Baltimore: Johns Hopkins University Press, 1997). The now archaic,

usually frowned upon term "Jewess" nonetheless guarantees that a particular double identity, both Jewish and feminine, remains intertwined, resistant to the split effacement that is made possible by the term "Jewish woman."

5. Weissberg's scholarly edition of *Rahel Varnhagen* clearly establishes the extent to which Arendt's text is a self-conscious construction, as a narrative and as a publication. Weissberg documents Arendt's attempts in the 1960s to have the manuscript retroactively considered as her *Habilitation;* the postwar monetary reparations Arendt would be entitled to from the German government would be substantially more if she could show she had completed advanced academic training, rather than merely a thesis and a private scholarly project. In 1971 the West German government granted (on appeal) Arendt's claim for reparations for a lost German academic career; the verdict described Arendt as a "truly exceptional case" and dated her *Habilitation* (with the Rahel manuscript) to 1933, even though Arendt had never formally applied for the *Habilitation* during that period. See Weissberg, *Rahel Varnhagen*, 38–41.

6. In this the Arendt "scandal" is like that surrounding Paul de Man. Both revelations shocked the academic community and prompted controversial reconsiderations of the link between the life and the work. But the disclosure of de Man's youthful association with fascism was an intellectual scandal: he wrote for an antisemitic newspaper. What came under scrutiny was the connection between his early writings and his later work, and his suppression of his early political associations. In Arendt's case, the disclosure is of her youthful affair with a famous married man who later associated himself with fascism: the scandal is sexual, and she is tainted not by her own actions but by her lover's later ones. What has come under scrutiny is not her intellectual work but her personal life and her suppression of its evidence. But women especially are well aware of the extent to which they are judged by their sexual reputation, and keeping quiet about an early romance is not the same as keeping quiet about one's political affiliations. Feminist scholars particularly seem to have made every effort not to hold Arendt to account for her sexual history by overprivileging the affair, and there has been a certain backlash against work that is seen as dealing in a theoretically vulgar fashion with so delicate an issue. This seems to be true of the response to Elzbieta Ettinger's *Hannah Arendt / Martin Heidegger* (New Haven, Conn.: Yale University Press, 1995), for instance.

For all the wonder that news of the affair initially prompted, there has been a kind of awkward reluctance to address it. This may in general be truer of the English-language scholarly community than of scholars in Europe; see for instance the combined engagement with Arendt's life and philosophy that characterizes the variety of articles in the edition of *magazine littéraire* devoted to "Hannah Arendt: philosophie et politique," 337 (November 1995). The articles deal with different aspects of Arendt's life as a woman political philosopher who, naturally enough, had close relationships with a variety of men and women who shared diverse political sympathies. See especially Catherine Clément's matter-of-fact feminist response to Ettinger's characterization of Arendt as a misled young thing even in middle age, "Hannah Arendt / Martin Heidegger: histoire d'un grand amour" (25–26). See also Jean-Michel Palmier's review of Elfriede Jelinek's drama *Totenauberg*, "Arendt / Heidegger: une rencontre imaginaire" (26–27). Structured around a postwar conversation between two anonymous protagonists who are clearly intended to be Arendt and Heidegger, the work poses exactly the kind of questions one would guess might have arisen between two such people who share an old intimacy but have made very different political and intellectual choices, as they walk on a mountainside in an Alpine resort area that is all too reminiscent of Todtnauberg, Heidegger's mountain retreat.

7. Young-Bruehl identifies this as Arendt's university student nickname, an allusion to her brilliance that might also have referred to her unavailability. See Young-Bruehl, *Hannah Arendt*, 99.

8. This problem is exacerbated because there is relatively so little written in English on Rahel Varnhagen that her name and reputation are unfamiliar to scholars outside of German studies; as a result Arendt's book has been further marginalized in the academic discourse. For an early (1913), rather dated exception to this absence, first published in Swedish, that asserts the significance of Rahel's story and writing for "modern" women, see Ellen Kay, *Rahel Varnhagen: A Portrait*, trans. Arthur G. Chater, with an introduction by Havelock Ellis (New York: G. P. Putnam's Sons, 1913).

9. The reverberations from this piece of news in Young-Bruehl's book had never really settled and were reanimated by Ettinger's publication of new letters in *Hannah Arendt/Martin Heidegger*. Both books were invaluable; because the relevant correspondence was restricted, they contained virtually the only generally available information on the relationship. This is not to say, however, that they therefore provide sophisticated interpretations. Ettinger's study, which focuses specifically on the relationship, is the more frustrating, since it perpetuates a fairly simplistic and even prurient critical attitude: the easy outside insight that Arendt, at least, should have repudiated the whole thing as a big mistake. In this context of heightened interest and limited information, the recent publication of the complete extant Arendt/Heidegger correspondence has been invaluable to scholars. See *Hannah Arendt/Martin Heidegger: Briefe 1925 bis 1975*, ed. Ursula Ludz (Frankfurt: Vittorio Klostermann, 1999).

10. Young-Bruehl notes that Heidegger finally told his wife about the affair, calling Arendt "the passion of his life," after the two had met again in 1950, after the war. It isn't clear that Heidegger's wife didn't know about the affair, but his explicit confession prompted a jealous outburst on her part; describing this, Arendt rather disingenuously labeled her rival "simply stupid" (letters from Arendt to Hilde Fränkel, quoted in Young-Bruehl, *Hannah Arendt*, 247). Ettinger's book does make clear that Arendt never ceased regarding Elfride Heidegger as a rival; her rejection of feminist or psychoanalytic interpretations of the dynamics of such a triangle enabled her to maintain a version of the romantic dyad, while assigning the "stupid" wife all the blame.

11. This experience of a peculiarly overlapping dichotomy between one's public and private worlds, in which the private both guarantees the public and must be completely hidden if the worth of the public is to be maintained, marked Arendt's thinking about social identity and politics. Her thinking on these subjects is most evident in *The Human Condition* and *On Revolution*, but her discussion of Proust's depiction of the public secret of homosexuality in *Remembrance of Things Past* also explores this sense of impossibly intertwined public and private lives. See "Between

NOTES TO PAGE 52

NOTES TO PAGE 52

Vice and Crime," in *Antisemitism*, vol. 1 of *The Origins of Totalitarianism* (79–88), and my discussion of it in chapter 5.

12. Dagmar Barnouw credits the Zionist Kurt Blumenfeld with introducing Arendt to the writings of Bernard Lazare and his formulations of the Jewish "pariah" (self-identified political outsider and critic) and the "parvenu" (assimilationist who denies and seeks to escape the pariah identity that is imposed from outside). See Barnouw, *Visible Spaces: Hannah Arendt and the German-Jewish Experience* (Baltimore: Johns Hopkins University Press, 1990), 38–39. Barnouw very effectively brings out the extent to which the Varnhagen project was for Arendt an examination of a consciousness torn between pariah and parvenu attitudes; but like most other commentators, she treats the whole book as though it were written from the political perspective of its last two chapters. In this chapter I argue that most of the book is written from the painful emotional perspective of the feminine parvenu and is a portrait of feminine assimilationist strategies and desires, despite Arendt's own assertions that it is about a generalized German Jewish situation.

13. This is true of the brief discussion Young-Bruehl gives of the *Rahel* text ("Biography as Autobiography," in Young-Bruehl, *Hannah Arendt*, 85–92). It is also true of Deborah Hertz's excellent analysis in "Hannah Arendt's Rahel Varnhagen," in *German Women in the Nineteenth Century*, ed. John C. Fout (New York: Holmes & Meier, 1984), 72–87. Hertz examines *Rahel Varnhagen* for indications of Arendt's own intellectual history (80), but she focuses primarily on Arendt's concern with Jewish social history and identity. Liliane Weissberg, in "Stepping Out: The Writing of Difference in Rahel Varnhagen's Letters," *New German Critique* 53 (1991): 149–62, gives a very insightful analysis of Rahel's writing about metaphors of national and Jewish identity. Weissberg deftly uses Arendt's conceptual definitions of antisemitism and of pariah and parvenu consciousness to locate her own discussion of Rahel's somatization of Jewish, as opposed to German, identity.

Other recent studies, including Richard Bernstein's *Hannah Arendt and the Jewish Question* (Cambridge: MIT Press, 1986); Hanna Pitkin's "Conformism, Housekeeping, and the Attack of the Blob: The Origins of Hannah Arendt's Concept of the Social," in *Feminist Interpretations of Hannah Arendt*, ed. Bonnie Honig (University Park: Pennsylvania State University Press, 1995), 51–81; and Seyla Benhabib's "The Pariah and Her Shadow: Hannah Arendt's Biography of Rahel Varnhagen," also in Honig, *Feminist Interpretations*, 83–104, and included in longer form in Benhabib's *The Reluctant Modernism of Hannah Arendt* (Thousand Oaks, Calif.: Sage Publications, 1996), similarly emphasize that Arendt found in Rahel's life story a way to theorize an emphatically Jewish experience. This is in keeping with Arendt's own assertions, especially in her correspondence with her former professor Karl Jaspers, that she was investigating Rahel's life as a life defined by, although not founded upon, its Jewishness. Both Bernstein and Benhabib quote letters between Arendt and Jaspers about the work, letters in which Jaspers expresses his concern that Arendt is overemphasizing Rahel's perception of her Jewishness, at the expense of other perceptions, for her own reasons. Benhabib and Pitkin both link Arendt's work on the Varnhagen project to her personal experiences. Benhabib describes the "mirror effect" of the text, in which "the one narrated about becomes the mirror in which the narrator also portrays herself" (Benhabib, "The

Pariah and Her Shadow," 90), but in the later, expanded version Benhabib closes down the possibility that this is a particularly feminine, Jewish reflection, emphasizing instead the experience of being a Jew in difficult historical times. This is the expanded version: "The one narrated about becomes the mirror in which the narrator seeks to understand and interpret herself. Retelling and reconstructing Rahel Varnhagen's life story was clearly a medium for Hannah Arendt to reflect upon aspects of her own identity as a German Jew" (Benhabib, *Reluctant Modernism*, 10). The rest of the expanded paragraph goes on to make clear that Benhabib now has in mind a Jewish, but not a gendered, personal identification, although further on in the essay she does note that even Arendt acknowledges Rahel's assimilationist strategies as necessarily feminine. Pitkin points to the Varnhagen book as evidence of Arendt's having learned from her relationship with Heidegger. Ironically, in emphasizing Arendt's identification with Rahel as a *Jewish* woman, these authors seem to overlook her possible identification with Rahel as a Jewish *woman*. Nonetheless, none of these authors view the text itself as offering alternative interpretive possibilities—as not a finished result of lessons learned, but itself a lesson in learning.

14. See Arendt, "Berlin Salon," trans. Robert Kimber and Rita Kimber, in Hannah Arendt, *Essays in Understanding*, ed. Jerome Kohn (New York: Harcourt Brace, 1994), 57–65.

15. See Sybille Bedford, "Emancipation and Destiny," *Book Notes*, 12 December 1958, 22–23 (quoted in Young-Bruehl, *Hannah Arendt*, 86–87).

16. Arendt's style in *Rahel Varnhagen* is more reminiscent of Virginia Woolf's in *To the Lighthouse* than of Arendt's own usual tone. Both authors seem to be writing as though muffled, through a secret knowledge that cannot be spoken, although it fully directs their speaking a scenario of rarefied emotion. For Woolf, that knowledge is of the difficult experience of her childhood, including the problem of her mother's authoritative but disengaged presence. For Arendt, the knowledge is of her abbreviated affair with Heidegger, her professor. For both women authors, keeping the secret is as much about loyalty to the other as telling the emotional truth of it is about loyalty to the self. See the discussion of Woolf's writing in the context of her early life in Louise DeSalvo, *Virginia Woolf: The Impact of Childhood Sexual Abuse on Her Life and Work* (Boston: Beacon Press, 1989).

17. See Weissberg, "Writing on the Wall," *New German Critique* 36 (1985): 157–73. Weissberg discusses the contradiction, apparent in Rahel's letters, between her education and her own protestations of ignorance: "Her letters to David Veit are filled with reports about lessons—English, French, waltz dancing—as well as autodidactic attempts to master classical literature and philosophy" (165), even as she complains that she will never master a good style.

In his biography of Karl August Varnhagen (*The Unseasonable Democrat: K. A. Varnhagen von Ense [1785–1858]* [Bonn: Bouvier Verlag Herbert Grundmann, 1985]), Terry Pickett actually provides fairly specific accounts of Rahel's elastic relationship with her family before her marriage; after her father's death, her brothers supported her without overly restricting her independence, whether she was living at home with her mother, on her own, or traveling, and despite the family's financial difficulties due to war and recession. Pickett's work is interesting in that, as a biography of Varnhagen the man of liberal political involvement, it treats Rahel as a secondary character. In comparison to other descriptions of her as a woman of great, natural sensitivities, in Pickett's account Rahel comes across as petulant, demanding, and all too self-involved; the terms he uses echo Arendt's own later critique (in *On Revolution*) of the politically destructive insistence on pure intentions. "She was her own heroine. Viewing herself as a kind of natural force, full of sincerity and therefore authentic, Rahel created a paradigm of the bourgeois view of experience: private innocence versus public corruption" (Pickett, *Unseasonable Democrat*, 25). Like the German scholar Werner Greiling, Pickett's work emphasizes Varnhagen's career as a diplomat, a journalist, and a supporter of Jacobinist and radical democratic writers, and further calls into question Arendt's dismissive characterization of this public, political man as the boorish attendant to the private world of his wife.

18. "Das Licht der Öffentlichkeit verdunkelt alles und gibt das so Verdeckte als das Bekannte und jedem Zugängliche aus." ["By publicness everything gets obscured, and what has thus been covered up gets passed off as something familiar and accessible to everyone."] See Martin Heidegger, *Sein und Zeit* (Tübingen: Max Niemayer Verlag, 1963), 127; English translation from Martin Heidegger, *Being and Time*, trans. John Macquarrie and Edward Robinson (New York: Harper & Row, 1962), 165.

19. From Arendt's 1925 personal essay "Die Schatten."

20. Young-Bruehl and others emphasize that the book is divided into a central discussion of Rahel's dreams, and the surrounding material. Given the interiority of most of the book, I believe Arendt's discussion of the dreams is perfectly in keeping with the tone she is taking in the rest of the text, except for the last two chapters. Thus, while Young-Bruehl finds the dream material out of keeping with Arendt's usual emphasis on politics, I find the emphasis on politics in the last two chapters out of keeping with the dreamlike quality of the rest of the book, which is itself entirely (except for the last two chapters) out of keeping with the rest of Arendt's published work.

21. Arendt identifies these influences on the book's final chapters in a 1952 letter to Jaspers. "I wrote the end of the book very irritably in the summer of 1938, because Blücher and Benjamin would not leave me in peace until I did. It is written throughout in terms of the Zionist critique of assimilation which I accepted then and which I have not until this day modified very much" (quoted in Young-Bruehl, *Hannah Arendt*, 91). Unfortunately, the referent is a bit unclear; certainly, the end of the book is "written throughout" in terms of a Zionist critique of assimilation, but to ascribe such a perspective to the whole book would be rather ingenuous. Nonetheless, this is how the book has been presented; it is not, however, how the book reads.

22. The essays on Jewish identity are collected in Hannah Arendt, *The Jew as Pariah: Jewish Identity and Politics in the Modern Age* (New York: Grove Press, 1978—hereafter *Pariah*). The individual pieces in the collection were all originally published between 1942 and 1966.

23. Arendt suppresses the sections of the deathbed utterance that would place Rahel's pariah identity in doubt. Although Arendt was herself terribly critical of Varnhagen's editorial elisions of Rahel's Jewish connections, this is not the only quotation of Rahel's that Arendt edits to suit her purpose. See Weissberg, *Rahel Varnhagen*, 13–17.

24. Barnouw emphasizes that Arendt combines an analysis of Jewish and woman's identity in *Rahel Varnhagen*, but she understands it as Arendt having "lent her voice to Rahel" (Barnouw, *Visible Spaces*, 70), rather than borrowing Rahel's voice for herself. The difference is that, to the extent that Arendt is understood to be lending her voice to Rahel, it is presumed to be the voice of the last two chapters, the critical political voice of the pariah. To the extent that Arendt borrows Rahel's voice it is the shared voice, and experience, of the parvenu.

25. Elizabeth Kamarck Minnich comes close to providing such a model in "Hannah Arendt: Thinking as We Are," in *Between Women*, ed. Carol Ascher, Louise DeSalvo, and Sarah Ruddick (Boston: Beacon Press, 1984), 170–85. Minnich, a feminist and a student of Arendt's, discusses Arendt as a model of feminist thinking and practice, as both a teacher and a writer. Minnich specifically discusses *Rahel Varnhagen* as elucidating Arendt's concern with feminine identity, and Arendt herself as a model of a feminine pariah: independent, iconoclastic, self-consciously affirming of her social identity without being bound by the conventions and conceptions associated with it.

26. Heinrich Blücher to Hannah Arendt after her mother's death, as quoted in Young-Bruehl, *Hannah Arendt*, 236.

27. For an extremely concise explication of the politics of écriture feminine, see Xavière Gauthier, "Is There Such a Thing as Women's Writing?" *Tel Quel* (summer 1974); reprinted in *New French Feminisms*, ed. Elaine Marks and Isabelle de Courtivron (New York: Schocken Books, 1981), 161–64. For analyses of Rahel's "female" writing of difficult feminine experience, see Marianne Schuller, " 'Unsere Sprache ist unser gelebtes Leben': Randmerkungen zur Schreibweise Rahel Varnhagens," in *Rahel Varnhagen: Gesammelte Werke*, vol. 10 (Munich: Matthes & Seitz, 1983), 43–59; and also Uwe Schweikert, " 'Am jüngsten Tag hab ich Recht': Rahel Varnhagen als Briefschreiberin," in *Rahel Varnhagen: Gesammelte Werke* 10:17–42.

28. See Arendt, "On the Emancipation of Women," trans. Elisabeth Young-Bruehl, in *Essays in Understanding*, 66–68. First published in German in *Die Gesellschaft* 2 (1933), the essay reviews *Das Frauenproblem der Gegenwart: Eine Psychologische Bilanz* (Contemporary Women's Issues: A Psychological Balance Sheet), by Alice Rühle-Gerstel.

29. Young-Bruehl describes Arendt's deep displeasure, when she was offered a full professorship at Princeton, that the university had publicly emphasized her status as the first woman there to hold that rank (Young-Bruehl, *Hannah Arendt*, 272–73). Although Arendt claimed not to want to be treated as an "exception woman," her refusal to consider the structural arrangements that put her in such a position, combined with her resistance to making common cause with other women as women, undercuts the strength of her claim.

30. See Weissberg's detailed analysis of Arendt's strategy, both professional and economic, for publishing the book in the context of postwar German reparations (Weissberg, *Rahel Varnhagen*, 41–54).

FIVE. FINDING A VOICE

1. Arendt's is a resolutely Eurocentric focus. Anne Norton criticizes Arendt's dismissal of Africans from her discussion of "the scramble for Africa," and Seyla Benhabib defends Arendt from Norton's criticism on the grounds

that Arendt is concerned not to accept (an essentializing version of) a homogenized Africa and that Arendt is more concerned with the effect the colonial project had on European self-conception. That this defense is accurate does not, I think, negate Norton's criticism. See Anne Norton, "Heart of Darkness: Africa and African Americans in the Writings of Hannah Arendt," in *Feminist Interpretations of Hannah Arendt*, ed. Bonnie Honig (University Park: Pennsylvania State University Press, 1995), 247–61; and Seyla Benhabib, *The Reluctant Modernism of Hannah Arendt* (Thousand Oaks, Calif.: Sage Publications, 1996), 85. For discussions of the relation between race and otherness in the history of European self-consciousness, see Julia Kristeva, *Strangers to Ourselves*, trans. Leon Roudiez (New York: Columbia University Press, 1991), originally published as *Étrangers à nous-mêmes* (Paris: Fayard, 1989). See also Tzvetan Todorov, *On Human Diversity: Nationalism, Racism, and Exoticism in French Thought*, trans. Catherine Porter (Cambridge: Harvard University Press, 1993), originally published as *Nous et les autres* (Paris: Seuil, 1989).

2. For a sensitive account of Arendt as a refugee who identified herself as one without identifying with the refugee community, see " 'I Somehow Don't Fit': Hannah Arendt," in Anthony Heilbut, *Exiled in Paradise: German Refugee Artists and Intellectuals in America from the 1930s to the Present* (New York: Viking Press, 1983), 395–437. Heilbut particularly emphasizes Arendt's self-conscious politicization of the emigré experience and her extraordinary attentiveness to the expression of power through language.

3. Arendt had brought with her the printed copy of her dissertation, *Der Liebesbegriff bei Augustin* (Berlin: J. Springer Verlag, 1929), and she had been publishing essays in German and English, but *The Origins* gave her much wider public recognition than anything she had written before.

4. Walter Benjamin, "Theses on the Philosophy of History," in Walter Benjamin, *Illuminations*, ed. Hannah Arendt (New York: Schocken Books, 1969), 257–58. In her notes at the back of *Illuminations* Arendt mentions having received a manuscript copy of the "Theses on the Philosophy of History" from Benjamin before he died, and references to Benjamin and his work appear in her correspondence while she was writing *The Origins* in America. Benjamin's narrative theory of history as storytelling and the provision of meaning is implicit in the organization of *The Origins*, as well as explicit in her concern, expressed during the same period in her letters, that Benjamin's work be collected, edited, and published. See especially her correspondence with Gershom Scholem in the Hannah Arendt collection at the Library of Congress, in which she repeatedly urged Scholem to prepare Benjamin's writings for posthumous publication. Even Scholem admitted that Benjamin carried, for Arendt, a remarkable intellectual weight, unusual at the time. See Gershom Scholem, *Walter Benjamin: The Story of a Friendship*, trans. Harry Zohn (Philadelphia: Jewish Publication Society of America, 1981), 191. Seyla Benhabib also notes the resonance with Benjamin's *The Origin of German Tragic Drama*; see Benhabib, *Reluctant Modernism*, 64.

5. *The Origins* was initially to have been titled *The Burden of Our Times*, which would have emphasized the personal, emotional weight of the historical analysis. See Benhabib, *Reluctant Modernism*, 64.

6. This question comes up especially in reviews of later editions of the book. See the file on *The Origins of Totalitarianism*, Hannah Arendt Papers,

Library of Congress, Washington, D.C. Arendt devotes much of her argument in *Antisemitism* to explaining the historical reasons that made the Jews the most obvious and generally noticeable European other. While they were more common than other dispersed national communities (like the Gypsies), the Jews were identified as other not because of what they did (like the communists or homosexuals) but because of a fact of birth that determined who they were. They were marked by an identification of their (supposedly) essential bodies, rather than their lives: a mysteriously embodied otherness that was only exacerbated by their different religious practices or historical community identity.

7. *Origins*, xvi. This is a paraphrase of Arendt's own phrasing; note that she herself avoids the specificity of dates.

8. Arendt's quotation is from an interview with Gunther Gaus, published as "Was bleibt? Es bleibt die Muttersprache," in Günther Gaus, *Zur Person* (Munich: Feder, 1964), translated in Elisabeth Young-Bruehl, *Hannah Arendt: For Love of the World* (New Haven, Conn.: Yale University Press, 1982), 3.

9. See Bernard Crick's discussion of the personal and passionate commitment behind the work, in Bernard Crick, "On Rereading *The Origins of Totalitarianism*," in *Hannah Arendt: The Recovery of the Public World*, ed. Melvyn Hill (New York: St. Martin's Press, 1979), 27–47.

10. In *On Revolution* Arendt uses the Billy Budd story as an exemplary narrative of political responsibility and choice, and she identifies Captain Vere as the appropriate model of an articulate, knowing political actor. Billy Budd, although morally innocent or good, is unable to speak or speak clearly. He is therefore unable to tell his own story and unable to use language to enter the political realm of agency; he is limited to the alternatives of passivity and violence. Because of his lack, Arendt rather ruthlessly rejects Billy Budd as a model, and resists the seemingly natural tendency to empathize with him. She comes down firmly on the side of rationally articulated justice, even if at the expense of a silent or silenced victim.

Billy's lack is primarily his inability to master language, but it can be understood, secondarily, to be his lack of a phallus in the Lacanian sense. Throughout the story, Melville describes Billy Budd as the beautiful sailor (his nickname is Beauty, and the story itself was originally called *Baby Budd*). Billy's blond beauty, his youth, and even his cheerful loyalty—all combine to negate his significance as a conventionally masculine character. Arendt, who has often been noted to have valued traditionally masculine virtues over emasculated or feminine ones, can also be understood as rejecting Billy as a model because his inarticulateness is inextricable from his ineffective masculinity. He is neutered, in language as well as in gender.

11. Quite a bit has been written about Arendt's identity as a Jewish writer, but one of the most acute analyses of her own understanding of the relationship between (her) social identity and (her) political analysis is found in Amos Elon's "The Case of Hannah Arendt," *New York Review of Books* 44, no. 17 (6 November 1997): 25–29. Elon's essay is an insightful investigation of the extent to which Arendt's analyses of Jewish history and identity got her into trouble, not because of her facts, but because of her tone, which was resolutely independent rather than empathic. The tone is what sets her work apart from other works in the

NOTES TO PAGES 65-71

area that has come to be known as Holocaust Studies, and from the community politics that underlie this new field. For a discussion of how this field functions as the moral legitimation of the policies of the modern state of Israel, see Norman Finkelstein, "Daniel Jonah Goldhagen's 'Crazy' Thesis: A Critique of *Hitler's Willing Executioners*," *New Left Review* 224 (July / August 1997): 39–87. Finkelstein points out that several of the foremost scholars whose substantive work overlaps and comes into conflict with the ideological project of Holocaust Studies have essentially been excommunicated from the canon and the community; see Finkelstein, 83 and n. 75.

12. See " 'Eichmann in Jerusalem': An Exchange of Letters between Gershom Scholem and Hannah Arendt," in *Pariah*, 247. Arendt's letter to Scholem was originally published by *Encounter* magazine; his letter to her, with a commentary, was reprinted in Gershom Scholem, *On Jews and Judaism* (New York: Schocken Books, 1978), 298–306. The letters were written in June and July 1963.

13. For a discussion of the relation between antisemitism and another abrupt, jerky style of literary phrasing, see Julia Kristeva's *Powers of Horror*, trans Leon S. Roudiez (New York: Columbia University Press, 1982), chapters 9, "Ours to Jew or Die," and 10, "In the Beginning and without End," 174–206. Kristeva places both Céline's ideology and his style in relation to a paternal and symbolic law, against which they are reactions. In this regard, consider also the notorious antisemitism and stylistic parataxis of Ezra Pound.

SIX. THE CHARLATAN: BENJAMIN DISRAELI

1. Nineteenth-century secular antisemitism developed in relation to the nation-state; Arendt is not interested in earlier religious anti-Jewish attitudes because they are directed at an unassimilated religious and national group, located within a Europe that was composed of absolutist or fragmented states. For her distinction between the "secular, nineteenth-century ideology" of antisemitism and "earlier religious Jew-hatred," see *The Origins*, xi–xii.

2. Arendt notes that Nietzsche first coined the term the "good European" (*The Origins*, 23), but elsewhere she describes her teacher Karl Jaspers as a "citizen of the world." The difference between the "good European" and the "citizen of the world" is the difference between the political sphere of the nineteenth century and that of the twentieth. Nietzsche aims for cosmopolitanism; Jaspers for solidarity in global politics. For Arendt's discussion of Jaspers, see "Karl Jaspers: Citizen of the World?" in *Men in Dark Times* (New York: Harcourt Brace Jovanovich, 1955), 81–94.

3. The logic of Arendt's position can be better understood if one considers the graphs in Pierre Bourdieu's *Distinction*. Bourdieu plots economic capital and cultural capital separately, as determinants of individual identity, and investigates the extent to which the interests of economic capital and cultural capital intersect or conflict. According to Bourdieu's analysis, Arendt's position plots out very nicely: very high on cultural capital, relatively low on economic capital, she would feel very little in common, culturally or economically, with the working class but would be hostile to the prerogatives of business. She has high capital, but her capital is cultural; thus she would be sympathetic to any political regime that limits the power of economic capital but maintains the power of

cultural capital. The particular elitism of her position is quite typical of intellectuals and higher cultural practitioners, who have more in common with the upper business class than with the working class (alliances with others who hold high capital), but who also realize that, in a capitalist culture, economic capital usually garners more power than cultural capital (rivalry with those whose capital is different). The fact that Arendt would probably hate Bourdieu's analysis doesn't necessarily undermine its aptness. See Bourdieu, *Distinction: A Social Critique of the Judgement of Taste*, trans. Richard Nice (Cambridge: Harvard University Press, 1984), 128–29.

4. Prior to publishing *The Origins*, Arendt developed these terms in various essays, some of which were collected in *The Jew as Pariah: Jewish Politics and Identity in the Modern Age*, ed. Ron H. Feldman (New York: Grove Press, 1978), especially "Part I: The Pariah as Rebel." See also part I, "Between Pariah and Parvenu," of chapter 3, "The Jews and Society," in *The Origins*, 56–68.

5. Arendt defines them in terms of Jews and Jewishness, but the analysis can be extended to any discussion of social and political marginality and difference. The categories are particularly useful in political examinations of identity that involve gender, race, or colonialism and are related to the descriptions of identity as a response to an oppressive political and cultural milieu that are examined in subaltern studies.

6. See especially the discussions about Heinrich Heine, Bernard Lazare, Charlie Chaplin, and Franz Kafka in "The Jew as Pariah: A Hidden Tradition," in *Pariah*, 67–90, first published as an article under the same title in *Jewish Social Studies* 6, no. 3 (April 1944): 99–122.

7. Arendt repeatedly (and affectionately) calls Disraeli a "charlatan" in her discussion of him. See *The Origins*, 68–79.

8. Arendt also shows a marked diffidence, in *The Origins*, toward Bernard Lazare, another Jewish pariah she describes in much more detail elsewhere. Although it was through appropriation of Lazare's conception of the pariah and the parvenu that Arendt extricated herself from an exclusively emotional identification with Rahel, both Rahel and Lazare remain too intimate to her own intellectual self-understanding to be easily figured in this particular text. They are too much like Arendt herself, in their relation to their community and their world, to be easily available to Arendt as an alternative public mask or voice. I address Arendt's specific avoidance, in *Antisemitism*, of any extended discussion of Lazare later in this chapter.

9. Arendt notes that she takes that phrase from W. F. Monypenny and G. E. Buckle, *The Life of Benjamin Disraeli, Earl of Beaconsfield* (New York: Macmillan, 1929), 2.292–93.

10. Internal quotation from Morris S. Lazaron, "Benjamin Disraeli," in *Seed of Abraham* (New York: The Century Co., 1930), 260.

11. Internal quotation from Horace B. Samuel, "The Psychology of Disraeli," in *Modernities* (London: Kegan Paul, Trench, Trubner & Co., 1914).

12. Internal quotation from Sir John Skelton, in Monypenny and Buckle, *Life of Disraeli*, 70.

13. See the numerous contemporary judgments of Disraeli, emphasizing mistrust of his strangeness, foreignness, and Orientalism, included in Boris Segalowitsch, *Benjamin Disraelis Orientalismus* (Berlin: Verlag Kedem, 1930).

14. Disraeli was able to move himself to the center of the British political scene by involving himself in the process of extending the margins of British

power. In doing so, he guaranteed the authority and the exceptionalism of his own voice by providing himself with a much more frightening and distant exoticism relative to which he could position himself. This dynamic of exceptionalism, which Disraeli seems to have worked between himself, as a British Jew, and the non-British, non-Jewish peoples of the Empire is remarkably similar to the dynamic of exceptionalism that Arendt describes as having also gone on between Jews. Assimilated European Jews defined themselves as European and civilized by comparison to their backward, less assimilated, less European, more Eastern or Oriental coreligionists. (For a discussion of this dynamic, see, for instance, Bernard Lazare's accusation regarding the Jewish community's comparative identities, in *The Origins*, 117.) The difference is not only that Disraeli defined himself in relation to non-Jews; more significantly, he did so in order to participate in two identities, making himself appear more Oriental rather than less, while at the same time remaining thoroughly civilized and assimilated.

15. Internal quotation from Monypenny and Buckle, *Life of Disraeli*, 1507.

16. Conversely, others have argued that Disraeli's political interest in the Jews was wholly self-serving. See, for instance, Abraham Gilam's *Benjamin Disraeli and the Emancipation of the Jews* (Kingston, Ontario: Queen's University Press, 1980).

17. Proust himself she holds in high esteem, but she regards him as a chronicler and not a noteworthy personality in his own right. His decadent salons fascinate Arendt because they contain the open secrets of parvenu identities; Jews, homosexuals, and courtesans mingle with the nouveau riche and the remnants of the old aristocracy. Arendt's criticism is of a cosmopolitan society that refuses the political possibilities of its own self-representation. But her description of Proust's late nineteenth-century salon societies, in which nothing is ever openly admitted and everything is conveyed by a secret language of nod and glance, sounds much like the salons described in the early nineteenth-century novels of Stendhal. Stendhal's first novel, *Armance*, deals with the problem of requited, but unacknowledged, love in a salon that is exclusively aristocratic and in which the alternative society of the new liberal political class is explicitly disdained and suspected. These aristocratic reactionaries do indeed function according to codes of behavior that seem to preclude individual agency, but theirs is also a homogeneous social and political group. Since Arendt is primarily concerned with the problem of representing social identities in a mixed society, she is less interested in the decadent exclusivity described by Stendhal than in the decadent cosmopolitanism described by Proust. See Stendhal (Marie-Henri Beyle), *Armance*, trans. C. K. Scott-Moncrieff (New York: Premier Books, 1960), first published in French in 1827, first published in this English translation in 1928.

18. This is one of the terms used in the standard Proust translation by Moncrieff and Kilmartin; for the most part, however, Proust simply refers to "vice." But Proust does explicitly equate the social dynamic of a hidden and revealed sexual identity with the social dynamic of Jewish identity, and especially the uneasy parvenu politics of the Dreyfus case. See Marcel Proust, *Remembrance of Things Past*, trans. C. K. Scott Moncrieff and Terence Kilmartin (New York: Random House, 1982). Moncrieff's translation (the Moncrieff and Kilmartin edition is from a revised French edition) was first published (in separate volumes) between 1924 and 1930.

19. Arendt does not define what she means by a Jewish "origin" that implies political responsibility. One can only assume that she means the ancient Jewish nation, its diaspora, and its continuity through the self-conscious national identity of its individual members.

20. In the last section of the chapter, "The Pardon and Its Significance," Arendt rather bitterly calls the whole affair a comedy (*The Origins*, 119).

21. See the discussion of Lazare's efforts on behalf of Dreyfus, and the restraints the family imposed on him, in Michael R. Marrus, *The Politics of Assimilation: A Study of the French Jewish Community at the Time of the Dreyfus Affair* (Oxford: Clarendon Press, 1971), especially chapter 7, "Bernard Lazare and the Origins of Jewish Nationalism," 164–95.

22. See "The Jew as Pariah: A Hidden Tradition," in *Pariah*, 67–90. See also "Herzl and Lazare," in *Pariah*, 125–30, in which Arendt laments Lazare's loss of historical preeminence to Theodore Herzl. "Herzl and Lazare" was excerpted from "From the Dreyfus Affair to France Today," *Jewish Social Studies* 4, no. 3 (July 1942): 235–40.

23. See Marrus, *Politics of Assimilation*, 164–95. Note also that Proust describes how the Dreyfus case, to the extent that it is political, is viewed by French society as an infringement on taste. See the Duchess de Guermantes's complaint that Dreyfus can't have done much to prove his innocence because his letters from his island prison are in such bad style (Proust, *Remembrance*, 2.246).

24. Internal quotation from Bernard Lazare, *Job's Dungheap*, ed. Hannah Arendt (New York: Schocken Books, 1948), 97.

25. See N. H. Frankel, ed., *Unknown Documents on the Jewish Question: Disraeli's Plan for a Jewish State (1877)*, trans. Theodore Gaster (Baltimore, Md., and Tel Aviv, Palestine: Schlesinger Publishing, 1947). The pamphlet exists in the collections of several research libraries, including the Leo Baeck Institute and the University of Chicago, even though the main Disraeli bibliography lists it as "not traced." See R. W. Stewart, *Benjamin Disraeli: A List of Writings by Him, and Writings about Him, with Notes* (Metuchen, N.J.: Scarecrow Press, 1972), 140.

26. In the Foreword to his own edition, N. H. Frankel notes, "Except for the copy in the present writer's possession, the pamphlet in which this plan is set forth, has altogether disappeared from circulation, nor is there any mention of it in standard works of reference. The copy in question was tucked away among a number of extremely interesting documents belonging to the Austrian statesman, Leon Ritter von Bilinski." Frankel goes on to explain how the original pamphlet came to him, while the "Memoranda of Leon Ritter von Bilinski: Concerning Disraeli's Project of a Jewish State in Palestine" within the pamphlet explains how the pamphlet came into the hands of the Austrian Finance Minister. See Frankel, *Unknown Documents*, 3–5, 21–23. It is possible that the entire pamphlet is a clever forgery. In that case, however, it is a very ambiguous one, since it argues (through Disraeli) for a Jewish national state under British protection (presumably to pressure the British), and (through Bilinski and others) against Jewish national interest in such a state (presumably to pressure Jews not to support such an option).

27. See the title page(s) of the original pamphlet, "Die judische Frage in der orientalischen Frage," reprinted in the 1947 Frankel edition on pp. 27 and 29.

28. According to the pamphlet, it was deemed more suitable for the project to seem to have spontaneously arisen among the Austrians, who had no

territorial interest in Palestine, than to have originated in England, or through the British Embassy, let alone the British Prime Minister. Before the proposal was distributed, however, news of its contents leaked out, and the negative response caused the British Embassy to have it suppressed. The Berlin Congress convened and concluded with no formal discussion of the Jewish Question. See Frankel, *Unknown Documents*, 3–5. Note that the United Nations General Assembly Resolution supporting the creation of an independent, binational Arab and Jewish state was passed in November 1947.

29. This position is almost unique in its explicit advocacy of both Jewish national and Great Power imperial interests. The emphasis on British political and cultural / linguistic hegemony is out of keeping with later Zionist advocations of a Jewish homeland, while the emphasis on a Jewish national homeland is out of keeping with most British imperial positions.

30. That Disraeli's stance on public issues dealing with Jewish interests was very much calculated, and never at political expense, is emphasized in Gilam, *Benjamin Disraeli*.

31. For a discussion of Arendt's own intellectual relationship to the Jewish Zionism of Theodore Herzl, see Shiraz Dossa, "Hannah Arendt on Political Zionism," *Arab Studies Quarterly* 8, no. 3 (summer 1986): 219–30.

SEVEN. RACE AND ECONOMICS

1. Arendt's concern, in *The Origins*, with South African racial politics prefigures the international significance that accompanied the struggles over South African apartheid decades later. As I have already indicated, I believe Anne Norton is right to criticize Arendt for ignoring the perspective of black Africans. Nonetheless, Arendt was prescient in recognizing that South Africa would hold particular significance for Europe (and the West); rereading *The Origins* from a contemporary perspective, I find it remarkable that she gives so much (even if still inadequate) attention to an issue that would indeed develop into a major site of late twentieth-century struggles over the politics of social identity. For an account of why this particular struggle gained such moral weight in the West, see Audie Klotz, *Norms in International Relations: The Struggle against Apartheid* (Ithaca: Cornell University Press, 1995).

2. Edward Said, *Orientalism* (New York: Random House, 1979). Said's work has of course opened up a whole field of subsequent study and argument, and can be understood to have been fundamental in providing a context in U.S. scholarship for the work of the Subaltern Studies Collective, work that has had theoretical significance far beyond the borders of its geographical focus. For work that reconsiders the colonial project on the subcontinent from the subalterns' perspective, see publications by the Subaltern Studies Collective, originally published through the journal *Subaltern Studies* (Delhi: Oxford University Press). Some essays were reprinted in *Selected Subaltern Studies*, ed. Ranajit Guha and Gayatri Chakravorty Spivak (New York: Oxford University Press, 1988). Several of the most significant texts associated with the collective include Ranajit Guha, *Elementary Aspects of Peasant Insurgency in Colonial India* (Delhi: Oxford University Press, 1994), originally published in 1983; Partha Chatterjee, *The Nation and Its Fragments: Colonial and Postcolonial Histories* (Princeton: Princeton University Press, 1993); Gayatri Chakravorty Spivak, "Can the Subaltern Speak?" in *Marxism*

and the Interpretation of Culture, ed. C. Nelson and L. Grossberg (Basingstoke: Macmillan Education, 1988), 271–313.

3. This analysis presumes that the political realm was originally separate from economic concerns; although this is Arendt's understanding (and the one she enunciates, with some nostalgia, in *The Human Condition*), it reveals a rather glaring ignorance of the whole discipline of political economy. While Arendt did assert that she had come "late" to an appreciation of politics from her early training in philosophy, the scope of her writing indicates that her understanding of politics remained almost entirely philosophical. *The Human Condition*, after all, originated as Arendt's investigation of Marx.

4. This is certainly the case for Germany. Nineteenth-century unification of the various German states, principalities, and independent cities had as much to do with the rationalization of trade and taxation as it did with state-building. See Theodore S. Hamerow, *Restoration, Revolution, Reaction: Economics and Politics in Germany, 1815–1871* (Princeton, N.J.: Princeton University Press, 1972).

5. Internal quotation from S. Gertrude Millen, *Rhodes* (London: Chatto & Windus, 1933), 138. Arendt's unfortunate hostility to the entire Frankfurt School means that her criticism of Rhodes's frustration in not being able to "annex the planets" completely ignores Horkheimer's analysis of just such desires, which he integrates into a larger critique of rationalized capitalist society. See "The Revolt of Nature," in Max Horkheimer, *Eclipse of Reason* (New York: Oxford University Press, 1947), 92–127. For a more recent discussion of similar themes, see Cornelius Castoriadis, "Reflections of 'Rationality' and 'Development,'" *Thesis Eleven* 10/11 (November/March 1984–85): 18–36.

6. Nonetheless, those who will eventually become the primary European victims of the totalitarian desire to dominate all possibility are markedly absent from Arendt's discussion in *Imperialism*. She explicitly notes the lack of a Jewish role in the imperialist adventure; Arendt argues that the Jewish financiers were hesitant to become deeply involved in imperialist projects. They engaged in economic speculation, but instead of pursuing expansion for expansion's sake they retained a more traditional idea of the relation between power and finance. Thus they were no competition for the new imperialist radicals:

> Very instructive in this respect is the career of Cecil Rhodes in South Africa, who, an absolute newcomer, in a few years could supplant the all-powerful Jewish financiers in first place.... Somehow the government's reluctance to yield real power to Jews and the Jews' reluctance to engage in business with political implications coincided so well that, despite the great wealth of the Jewish group, no actual struggle for power ever developed after the initial stage of gambling and commission-earning had come to an end.
>
> (*The Origins*, 136)

7. For Arendt's discussion of the mob as an inseparable byproduct of bourgeois society, see *The Origins*, 155. Her definition of the mob as an antipolitical body that is abjected from society, despite its essential links with the social, carries overtones of her later discussion of the abject, miserable poor in *On Revolution*.

8. Indeed, in Arendt's view Gobineau turns to race thinking in order to explain his own superfluousness: a ruler who no longer rules (*The Origins*, 170–75).

9. For Arendt's discussion of Darwin's evolutionary theory as being both politically charged and politically neutral, in that it was equally available to progressive or reactionary opinion, see *The Origins*, 178.

10. *The Origins*, 170–75. The edition Arendt uses is Arthur de Gobineau, *Essai sur l'inégalité des races humaines* (Paris: P. Belfond, 1967), originally published 1853–55. See also Joseph Arthur Gobineau, *Selected Political Writings*, ed. Michael D. Biddis (New York: Harper & Row, 1970).

11. Arthur Gobineau to his father, 20 February 1839, as quoted in Michael D. Biddis, *Father of Racist Ideology: The Social and Political Thought of Count Gobineau* (New York: Weybright and Talley, 1970), 17. Biddis's discussion of the relationship between the circumstances of Gobineau's life and the development of his social theories, particularly the possible relationship between the domestic irregularities of his parents and his own later social rigidity, is extremely insightful.

12. Gobineau was also a frequent correspondent of Alexis de Tocqueville's and wrote extensively on the Orient, texts that are still regarded with a mixture of skepticism and respect. In particular, see Arthur de Gobineau, *Lettres Persanes* (Paris: Mercure de France, 1957).

13. For a discussion of Arendt's own textual Eurocentrism, see Shiraz Dossa, "Human Status and Politics: Hannah Arendt on the Holocaust," *Canadian Journal of Political Science* 13, no. 2 (June 1980): 309–23, esp. 318–23. Dossa makes an extremely perceptive analysis of *The Origins* specifically, and of Arendt's normative political theory in general. He brings out, for instance, the degree to which Arendt's cultural values sometimes edge into racial association (in particular, she often associated her category of *animal laborans* with blacks). See also pages 252–59 of Anne Norton, "Heart of Darkness: Africa and African Americans in the Writings of Hannah Arendt," in *Feminist Interpretations of Hannah Arendt*, ed. Bonnie Honig (University Park: Pennsylvania State University Press, 1995). Norton is appropriately critical of Arendt's Eurocentric racism, but she does not particularly explore Arendt's theorizing about the political role of race.

14. Internal quotation from Joseph Conrad, *Heart of Darkness* (New York: Penguin Books, 1994), 72, which Arendt there describes as "the most illuminating work on actual race experience in Africa," with no apparent distinction given as to whose experience is being illuminated.

15. Arendt asserts that "the two continents . . . without a culture and a history of their own" had been openly available for colonization and annexation to the European heritage (*The Origins*, 186). In a footnote she adds that "colonization of America and Australia was accompanied by comparatively short periods of cruel liquidation because of the natives' numerical weakness" (*The Origins*, 187); there is absolutely no acknowledgment that this eventual "numerical weakness" can accurately be explained as the result of genocide. But the assertion that lands deemed appropriate for colonial settlement are "empty," no matter how many people might be living on them, is a standard feature of imperialist discourse. For an equivalent assumption about the open availability of Africa for the white European presence, recall the anecdote concerning Perry Miller (himself a noted Americanist and advocate of the notion that North America was empty and available for colonization) and the emptiness of the African landscape in Jane Tompkins, " 'Indians': Textualism, Morality, and the Problem of History," in *"Race," Writing, and Difference*, ed. Henry Louis Gates (Chicago: University of Chicago

Press, 1986), 59–77. For a further discussion of the role of the other in European perceptions of the presence of the indigenous population in the African landscape, see Mary Louise Pratt, "Scratches on the Face of the Country; or, What Mr. Barrows Saw in the Land of the Bushmen," also in Gates, *"Race," Writing, and Difference,* 138–62.

16. Arendt makes no mention of the earlier southern European colonization of Central and South America. Not only were these areas not empty of population or history; they also developed a Creole culture Arendt apparently finds unsuitable for her argument.

17. Asia is dismissed as an area where the European presence was simply a matter of trade stations; Arendt seems to consider it to begin with the Indian subcontinent and to extend eastward into areas she does acknowledge to have an indigenous civilization, and therefore finds not particularly appropriate for discussion (*The Origins,* 186–87).

18. In Arendt's account, power and civilization apparently range outward from their European center and never travel in the reverse direction. Of the "Dark Continent of Africa," she writes: "Its northern shores, populated by Arabic peoples and tribes, were well known and had belonged to the European sphere of influence in one way or another since the days of antiquity" (*The Origins,* 187). Since during antiquity the relevant sphere of influence was not "Europe" but the Mediterranean, and during the Middle Ages the sphere of intellectual and cultural influence extended from Islamic Asia and North Africa into Europe through Spain, Provence, and Italy, this is an odd statement, to say the least. In this same section, Arendt also characterizes the repeated invasions of North Africa, the Levant, and western Asia during the Crusades as attempts to convert the inhabitants and incorporate the territory, rather than recognizing them as the religiously justified looting expeditions they often were. She further describes North Africa as "[t]oo well populated to attract settlers, and too poor to be exploited" (*The Origins,* 187), a remark that seems inexplicable given the modern colonial history of that region. For an excellent account of the origins of troubadour (and the tradition of European lyric) poetry in the formal and substantive conventions of Arabic mystical and love poems, a tradition that evolved as it moved from North Africa through Moorish Spain, through Provence, and into Italy, see Robert Briffault, *The Troubadours,* trans. Robert Briffault (Bloomington: Indiana University Press, 1965), first published in France in 1945. For accounts of the influence of this area on Europe, or the non-European version of European influence, see Amin Ma'alouf, *The Crusades through Arab Eyes,* trans. Jon Rothschild (London: Al Saqi Books, 1984).

19. Arendt shifts here between using "absolute values" to indicate absolute moral values and prohibitions and using economic "absolute value" to stand for a looked-for stability that is wholly specious. The second use (in which "absolute value" is singular) is for her an indication of an obvious impossibility, since it would be a search for a fixed law of value in a market of things rather than a stable relationship of values in a human world.

20. Internal quotation unknown.

21. Internal quotation from Paul Ritter, *Kolonien im deutschen Schriftum,* 1936, Preface.

22. For an intriguing application of Arendt's ideas about the frustration of individual strength in the modern world, see G. S. Fraser's use of *The*

Human Condition in a discussion of the antidemocratic political personality of Ezra Pound. Fraser, through Arendt, identifies Pound's reactionary politics as the strong individual's unfortunate response to the
conforming power of modern society. See G. S. Fraser, *Ezra Pound*
(London: Oliver and Boyd, 1960), 5–9.

23. That the theoretical construct "state of nature" is always a projection of contemporary norms seems too obvious a point to belabor at this late date.

24. Internal quotation from Conrad, *Heart of Darkness*, 51.

25. In *The Human Condition* Arendt does not necessarily absolutely condemn
slavery, provided it is redeemed by the achievements of the culture it
supports. For Arendt, this achievement is best represented by the political life of the polis: a world supported by slaves but in which the fullest
development of (limited) democratic political self-representation did
occur among those who were citizens. The problem with slavery in
South Africa is that it was not redeemed. Instead of a glorious people
enslaving others out of their own secure knowledge of their own value
and authority, the Boers adopted slavery out of fright, and their meager
self-respect was only further diminished by a mastery that produced
nothing worth writing home about.

26. Arendt's selective application of nationality as exclusively European (while
non-European movements are identified as communitarian or funda-
mentalist) is all too often reflected in recent studies of nationalism. See
Eric Hobsbawm, *Nations and Nationalism since 1780: Programme, Myth,
Reality* (Cambridge: Cambridge University Press, 1990). For an alternative approach to the question of nationalism, which is also an analysis of a specific non-European society, see Benedict Anderson, *Imagined
Communities: Reflections on the Origin and Spread of Nationalism* (New
York: Verso, 1983).

27. Writing about the organized warfare among black Africans that she has
apparently read about, Arendt nonetheless forcefully excludes black
African history from human history: "Since discipline and military
organization by themselves cannot establish a political body, the
destruction remained an unrecorded episode in an unreal, incomprehensible process which cannot be accepted by man and therefore is not
remembered by human history" (*The Origins*, 192–93). Aside from the
problem of a historical incident that is unrecorded and unremembered
but that she still knows enough about to write about, what is particularly shocking about this statement is its wholehearted participation in
the denial of humanity to the Africans. Black history "cannot be
accepted by man" (so who or what are the Africans?) and "therefore is
not remembered by human history" (so who remembers it, and just
what kind of history then can it be, if not human?). Her statements here
are of course reminiscent of John Stuart Mill's notorious assertions, in
On Liberty, that some peoples are simply without history.

28. Nor does she discuss its resemblance to her category of labor. Threading
through Arendt's economic analysis of South African society is the
labor-based perspective of a very Hegelian version of Marx. Although
she is no Marxist, and hers is not strictly an economic analysis, Arendt's
discussion of the Boers and of South Africa's development into a state
in which only black men labor owes much to her own adaptation of a
Marxian analysis. Her critique of Marx is developed in *The Human Condition*, her second book, but the basic elements of that analysis are
already present here. While most critics note that *The Human Condition*

was Arendt's critique of Marxism, few acknowledge the extent to which *The Origins* makes use of a Marxian analysis to evaluate the depoliticized significance of the bourgeoisie. For a refreshingly insightful approach to Arendt's discussion of class, politics, and her debt to Marx, see the chapter "Politics as Identity-Disclosing Action," in John McGowan, *Hannah Arendt: An Introduction* (Minneapolis: University of Minnesota Press, 1998), 34–95, especially 56. What Arendt adapts most directly from Marx (although for her it is not the central focus) is a sense of the redeeming power of work: through work, one creates oneself and one's world. For the most striking instance of this redemptive quality of work in Karl Marx's own writing, see the almost lyrical description of the transformation of Nature through Labor in the opening pages of chapter 7, "The Labour-Process and the Process of Producing Surplus Value," in Karl Marx, *Capital*, trans. Samuel Moore and Edward Aveling (New York: International Publishers, 1984), 1.173–79.

29. I am gesturing here toward Homi Bhabha's phrase about those who are "not quite white," in "Of Mimicry and Man: The Ambivalence of Colonial Discourse," *October* 28 (spring 1984): 125–33. For further elaboration of this aspect of his work, see "The Other Question—the Stereotype and Colonial Discourse," *Screen* 24, no. 6 (November–December 1983): 18–36, and "Sly Civility," *October* 34 (fall 1984).

30. Unlike the Boers, and later the imperialists, who evade and destroy the standards of the European world in the name of economic profit and national interest, the Jews begin, almost in spite of themselves, to try to re-create those standards. Thus the Jews, of all the major European peoples the most marginal, also become, in Arendt's text, the most representative of a specifically European identity. The European Gypsies, for instance, were also an intra-European people without a homeland and occupied an even more marginal position in terms of European cultural identity than the Jews. But the Gypsies were nomads, and thus, although Arendt never mentions them, one suspects that she might consider them nearly as savage, in not creating a stable, fixed (and urban) world for themselves, as the Africans. As the traditional People of the Book, the Jews, in Arendt's mind, may have a particular claim to narrative, or civilization, even though their original history is also nomadic.

31. Clearly, Arendt can conceive of a politics of antiracism when she is considering Jewish identity; the whole weight of her analysis in *Antisemitism*, especially the discussions of the Dreyfus affair, bears testimony to this. But her very appreciation of the validity of a politicized Jewish identity makes more remarkable her blindness to this possibility for other races. Arendt has painted herself into a political corner: her awareness of the dangers of mixing race and politics has made her overly suspicious of even antiracist politics. When considering Jewish political identity, she gets around this problem by theorizing the role of the individual pariah. But when considering African identity, she is left vaguely gesturing toward the possibility that working-class identity (and politics) will eventually do the trick. Yet reading these sections, one is left with the uncomfortable feeling that for Arendt, no matter how hard the black Africans work, they apparently will remain at labor, while the Jewish Europeans work to build a human world.

32. The phrase "the Great Game" became common currency for the intricate, hidden play of far-flung imperial power. For an excellent analysis of the

historical reality and contemporary legacy of the intrigues for imperial control of Asia, see Peter Hopkirk, *The Great Game: The Struggle for Empire in Central Asia* (New York: Kodansha International, 1994).

33. Arendt identifies the imperial character with Cecil Rhodes and Lord Cromer. Cromer, the exemplary bureaucrat, modestly forgoing fame for influence, and Rhodes, the national entrepreneur, running South Africa like a business (with the recalcitrant Boers as minority board members), seem like completely opposite types. But Arendt finds remarkable both men's discovery of bureaucratic intrigue as a key to imperialist rule. She attributes this to both rulers' sense of royal dislocation: they were Englishmen in Africa (North and South) who regarded where they were (Egypt and South Africa) only as a stop on the way to somewhere else (India for Cromer, and the world for Rhodes). Egypt and South Africa were only way stations; they functioned as places for men from somewhere else to stay in while they consolidated power elsewhere.

For Rhodes, worldwide expansion was a type of megalomania. Willed in the form of an international (Aryan) young men's secret society that would establish worldwide a ruling elite of individuals imbued with the "Founders' purpose," the society was institutionalized after his death as the exclusive, but not covert, Rhodes Scholarships. See *The Origins*, 214–15. (Internal quotation of Rhodes's description of himself as the "Founder" from Basil Williams, *Cecil Rhodes* [London: Constable and Company, 1921]). For Cromer, India always remained the destination of imperialist purpose, and Egypt was only the intermediate means. It was a destination at which he agreed never to arrive, however, when in 1894 he declined the appointment of Viceroy of India, preferring to remain as British Consul General in Egypt, all-powerful but doubly behind the scene.

In the end Cromer and Rhodes both preferred to remain in the middle of their own tangled webs of imperialist schemings. They wanted the imperial stage to be available only for puppets, and they wanted to be the ones pulling the strings. Their passion for control effectively canceled out any competing desire they may have had for self-representation. Since for Arendt action is premised on free self-disclosure, the actor cannot also be the one who pulls the strings.

34. The bureaucracy of British imperialism provided for a stable order out of which legends could arise, not the least of which was the legendary quality of being British outside Britain. Arendt herself seems to have been somewhat convinced by this legendary quality; she is not nearly as interested in the imperial bureaucracy of Austria-Hungary, for instance, let alone the Ottomans.

35. Said quotes Disraeli and then comments further, "When Disraeli said in his novel *Tancred* that the East was a career, he meant that to be interested in the East was something bright young Westerners would find to be an all-consuming passion; he should not be interpreted as saying that the East was *only* a career for Westerners" (Said, *Orientalism*, 5).

36. Arendt's reference is to Rudyard Kipling, "The First Sailor," in *Humorous Tales* (1891). "The First Sailor" is also collected in *The Writings in Prose and Verse of Rudyard Kipling*, vol. 32, *A Book of Words: Selections from Speeches and Addresses Delivered between 1906 and 1927* (New York: Charles Scribner's Sons, 1928), 167–86. In this collection "The First Sailor" is delivered as an address "To some Junior Naval Officers of an

NOTES TO PAGES 107–111

East Coast Patrol: 1918," a circumstance which indicates that the story's biblical style was very much intended to be self-applied by its audience.

37. Similarly, Friedrich Nietzsche's *Thus Spoke Zarathustra* does not have the authority of the biblical prophet stories, but it is significant for its attempt to recycle the form of those stories with a revised content.

38. Arendt's reference is to Rudyard Kipling, "The Tomb of His Ancestor," in *The Day's Work* (1898).

39. Note that this is a story of Anglo-Indian nobility, told by an Anglo-Indian. It reveals Anglo-Indians' assumptions about their role in India, not an absolute truth about that role. For an explicit declaration of the assumptions inherent in the imperial project, see, for instance, another work of Kipling's, the poem "The White Man's Burden," in *The Writings in Prose and Verse of Rudyard Kipling*, vol. 21, *The Five Nations* (New York: Charles Scribner's Sons, 1925), 78–80. It would be curious to read an Indian's account of how the natives view their "protector." For a version of how such a story might differ from Kipling's, see, for instance, "The Hunt," in Mahasweta Devi, *Imaginary Maps: Three Stories*, trans. Gayatri Chakravorty Spivak (New York: Routledge, 1995).

40. "Foggy prosaic London" is a quote from Arendt's description of Disraeli's own dual role, in which he lived in one ordinary place but presented himself as belonging to another world of fairy tales and empire. See *The Origins*, 69.

41. Rudyard Kipling, *Kim*, ed. Edward Said (Harmondsworth, Middlesex: Penguin Books, 1987).

42. Internal quotation from Kipling's *Kim*; Arendt does not specify an edition.

43. Internal quotation from T. E. Lawrence, *Letters*, ed. David Garnett (New York: Doubleday, Doran, 1939), 244. Written in 1918, the letter also appears in *T. E. Lawrence: The Selected Letters*, ed. Malcolm Brown (New York: Norton, 1989), 149–50.

44. That the glory of Lawrence's role depended on his ability to unify British imperialist designs and Arab nationalism, and his ability to convince himself as well as others of the validity of that volatile combination, is brought out in an essay on Lawrence by André Malraux, "N'Était-ce donc que cela?" *Saisons* 3 (winter 1946–47): 9–24. Malraux argues that Lawrence's disillusionment with his own myth occurred as he observed, after the revolt, both British nonsupport for an independent Arab state and the Arabs' own disinclination to transform their passionate hatred of the Ottoman Turks into the more disciplined process of state foundation. The Arabs had achieved their own liberation, but they could not, for various reasons, manage the foundation of a state. They could only achieve half of the two-part process Arendt describes in *On Revolution* as necessary for a successful revolution, and thus the Arab Revolt remained, according also to Malraux, no more than that.

45. From a letter to Vyvyan Richards, written from Cairo, 15 July 1918, in *Selected Letters*, 149–50. "Frankish" refers to a Crusade-era term among the Arabs for Europeans.

46. For a perceptive discussion of Lawrence as the last figure of noble adventure whose own actions contributed to his and the type's obsolescence, see William Pfaff, "The Fallen Hero," *New Yorker*, 8 May 1989, 105–15.

47. Letter to Col. A. P. Wavell on 29 August 1925, in *Selected Letters*, 289. After he enlisted in the RAF, Lawrence used several different alternative names, apparently finding no firm affinity with any of them.

48. Letter to Charlotte Shaw, 28 September 1925, in *Selected Letters*, 289–90.
49. Lawrence's last letter, to K. T. Parker, 12 May 1935, from Clouds Hill, his cottage in Dorset, is signed T. E. Shaw in *Selected Letters*, 540–41.
50. Internal quotes from T. E. Lawrence, *Seven Pillars of Wisdom: A Triumph* (Garden City, N.Y.: Doubleday, Doran, 1935), chapter 1.

EIGHT. THE BANALITY OF EVIL

1. The preface is dated June 1966. *Eichmann in Jerusalem* was published in 1963, and the furor surrounding *Eichmann* must surely have influenced Arendt's description of her perspective while writing the earlier book.
2. In *Totalitarianism* Arendt describes a movement concerned entirely with policy, not politics; citizens are reduced not merely to subjects but to replaceable units within a bureaucratic regime. Arendt's suspicion of the modern tension between politics and policy is idiosyncratic, but others share her preoccupation. Much of Michel Foucault's late work dealt explicitly with this relationship, while his earlier work often dealt with it implicitly. See several of the essays in *The Foucault Effect: Studies in Governmentality*, ed. Graham Burchell, Colin Gordon, and Peter Miller (Chicago: University of Chicago Press, 1991), especially Michel Foucault, "Politics and the Study of Discourse," 53–72, originally published in *Esprit* 371 (May 1968): 850–74; Michel Foucault, "Governmentality," 87–104, originally given as a lecture in 1978, first published (in Italian) in 1978; and Jacques Donzelot, "The Mobilization of Society," 169–79, originally given as a lecture in 1982.
3. My phrasing is an intentional allusion to Arendt's collection of essays on exceptional individuals: Rosa Luxemburg, Pope John XXIII, Karl Jaspers, Isak Dinesen, Walter Benjamin, and so on. See Hannah Arendt, *Men in Dark Times* (New York: Harcourt Brace Jovanovich, 1968).
4. Arendt's intention to extend her work on totalitarianism is mentioned in the essay "From the Pariah's Point of View," in Elisabeth Young-Bruehl, *Mind and the Body Politic* (New York: Routledge, 1989), 14.
5. Although Arendt is not a postmodern theorist (being rather very much a theorist of modernity, observing the end of her own era), her awareness of the closure of certain historical modernist projects sets her at the self-conscious beginning of what is now called postmodernity.
6. *Eichmann in Jerusalem: A Report on the Banality of Evil* (New York: Viking Penguin, 1963) was first published as a five-part serial in the *New Yorker* under the title "A Reporter at Large: Eichmann in Jerusalem," in February and March 1963. The subtitle "A Report on the Banality of Evil" was added for the book publication. See Richard J. Bernstein, *Hannah Arendt and the Jewish Question* (Cambridge: MIT Press, 1996), 154–78. *The Life of the Mind* (New York: Harcourt Brace Jovanovich, 1977) was published in two volumes, *Thinking*, and *Willing*, with the third volume, *Judging*, unfinished at the time of Arendt's death. Preliminary notes for the third volume were published as *Lectures on Kant's Political Philosophy* (Chicago: University of Chicago Press, 1982).
7. The political ambitions of the nineteenth-century pan-movements were modeled directly on British imperial power, except that instead of spreading over the seas, they intended to rule the land. Arendt quotes contemporary Alldeutschen and Slavophile writers who express this direct comparison between their continental ambitions and England's overseas empire. See *The Origins*, 223. Arendt's insistence, in mid-century, on this linkage between pan-German movements and what must then have

seemed to be an all but moribund pan-Slavism appears in late century, after the wreckage of the former Yugoslavia, to be sadly accurate.

8. Unfortunately, however, this is another instance when Arendt simply seems to presume that for Europeans to engage in racism outside of Europe is somehow quite different and more justified than engaging in racism among themselves:

> Continental imperialism truly begins at home. If it shared with over-seas imperialism the contempt for the narrowness of the nation-state, it opposed to it not so much economic arguments, which after all quite frequently expressed authentic national needs, as an "enlarged tribal consciousness" which was supposed to unite all people of similar folk origin, independent of all history and no matter where they happened to live. Continental imperialism, therefore, started with a much closer affinity to race concepts, enthusiastically absorbed the tradition of race thinking, and relied very little on specific experiences. Its race concepts were completely ideological in basis and developed much more quickly into a convenient political weapon than similar theories expressed by overseas imperialists which could always claim a certain basis in authentic experience.

> (*The Origins*, 223–24)

Arendt's moral exculpation of European extracontinental expansion as based on "authentic national needs" (without identifying those needs as produced by a capitalist system of economic competition and expansion) and European extra-European racism as based on "authentic experience" (without identifying the race thinking behind that statement) is simply wrong and doesn't even acknowledge the obvious factor that contributed to the growth of the pan-movements: ideologies of national resistance against the internal, multinational European empires. Against multinational empires (based on blood line or ideology) nothing is so effective and so potentially dangerous as a political movement based on an essentialized national ethnicity. Precisely because of this, Arendt's analysis of the problem of racism in the pan-movements is important, despite her lapses.

The phrase "enlarged tribal consciousness" is translated from Emil Deckert, *Panlatinismus, Panslawismus und Panteutonismus in ihrer Bedeutung für die politische Weltlage* (Frankfurt am Main: H. Keller, 1914), 4.

9. Arendt understands the pan-movements as having developed among those peoples who had not achieved the full political emancipation of an established nation-state, especially in multinational empires like Austria-Hungary and Russia (*The Origins*, 227). In such a situation, and in an international context of imperialist race thinking and expansion, it was easy enough for nations without states, as subjects without citizenship, to seek the larger status of tribes.

Postwar history provides other examples of pan-movements. The slow economic and political unification of the European Economic Community has raised questions of the development of a version of a "fortress Europe" mentality in which increased homogenization within Europe is countered by a loosening of the traditional ties individual nations had maintained with their extranational communities (i.e., French relations with the Francophone nations outside of Europe being deemphasized in favor of relations with non-Francophones inside Europe). On the other hand, the ideologies and policies of the Israeli state fit a pan-Jewish model, in which regional and historical dif-

ferences in Jewish identity are effaced in favor of a myth of essentialized, threatened Jewish existence.

10. Arendt's discussion of pan-national tribalism and Jewish tribalism is more
fully developed in section 1, "Tribal Nationalism" (*The Origins*,
227–43).

11. Arendt's own personal antipathy to what she describes as "tribal nationalism"
may also be linked with the tradition of secular, assimilated German
Jewish experience that defined her own European history; for German
Jews, the models for the backward, xenophobic, insular tribe were the
communities of *shtetl* Jews to the East. For a German Jew like Arendt,
even one politically aware of her own parvenu tendencies, the un-
emancipated, Yiddish-speaking Jews to the East, whose strict observance
of religious prohibitions helped keep them a people apart, represented
both the antisemites' caricature and the home version of a politically
problematic tribal nationalism.

In *The Political Consequences of Thinking* (Albany: State University of
New York Press, 1997), Jennifer Ring investigates the apparent contradiction between Arendt's Germanness and her Jewishness; Ring holds
that although Arendt identified politically as a Jew, she identified intellectually as a German, and this split identity contributed to her own isolation within the American Jewish intellectual community. While Ring
admirably emphasizes the extent to which Arendt's gender functioned
as a barrier in the cozy masculine society of the New York Jewish intellectuals, she misses two important aspects of Arendt's intellectual identification. One is that Arendt did not simply split the poles of her
thought into the intellectual (German) and the political (Jewish) but
linked and balanced them through a serious engagement with cultural,
especially literary figures, many of whom were, like herself, assimilated
German (speaking) Jews. These figures include Heine, Kafka, and Benjamin, as well as non-German Jews and German and non-German
Gentiles. If the philosophical tradition with which Arendt identified
was German Gentile and her political identification was with pariah
Jews, this apparent bifurcation is mediated by the remarkable emphasis, both intellectual and political, she gives to this mixed group of cultural producers. It is precisely this triple identification—with German
Gentile philosophy, Jewish political pariahdom, and the mediating
ground of German/Jewish literary culture—that makes Arendt such a
powerful thinker of social identity in general rather than simply of Jewish identity per se. The second point Ring misses is the extent to which
Arendt's high culture cosmopolitanism (her identification through art
with a denationalized individuality) was specifically typical of German
Jews, while the profile of Jewish identity in the United States has come
to be associated with the heritage of Eastern European Jewish migra-
tion. In *Hannah Arendt and the Jewish Question*, Bernstein includes a
quote (from Young-Bruehl, *Mind*, 204) that in part provides Arendt's
own very secular response to the "Germanness" of her thought: "We
[Jews] lack an intelligentsia which has been grounded in history and
educated through a long political tradition" (Bernstein, *Hannah Arendt*,
89–90).

12. Julia Kristeva, *Powers of Horror: An Essay on Abjection*, trans. Leon S. Roudiez
(New York: Columbia University Press, 1982).

13. This is all the more striking because Kafka, like Walter Benjamin and Bernard Lazare, is a recurrent figure in much of Arendt's work, indicating

that the lack of attention he receives here is not due to a lack of interest on her part.

14. Franz Kafka, *The Castle*, trans. Willa and Edwin Muir (New York: Alfred A. Knopf, 1968), 243–300. Originally published in German in 1926.

15. In situations of absolute extremity, Arendt seems to regard the refusal to cooperate as the only honorable, even if doomed, possibility remaining. It is this belief in the complicity of cooperation that got her into such trouble with the Jewish community over *Eichmann in Jerusalem*. Specifically, she expresses a marked disapproval throughout the book for the Jewish ghetto committees' cooperation with the Nazis' demands for efficient self-annihilation.

16. Arendt's discussion of European collapse barely mentions economic factors. According to her, the threat to the nation-state system was not an international depression but the release into that system of excess populations: the problem was bodies, not money. The nation-state broke down, not under the weight of the contradictions of modern capitalism, but under the redistributed weight of the contradiction of its own structure. The interest of the nation and the state, always in contradiction to each other but unified by constitutional government and the rule of law, broke apart once the sovereignty of national will (and blood) was elevated above "all legal and abstract institutions" (*The Origins*, 275). For major texts besides Hobsbawm and Anderson within the debate on nation-state identity, see Ernest Gellner, *Nations and Nationalism* (Ithaca: Cornell University Press, 1983); Partha Chatterjee, *Nationalist Thought and the Colonial World: A Derivative Discourse* (Minneapolis: University of Minnesota Press, 1986); Anthony D. Smith, *The Ethnic Origin of Nations* (Cambridge: Blackwell, 1986); and Anthony Giddens, *The Nation-State and Violence* (Berkeley: University of California Press, 1987).

17. It is remarkable how accurate this statement still is, almost one hundred years after the period about which it was written. The massive transfer of populations, even as refugees, still destabilizes states; witness the regional instability that has accompanied the ethnic cleansing of the states and regions of the former Yugoslavia.

The best long-term modern example of the political problem of statelessness probably centers on the Palestinians, most of whom are now in diaspora outside traditional Palestine. The very existence of their national identity is in question, but they have not been welcomed into any other state, and their presence as stateless refugees in the region has contributed to further disruption and statelessness.

18. Since the law can be applied only within a recognized jurisdiction, outside this area (which Arendt discusses at the level of the state) no law can be enforced; in effect, no law exists. This insight leads Arendt to some provocative statements on the relationship between human rights and citizenship:

> In other words, man had hardly appeared as a completely emancipated, completely isolated being who earned his dignity within himself without reference to some other larger encompassing order, when he disappeared again into a member of a people. From the beginning the paradox involved in the declaration of inalienable human rights was that it reckoned with an "abstract" human being who seemed to exist nowhere, for even savages lived in some kind of social order. If a tribal or other "backward" community did not enjoy human rights, it

was obviously because as a whole it had not yet reached that stage of civilization, the stage of popular and national sovereignty, but was oppressed by foreign or native despots. The whole question of human rights, therefore, was quickly and inextricably blended with the question of national emancipation.... The full implication of this identification of the rights of man with the rights of peoples in the European nation-state system came to light only when a growing number of people and peoples suddenly appeared whose elementary rights were as little safeguarded by the ordinary functioning of nation-states in the middle of Europe as they would have been in the heart of Africa. (*The Origins*, 291)

19. This is wishful thinking, or perhaps thinking based on Arendt's own rather exceptional experience with an unusually decent member of the German police. For an account of this incident, see Elisabeth Young-Bruehl, *Hannah Arendt: For Love of the World* (New Haven, Conn.: Yale University Press, 1982), 105–6.

20. See Arendt's discussion of criminality and fame as the only reliable providers of identity in a totalitarian situation, especially her mention that a stray dog with a name has a better chance of survival than one without one (*The Origins*, 286–87).

21. Having given little attention to the political barriers class erected in Europe, Arendt seems rather too ready to bemoan the political effects of the collapse of class distinctions. Although she is resolutely hostile to bourgeois perspectives, her unwillingness to consider class as a critical focus for political organizing leaves her implying that the working class would have been better off with some form of quiescent class solidarity rather than either working-class activism or nationalist classlessness.

22. In the contemporary context, the creation of a mass movement out of a "slumbering majority" may have more to do with cross-class economic crisis than with the "fall of protecting class walls," whatever that means. The end of organized state socialism in the Soviet Union and Eastern Europe has translated into the widespread delegitimization of socialism as a political alternative, while the tremendous economic dislocation that has accompanied the introduction of market economies has somewhat delegitimized liberalism, which has come to be identified with free market capitalism. This apparent failure of the two traditional main political ideologies (and the parties associated with them) to bring political and economic well-being to their citizens has left nationals of these states frustrated, disaffected, and ready to fill the political void with the mobilization of tribal nationalisms.

23. Instead of respecting their political leaders, the masses gave their enthusiastic admiration to the men who had accomplished something straightforward and tangible, like a transatlantic flight. Arendt mentions Bertolt Brecht's *Der Flug der Lindberghs* as a work in which modern identity is shown to have been reduced to the physical fact of what one does—the apex of heroic achievement being as impersonal as a record-breaking solo flight (*The Origins*, 331). She does not mention the work that may actually best represent the various social configurations she discusses, while not itself falling into the trap of irony or apologetics. Arendt never gave film the same cultural weight as literature, so she pays no notice to Jean Renoir's 1939 *La Règle du Jeu* (*The Rules of the Game*). Renoir's film portrays an upper-class milieu in which social

truths and hypocrisies become hopelessly confused, while petty criminals ally with decadent elites and the only innocent man is the one who has done something modern and meaningless: he has made a record-breaking solo flight, but we don't even know from where. The aviator is the apparent hero, but his personality is unformed, and his awkward intensity upsets the fragile balance of the social game and prompts chaos. He finishes the film by being shot dead in a case of mistaken identity. All the revelations are petty, the only open territory left in which to achieve an identity is the empty solitude of space, and once the confusion of bodies clears, at the center is death. Renoir's film, made during the Occupation, avoids any formal political critique, but is nonetheless a masterful representation of the end of any possible heroic mode of representation, and a near perfect illustration of Arendt's analysis of "The Temporary Alliance between the Mob and the Elite" (*The Origins*, 326–40).

24. The overwhelming praise given to Daniel Goldhagen's *Hitler's Willing Executioners: Ordinary Germans and the Holocaust* (New York: Alfred A. Knopf, 1996), despite the few lone voices who have pointed out that his research is neither so original nor so thorough, is testimony to the continuing desire to see the participants in totalitarian movements as monsters well apart from the rest of us. The moral of Goldhagen's story is relatively comforting: ordinary Germans were antisemitic monsters, and if we are not antisemitic monsters, we won't behave as ordinary Germans did. The moral of Arendt's work is much more disquieting: ordinary Germans were absolutely ordinary, and to the extent that we depoliticize ourselves in the same ordinary fashion, we might behave exactly as ordinary Germans did. For a critique of Goldhagen's thesis, see Norman Finkelstein, "Daniel Jonah Goldhagen's 'Crazy' Thesis: A Critique of *Hitler's Willing Executioner*," *New Left Review* 224 (1997): 39–87.

25. The phrasing comes from an even earlier period. Richard Bernstein (*Hannah Arendt*, 148–50) points out that in the correspondence between Arendt and Karl Jaspers in 1946, Jaspers takes issue with Arendt's characterization of the "monstrousness" of Nazi war crimes. In order to avoid any dangerous mythologizing of Nazi practices, Jaspers emphasizes their "banality." In a subsequent letter, Arendt agrees with Jaspers's efforts to demystify Nazi evil. Bernstein points out that both were deeply concerned to find an appropriate language in which to speak about events that seemed to be either unspeakable or transformed by language into different, more familiar categories (such as Shakespearean villainy). Bernstein effectively argues that while there may seem to be a theoretical difference in Arendt's conceptualization of totalitarian evil as either "radical" or "banal," this difference in phrasing actually reflects an ongoing search for a way of thinking and writing about a new form of political evil that encompassed both massive practice and lack of individual motive. See the chapter "From Radical Evil to the Banality of Evil: From Superfluousness to Thoughtlessness" in Bernstein, *Hannah Arendt*, 137–53. John McGowan makes an even stronger argument for the consistency in Arendt's political thinking, despite the particularities of her individual texts. McGowan's deceptively modest book offers an elegant synthesis of Arendt's entire oeuvre and a convincing argument for reading all her work as different approaches to the problem of the absence of political agency and the

presence of evil in the modern world. See John McGowan, *Hannah Arendt: An Introduction* (Minneapolis: University of Minnesota Press, 1998).

26. Bernstein points out that Arendt's own description of Schmidt's story also functions as a "dramatic moment" within the bleak context of her own Eichmann narrative. He suggests that the Schmidt anecdote provides an unresolved counterpoint within Arendt's analysis of evil (Bernstein, *Hannah Arendt*, 176–77). I am arguing that Arendt's analyses in *The Origins, Eichmann*, and *The Life of the Mind* should be considered as stages in a process and that the Schmidt example, unresolved in *Eichmann*, is the provocation for Arendt's discussion in *Thinking*.

27. Arendt distinguishes early in the volume between reason (*Vernunft*) and intellect (*Verstand*). Reason is concerned with meaning, which is what we search for when we think; intellect is concerned with cognition, which involves our search for knowledge. Thus there is no contradiction between knowing a lot and not thinking; there is no moral capacity to cognition. See *Thinking*, 14–16.

28. In the three projected volumes of *The Life of the Mind*, Arendt intended to explore the uneasy connection, which Schmidt achieves, between thinking, willing, and judging. The problem with the physician is that he doesn't pursue his thought process, doesn't continue to think, in his own mind, about his own role among others, and he is therefore unable to judge what he should do differently from anybody else.

29. A number of recent works have attested to the remarkable insistence, among inmates of the camps, on maintaining the remnants of the practices, and with them the distinctions, of normal life. There were unofficial schools, music groups, cookbooks, in which inmates recognized in themselves and each other the personal differences in expertise that uniform terror is meant to extinguish.

30. Arendt compares this totally dominated, disciplined self to Pavlov's dog; it is a bestial rather than a human image, but it serves her purpose (*The Origins*, 438).

31. Arendt emphasizes, however, that victimization (of the inmates) cannot in itself become the basis for a political identity, party, or movement. She writes that the fear we all should have of the fact of the camps should instead create an alliance, along the whole political spectrum, to oppose the system of totalitarian domination (which of course Arendt herself defined as being neither necessarily of the Right nor of the Left) (*The Origins*, 441–42).

32. The quotation is taken from David Rousset, *Les Jours de Notre Mort* (Paris: Editions du Pavois, 1947), 273.

NINE. POLITICS AS MASQUERADE

1. Arendt presumes that a politics of free action is premised on the firm segregation of work and labor from the sphere of free political action, and further presumes that labor and work are themselves absolutely distinct. But I specifically do not want to attempt here a detailed philosophical analysis of her categories of labor, work, and action. Other writers have already produced clear and useful analyses of Arendt's three categories and the relations between them. See especially the very subtle and complete discussion of labor, work, and action in André Enegrén, *La Pensée Politique de Hannah Arendt* (Paris: Presses Universitaires de France, 1984). In "Travail et oeuvre: Servitude naturelle et vio-

lence artificielle" Enegrén discusses the relationship between the necessary cycle of production and consumption that is labor, and Arendt's
emphasis on durability and worldliness as the mark of those objects that
are the product of work. For Enegrén, violence is the subduing of
nature through artifice, the erection of Arendt's common world out of
necessity and nature. I find that Arendt identifies violence much more
with necessity than against it. For her, work and artifice are the first
steps away from force and necessity and toward the ordered stability
that will eventually allow for free action. Despite my differences with
him, I find Enegrén's work to be one of the best general analyses of
Arendt's thought. For his discussion of her conception of action as it is
developed throughout her work, see the chapter "Une phénoménolo-
gie de l'action" in the same work, in which Enegrén discusses the significance for Arendt of plurality, the public space, and language. For
thoughtful analyses of labor, work, and action in *The Human Condition*
specifically, see chapter 3, "The Human Condition," in Margaret
Canovan's *The Political Thought of Hannah Arendt* (London: Methuen,
1974), esp. 55–65, and her revised discussion in chapter 4, "The
Human Condition," in *Hannah Arendt: A Reinterpretation of Her Political Thought* (New York: Cambridge University Press, 1992).

2. What is thoroughly excluded from Arendt's version of the Greek conception
of the political is violence, which she associates with strength rather
than power, and which in itself is always mute (*HC*, 26). Indeed, for
Arendt the distinction between heroic action and violence would seem
to be that action is inseparable from language, from either being speech
or being spoken about, while violence is mere force, which may, in and
of itself, just as well occur by stealth and in the dark, unseen and
unheard. For Arendt's distinctions between strength and power, see *OR*,
175, especially her description of power in the vocabulary of grammar
and syntax (language and action). See also her discussion of power, as
distinct from violence, force, and strength, in "On Violence," especially
section 2, 134–55, in *Crises of the Republic* (New York: Harcourt, Brace
& Jovanovich, 1969). Nancy Hartsock, in *Money, Sex, and Power* (Boston: Northeastern University Press, 1983), points to Arendt's unusual
theorization of power as an important reconceptualization for feminists. Arendt's conception of power presumes that it is multiple and diffuse rather than singular and unified. In this sense her conception of
power can be related to certain contemporary feminist and psychoanalytic conceptions of female, as opposed to male, sexuality. See for
instance Luce Irigaray, *This Sex Which Is Not One*, trans. Catherine
Porter and Carolyn Burke (Ithaca: Cornell University Press, 1985).

3. Arendt rather conveniently ignores the historical evidence that violence could
overwhelm speech in the Athenian as well as the barbarian empires. See,
for instance, "The Melian Dialogue," in Thucydides, *History of the Peloponnesian War*, trans. Rex Warner (New York: Penguin Books, 1972),
400–408. The presence of the immediate possibility of violence, a possibility that overwhelms language and all too often leaves its victims
mute, is fundamentally antipolitical. The Melians argue as much for a
serious discussion as they do for their lives, recognizing that the two are
linked; nonetheless, the Athenians dismiss both claims. Yet in an earlier, similar incident with the Mytilenes, the Athenians suffered a crisis
of civic conscience after the Athenian fleet had already set out to destroy
the city. In a second debate, the argument for the death sentence is

explicitly made as an argument against discussion and the persuasive powers of speech. The assembly votes against the death sentence (and against the argument against speech) and sends out a fast ship to overtake the fleet and rescind the order. See "The Mytilenian Debate," in Thucydides, *Peloponnesian War*, 212–23. Unfortunately for the Melians, no such act of mercy was forthcoming the second time around.

4. These are the various definitions of the Sanskrit etymology of *barbara*. As we have already seen, Arendt puts a great emphasis on the stammering body of Herman Melville's character Billy Budd, and in *The Origins* she herself adopts a stammering style.

5. Nonetheless, the analysis presumes that the private home is absolutely necessary for the common world; although Arendt's citizen may seem desperate to get out of it, he needs to be able to return to its secure location. For a description of how the concept of the home is itself rejected by the utopian architects of our contemporary society of mass production and consumption, see Kenneth Frampton's "The Status of Man and the Status of His Objects: A Reading of *The Human Condition*," in *Hannah Arendt: The Recovery of the Public World*, ed. Melvyn A. Hill (New York: St. Martin's Press, 1979), 116–17.

6. It is worth reflecting back on Robert Major's analysis of Arendt's conceptualization of the body as object (*der Korper*) rather than as living and lived (*das Leib*). Arendt thus disallows any possibility of public experience being mediated by bodily experience, a prohibition that may be not only unfortunate, but untenable. See Robert W. Major, "A Reading of Hannah Arendt's 'Unusual' Distinction between Labor and Work," in Hill, *Hannah Arendt*, 131–55.

7. Margaret Canovan gives an excellent explication of Arendt's double-sided understanding of "the social" as both the hegemony of economic values in all aspects of life and the sterile maneuverings of position and manners that constitute *ancien régime* court life. Both versions of society result in a politics that is engaged with derivative issues (economic outcomes, personal status) rather than the politics of worldly self-enactment and agency that Arendt values. See the discussion of "Society" in the chapter on "*The Human Condition*," in Canovan, *Hannah Arendt*, 116–22. Canovan also points out in this section that Arendt's understandings of society grow out of her work on totalitarianism and are further developed in *On Revolution*.

8. The political despotism associated with mass society can be that of an individual or that of majority rule. Bureaucracy, like majoritarian despotism she associates with "a kind of no-man rule." She adds that "the rule by nobody is not necessarily no-rule; it may indeed, under certain circumstances, even turn out to be one of the cruelest and most tyrannical versions" (*HC*, 40). For dramatic explications of the rule of "nobody" see Franz Kafka's *The Trial* or, more domestically, a country song by Kye Fleming and Dennis W. Morgan titled "Nobody" (Nashville: Tom Collins Music, 1982), in which the voice and person deceptively identified as "nobody" to the deceived-but-knowing wife is the husband's mistress.

9. Arendt's emphasis on political action as a process of self-representation totally ignores the overtly economic aspects of Greek political action. See, for example, Karl Polanyi's *The Livelihood of Man* (New York: Academic Press, 1977), in which the physical provision of bodily sustenance becomes the reason for national political engagements. See also Jean-

Pierre Vernant, *The Origins of Greek Thought* (Ithaca: Cornell University Press, 1982), 71–72. For a discussion of the relation between the displacement of Athenian labor onto noncitizens and the increased democratic freedom for the few, see the section "Women, Slaves, and Artisans," in Pierre Vidal-Naquet, *The Black Hunter: Forms of Thought and Forms of Society in the Greek World*, trans. Andrew Szegedy-Maszak (Baltimore: Johns Hopkins University Press, 1986), 159–245.

10. Take note especially of the footnote on the dissolution of rank among women in the household as a sign of their formal inequality when compared to men (*HC*, 72).

11. Although I examine Alcibiades as a prime example of an individual whose private behavior sustains and undermines his preeminent political position, one can easily find less controversial examples of recommendations to mind one's private manners for political success. See for instance Cicero, *On Duties*, ed. M. T. Griffin and E. M. Atkins (Cambridge: Cambridge University Press, 1991).

12. This is rather like Arendt's comments in *Imperialism* that black South Africans will achieve a political identity once they think of themselves as workers rather than as blacks. In both cases Arendt ignores the extent to which individuals who are politically defined by their social identity (be it gender or race) would have to have a parvenu consciousness to accept the premise that they must transcend and reject that identity in order to gain political emancipation.

13. For a contemporary analysis of the significance of private life for the ancient Greeks, and especially the Greek abhorrence of a subject's identification with a passive (slavish or feminine) sexuality, see Michel Foucault, *The Use of Pleasure*, vol. 2 of *The History of Sexuality*, trans. Robert Hurley (New York: Vintage Books, 1990). Foucault addresses a variety of topics, but for our purposes the most significant is his discussion of the conventions of discipline and power that structured male homosexual relationships in ancient Greece, in the section titled "Erotics." Foucault especially attends to the "Problematic Relation" (Greek homosexual relations between free youths and free men), in which the ambiguity of subject-object relations, of domination among peers, which Arendt so wishes to avoid that she banishes it from the world of citizens, is seen to have significant political implications when young men who have openly identified themselves with the passive or feminized sexual role later seek to assert themselves as citizens. See Foucault, *Use of Pleasure*, 185–225.

14. "The consequence of this was that on the one hand the 'active' and dominant role was always assigned dominant values, but on the other hand it was necessary to attribute to one of the partners in the sexual act the passive, dominated, and inferior position. And while this was no problem when it involved a woman or a slave, the case was altered when it involved a man. . . . In short, to delight in and be a subject of pleasure with a boy did not cause a problem for the Greeks; but to be an object of pleasure and to acknowledge oneself as such constituted a major difficulty for the boy. The relationship that he was expected to establish with himself in order to become a free man, master of himself and capable of prevailing over others, was at variance with a form of relationship in which he would be an object of pleasure for another" (Foucault, *Use of Pleasure*, 220–21).

15. That Arendt considers political life to be enacted stories in the space of appearance is indicated even by the section headings in her chapter

titled "Action": "The Disclosure of the Agent in Speech and Action" (sec. 24, 175); "The Web of Relationships and the Enacted Stories" (sec. 25, 181); "Power and the Space of Appearance" (sec. 28, 199); "*Homo Faber* and the Space of Appearance" (sec. 29, 207).

16. For a straightforward, thorough account of Alcibiades' life see Walter M. Ellis, *Alcibiades* (New York: Routledge, 1989), especially for a basic presentation of the circumstances of his early life, 1–23.

17. Sources differ on the date of Pericles' political ascendancy and therefore on the length of his political preeminence. Plutarch identifies his political predominance as lasting for forty years, from 469, but most scholars assume his power could not have consolidated before 461, and a conservative estimation places it at 446. Although this involves a difference of more than twenty years, the significant point is that Pericles exercised a dominant effect on Athenian politics for more than twenty years, and was active in the political life of the city for twice as long.

18. From Aristophanes' *The Frogs*, quoted in *Plutarch's Lives*, trans. John Dryden (New York: P. F. Collier and Sons, 1909), 124.

19. Aristophanes is himself particularly associated with the more freewheeling aspects of Athenian democratic culture. His satires were directed at recognizable public figures and situations, and he flourished as a playwright only so long as such public criticisms were permitted in the democracy.

20. Martha Nussbaum, *The Fragility of Goodness: Luck and Ethics in Greek Tragedy and Philosophy* (New York: Cambridge University Press, 1986). I am particularly grateful for Nussbaum's scholarly interpretation of classical symbolism. Although I disagree with her final interpretation of Alcibiades as a dangerous figure "very much at the mercy of fortune and irrational passions" (194), her discussion of the *Symposium* is invaluable to a nonclassicist for its detailed and sympathetic discussion of Alcibiades' presence and speech. Nussbaum does consider Plato's representation of Alcibiades to be an extraordinary argument for the positive, disruptive power and worldly contingency of passion and personal change. Although there are several book-length studies of Alcibiades, Nussbaum's analysis is unusual in that it seriously and sympathetically relates Alcibiades' private life and public actions.

21. Although in the modern tradition Socrates represents freedom of thought confronted by a repressive state apparatus, it is important to remember that in the Greek tradition he was generally associated with the antidemocratic politics that culminated in 411 in the coup that brought the bloody oligarchic government of the Four Hundred to power.

22. The lion, here a metaphor, seems to have become a metonym for Alcibiades. Recall the quotation from Aristophanes' *Frogs* mentioned earlier.

23. Both Nicias and Alcibiades himself, in their arguments to the assembly about the Sicilian expedition, make reference to Alcibiades' private life. See Thucydides, *Peloponnesian War*, 417, 419.

24. In his considerations of Greek culture, Nietzsche supposed that the collective value the Greeks placed on individual excellence could be maintained only through competitive striving among peers, a situation that would demand the banishment of any individual whose excellence so surpassed that of his fellows that his very presence fixed the game. Although Nietzsche, describing the Ephesians' banishment of Hemodorus, never refers to Alcibiades, and the Athenians never banished Alcibiades for excellence, much the same thing seems to have happened, in effect. See

"Homer's Contest," in Friedrich Nietzsche, *The Portable Nietzsche*, ed. Walter Kaufmann (New York: Penguin Books, 1982), 32–39.

25. This dialogue opens with Socrates' interlocutor joshing him about his preoccupation with the beautiful Alcibiades, who, it is pointed out, is now a man growing a beard, and whom Socrates insists he has abandoned for one more beautiful in wisdom: Protagoras. It is interesting to speculate on the rivalry and/or enmity Plato, the philosopher-scribe, may have felt toward the worldly Alcibiades. Alcibiades was the city's and Socrates' favorite; in the eyes of a younger admirer of the philosopher's, a member in a family of the antidemocratic opposition, Alcibiades must have cut a dashing, if appalling, figure-cum-legend.

26. Although the *Symposium* is a fictionalized dramatic account rather than a transcript of an interaction, Plato's representation of Alcibiades is especially pertinent precisely because of the poetic license taken in elaborating well-known public figures in a private scene. Since many of the specific references throughout the dialogue are verifiable in other sources, it is reasonable to accept that the characters were cast in the dramatic roles they played out more familiarly in daily life.

It is also important to keep in mind that this is Plato's representation of Socrates. The Socrates that Arendt takes as a model is the public thinker who interrogates certainties and offers brief, pithy recommendations. The Platonic Socrates is much more given to systems of thought that oppose a hierarchically ordered philosophical structure to the public truths of worldly experience.

27. For a clear analysis of the rigorous standards of behavior, intent, and identification that governed homosexual relations between youths and men, and the political implications of these relationships, see the section "Erotics" in Foucault, *Use of Pleasure*, 185–225.

28. At about the same time that the herms were mutilated, charges were brought that certain citizens were conducting profane, mock rituals of the Eleusinian Mysteries in their homes. Alcibiades was much more evidently involved in these mock rituals, which seem to have been held by some of the more daring and irreverent citizens. But Alcibiades' more verifiable involvement with the profanation of the Mysteries seems to have associated him in the public mind with the much more serious mutilation of the herms. For an analysis of Alcibiades' possible involvement in the profanation of the Mysteries and the relationship that had with his publicly assumed involvement with the mutilation of the herms, see Ellis, *Alcibiades*, 58–62.

29. In her discussion of Alcibiades' speech in the *Symposium* (Nussbaum, *Fragility of Goodness*, chapter 6, "The Speech of Alcibiades: A Reading of the Symposium"), Nussbaum makes much of Alcibiades' comparing Socrates to an inanimate Silenus statue-figure, the Greek homosexual erotic convention of greeting the beloved by touching his face and genitals, and the smashing of the herms' faces and genitals. Nussbaum makes clear that she thinks that, despite lack of other evidence, Alcibiades in fact did it.

30. For the authoritative collection of contemporary documents relating to Thucydides' *History of the Peloponnesian War*, see A. W. Gomme, A. Andrewes, and K. J. Dover, *A Historical Commentary of Thucydides* (Oxford: Clarendon Press, 1970). Gomme, Andrewes, and Dover point out (284–86) that there were linguistic associations between the words for constitution and the traditional religious observances and those for

the contravention of either: "It was not entirely a strange idea that a revolutionary conspiracy should advertise itself by mutilating statues. The more spectacular the crime, the stronger the impression of the numbers, power, and ubiquity of the conspirators; and when their chosen moment comes, the uncommitted individual may hesitate to act against them for fear that they have a majority on their side."

31. In *A Historical Commentary of Thucydides*, vol. 4, books 5–7, Gomme, Andrewes, and Dover organize a careful reconstruction of the various events associated with the scandal of the herms and the Mysteries. Drawing on a variety of sources, they have been able to construct a plausible version of who said and did what, when, and why. The evidence against those denounced, even after the prisoner Andokides' confession, was never particularly reliable, but Gomme, Andrewes, and Dover examine why a religious incident could have become something of a political witch-hunt. Although Andokides' confession quelled the general alarm, stopped further denunciations, and provoked the death sentence against those who were not cleared by him, Thucydides also indicates that the guilt of the accused was never firmly established. See Thucydides, *Peloponnesian War*, 447.

32. Gomme, Andrewes, and Dover note that although Alcibiades was immediately suspected, many of those accused by Diokleides (who was later executed for false testimony) were enemies of Alcibiades, while those accused by Andokides (who was himself a prisoner and who gained his own release by testifying) were Alcibiades and his friends. These authors therefore conclude that Diokleides' denunciations were politically motivated, capitalizing on what may simply have been a youthful prank, while Andokides' accusations, never disproved, might more likely have been true (Gomme, Andrewes, and Dover, *Historical Commentary*, 286–88). It seems just as likely, however, that Andokides was as problematically motivated as Diokleides, especially since his testimony won him his freedom and incriminated the other side. Andokides' personal motivations are taken note of in Plutarch's account of his confession:

> It happened that Andocides, amongst the rest who were prisoners upon the same account, contracted particular acquaintance and intimacy with one Timaeus, a person inferior to him in repute, but of remarkable dexterity and boldness. He persuaded Andocides to accuse himself and some few others of this crime, urging him that, upon his confession, he would be, by the decree of the people, secure of his pardon, whereas the event of judgement is uncertain to all men, but to great persons, such as he was, most formidable. So that it was better for him, if he regarded himself, to save his life by a falsity, than to suffer an infamous death, as really guilty of the crime. . . . Andocides was prevailed upon, and accused himself and some others, and, by the terms of the decree, obtained his pardon, while all the persons named by him, except some few who had saved themselves by flight, suffered death. To gain the greater credit to his information, he accused his own servants amongst others.
> (*Plutarch's Lives*, 129–30)

33. Eva C. Keuls, *The Reign of the Phallus: Sexual Politics in Ancient Athens* (New York: Harper & Row, 1985). The rest of the text is a detailed, if rather polemical, analysis of Greek masculine sexual violence and gynophobia

as evidenced by the representations of mythic and daily life on "porno-graphic" vase paintings.

34. The Adonia mourns the death of Adonis, the timid, beautiful young mortal lover of the goddess Aphrodite. He was said to have been gored to death by a wild boar, a traditional symbol of aggressive masculinity. In his description of the interconnected events, Plutarch specifically mentions the celebration of the Adonia: "When all things were fitted for the voyage, many unlucky omens appeared. At that very time the feast of Adonis happened, in which the women were used to expose, in all parts of the city, images resembling dead men carried out to their burial, and to represent funeral solemnities by lamentations and mournful songs" (*Plutarch's Lives*, 126).

35. One might conjecture that Aristophanes' three comedies—*Thesmophoriazu-sae* (Ladies' Day), *Lysistrata* (Women in Power), and *Ecclesiazusae* (Women in Parliament)—indicate the fear or knowledge that women might occasionally take power into their own hands. Although it is doubtful that respectable Athenian women were allowed to attend dramatic performances, they clearly were aware of the thematic details of works being performed. The *Thesmophoriazusae*, for instance, centers on the extreme displeasure of the ladies of Athens, expressed in the relative freedom of a women's festival (the Adonia), at the treatment of their sex in the various plays of Euripides. *Lysistrata*, the play about a women's sex strike to force an end to the Peloponnesian War, itself written after the desecration of the herms, can be interpreted as a reference to the sexualization of women's possible political action.

36. Keuls notes that Thucydides gives an exceptionally detailed account of the decisions that result in the Melian massacre and enslavement.

37. For the discussion, see Keuls, *Reign of the Phallus*, 16-32, 381-403.

38. Keuls points out that Athenian women are never suspected of political activity because of the circumspection of their supposedly entirely feminine lives, but she neglects to note that Alcibiades is implicated in political scandal precisely because of the flamboyant excess of his own behavior, which transgresses any singularly gendered specificity. Keuls rather simplistically identifies Alcibiades as the personification of Athenian phallicism; citing the many contemporary accounts of his personal lawlessness and political ambitions, she disregards the ambivalent implications of his ambiguously gendered persona.

39. I am indeed making reference here in general to Foucault, and particularly to Pierre Bourdieu. See Pierre Bourdieu, *Distinction: A Social Critique of the Judgement of Taste*, trans. Richard Nice (Cambridge: Harvard University Press, 1984), for an exhaustive inquiry into the regular social construction (through the habitus) of those attributes we take to be most personally unique.

Index

abjection, 26–27, 62, 86, 88, 92, 96–102, 112–15, 145, 150, 153; bodies, 19, 38–39, 45–46, 65, 101, 122, 134, 139–40, 142; and feminine shame, 49, 53, 59, 120; and the Jews, 117; Kristeva's conception of, 3, 15, 20–23, 25, 40, 118; and race, 24, 87, 97, 100–101, 106, as threat to the political, 24–27, 30, 34–37

Achilles, 151

action, 10, 15, 19, 26–27, 35, 62, 67, 78, 80, 87, 91, 95, 111, 114, 119–20, 125, 136, 150, 153; Arendt's political conception of, 2–5, 11, 23, 124, 142; labor, work, and, 11–12, 25, 104; the political actor, 34, 36, 38, 42, 76, 106, 108–9, 112, 137–38, 144, 152; speech and, 14, 16, 28, 31, 140; and thinking, 126–33, 154

Adams, John, 18, 21

Aeschylus, 144

agency, 12, 21, 35, 37, 50, 62, 114, 133–35, 146, 152–54; feminine, 40, 45, 47, 118, 120, 147, 149–50; individual agents, 13, 19, 27, 76, 108–10, 116, 124, 126, 130; through masquerade, 2–3, 5–6, 15, 47, 58; political, 1–6, 15, 59, 67–69, 78, 87–88, 106, 113, 115, 136, 147

Alcibiades, 3, 5, 136–54

antisemitism, 23, 52–56, 61, 64, 66–91, 117

Aphrodite, 145

Aristophanes, 143, 149

Aristotle, 5, 16

artifice, 3, 43, 46–47, 58, 77, 125, 152, 154; as artificial, 7; as human creation, 9, 15, 26, 32, 34, 36–37; as opposed to norm of naturalness, 27, 35, 38, 129; and self-representation, 38–40, 42, 45, 113, 128

assimilation, 56, 67–78, 81, 87, 91, 117

Athena, 50

Athens, 3, 5, 12, 25, 136–52

Augustine, 48, 63

Benjamin, Walter, 56, 63

bestiality, 22–23, 35, 95, 133

Bilinski, Leon Ritter von, 84; Frau Bilinski, 85

Billy Budd (Melville), 3, 26–32, 63–66, 78, 81, 119

black: Africans, 86, 97–106, 118; slavery, 24

Blücher, Heinrich, 56, 58

Blumenfeld, Kurt, 56

body, 7, 9–13, 16, 21–24, 33, 36, 37–39, 45–46, 62, 70, 98, 102–3, 106, 115, 118, 121; black, 86, 97, 100; gendered, 6, 10, 27, 40, 43, 47, 119; heavenly, 5, 7; Jewish, 84; laboring, 10, 11; miserable, 15, 23, 25; mother's, 9, 23; as threat to the political, 17–20, 137–42; totalitarian reduction to, 133–34; and violence, 30–31

body politic, 3, 70, 92, 93, 96

Boers, 87–88, 97, 100–106, 114–18, 152

bourgeois, 71, 87–93, 104–6, 115, 120–24

bureaucracy, 96–98, 104–13, 118–24, 130, 140

camps, 16, 90, 133

Céline, Louis-Ferdinand, 23

class, 1, 3, 14, 19, 47, 71, 90–94, 115, 121–22, 137, 140, 153

Clemenceau, Georges, 79, 80, 81

compassion, 14, 25–37, 65–66

Conrad, Joseph, 86, 88, 96–103

crime, 16, 32–35, 68, 77, 99–100, 121–23, 148

Cromer, Evelyn Baring, 1st Earl of, 109

Darwin, Charles, 94

Demange, Edgar, 79

Dionysus, 144, 146

Diotima, 146

Disraeli, Benjamin, 4, 62, 89, 91, 107, 137, 151, 154; contmporary opinion of, 67; as Jewish masquerade, 69, 72–79, 110; and plans for a Jewish state, 82–85; and race thinking, 95

Doane, Mary Ann, 2, 39, 40

Dostoevsky, Fyodor, 31

Dreyfus affair, 64, 68–72, 78–81, 118

écriture féminine, 47, 58, 59

Eichmann, Adolph, 66, 124, 126, 129, 131

Ellis, Walter, 151

embodiment, 91, 136, 145, 150; and identity, 15, 17, 68, 75, 104; as opposed to representation, 37; as physicality, 6–9, 11–14, 30, 36, 38, 92, 115, 140

enactment, 12, 15, 67, 126, 128; as performance, 3–4, 40, 89, 142; as self-creation, 13, 62, 67, 120, 137, 141

Epictetus, 134